Against Oblivion

After graduating from Manchester University in 1963, Jonathan Power worked for a year in the Ministry of Agriculture in Tanzania. In 1964 he went to the University of Wisconsin to write a thesis on migrant labour in Africa. Then, in 1966, he joined the staff of Martin Luther King.

Since 1967 he has been writing and broadcasting, as a regular columnist for the *International Herald Tribune*, and as a contributor of political comment to the BBC, the *New York Times, Washington Post* and *Encounter*. His interviews with people such as Zbigniew Brzezinski, Georgi Arbatov, Andrew Young, Willy Brandt, Indira Gandhi and Julius Nyerere have been printed in newspapers around the world. At present, he is editorial adviser to the International Commission on Disarmament and Security Issues, chaired by Olof Palme.

His previous books are *Development Economics* (1970), *World of Hunger* (1971) and *Migrant Workers in Western Europe and the United States* (1979). He has also made a number of films, including *It's Ours Whatever They Say*, which won the silver medal at the Venice Film Festival in 1972.

Jonathan Power is married and has three daughters, and lives in Islington, London.

Jonathan Power

Against Oblivion

Amnesty International's fight for human rights

Fontana Paperbacks

First published by Fontana Paperbacks 1981
Copyright © Jonathan Power 1981

Set in Lasercomp Apollo

Made and printed in Great Britain by
William Collins Sons & Co. Ltd, Glasgow

For Carmen, Miriam and Lucy. May they grow up in a world that honours and respects every human being.

Contents

Acknowledgments

I first began writing about human rights in my column in the *International Herald Tribune* after James Grant, then head of the Overseas Development Council (now director-general of UNICEF), invited me to spend a month in Washington taking a look at the new policies of the Carter administration. At almost every step I took, I found that Amnesty International had been there before me. So when David Baker of McGraw-Hill, a fervent *Herald Tribune* reader, suggested the theme of this book, his idea fell on well-tilled ground.

I have many other people to thank: the Ford Foundation for a number of trips to Third World countries; Mary White of the BBC who helped me with the early research and persuaded me over lunch one day that the moment when human rights seem to be getting a bashing from Western political leadership is a good time to write a book on Amnesty; Lynette de Rementeria who has been my able and thorough research assistant; Hilda Gage, my secretary who never lets up whatever the pressure; and Mary Clemmey, my literary agent, who, with an enthusiasm beyond the normal line of duty, not only has pushed the commercial prospects of the book forward, but has also been over every line of it with a critical eye and thus improved its content beyond measure.

The staff of Amnesty International deserve more than a word of thanks. I have demanded much of their patience and days of their time. The press officer, Richard Reoch, and his assistant, Lynn Jackson, have been invaluable.

I must also thank successive editors of the *International Herald Tribune*, Murray Weiss, Mort Rosenblum and Philip Foisie, for the constant encouragement they have given in allowing me to unfold many of my ideas on human rights in my weekly column.

Finally, a special thank you to Anne, who is my in-house critic and inspirer, whose political judgment is second to none and who always encourages me to do what I have decided to do better than I thought it could be done.

JONATHAN POWER   London, June 1981

Preface

Nearly half the 154 governments of the United Nations are believed to be holding prisoners of conscience – people imprisoned for their beliefs or origins, who have not used nor advocated violence. Over the last five years there have been allegations of the practice of torture in 60 nations. In more than 50 countries, citizens can be detained without trial or charge. In 134 countries the death penalty is in force, in many for politically stated offences.

This book is an attempt to look at the work of one organization, Amnesty International, and its efforts over twenty years of life to modify, diminish and in some cases end the rule of torture and false imprisonment, where the crime, if that is the word, has been nothing more than to criticize those who hold the reins of power in the country in which they live.

Amnesty's reach is global and the problem of choosing the countries and issues on which to concentrate in this book has not been easy. I hope, nevertheless, that the less than a dozen countries written about here give the reader something of the feel of this remarkable organization.

I have tried, whenever possible, to draw on my own experience, from my own journalistic travels over the last thirteen years. I have tried, too, to give it some measure of geographic and political balance.

The four Latin American countries chosen are all regimes of the right – Brazil, Guatemala, El Salvador, with the exception of Nicaragua. But then the continent is overwhelmingly of right-wing disposition. In Africa the two countries chosen are Tanzania and the Central African Republic. Tanzania since independence has been socialist. It would be difficult to put such a firm label on Bokassa's Central African Empire. Brutal is the only apt description.

In Asia, China selected itself. Amnesty's probings into this secretive hidden land are one of its most fascinating efforts.

In Europe it was impossible to ignore the Soviet Union, with its long record of persecution and iron-clad rule. But to find a Western country to act as a counterweight was not easy. In the end I settled on Western Germany which has produced in the Baader-Meinhof gang the single greatest internal challenge to a northern western democracy since the war and whose detention, imprisonment and trial drew Amnesty into deep water.

In the end, though, it must be an unsatisfactory list, for there are at least another dozen countries equally as interesting and equally as telling.

I should add that although Amnesty was helpful in supplying much of the information in this book, the organization did not commission it or ask that it be in any sense an official history; the views expressed are my own and do not necessarily reflect those of Amnesty International. I was not a member of the organization when I began to write it. Now I must get round to joining. Meanwhile – since I'm not very good at finding and filling in forms – I can make a simple decision as a mark of respect for the former political prisoners and those who campaign so tirelessly on their behalf that I have met in the course of researching and writing – to donate a percentage of my royalties on this book to that great and inspiring organization, Amnesty International.

1. The Story of Amnesty International

At 11 o'clock on the morning of Saturday, 28 February 1981, the telephone rang at Amnesty International's Secretariat in London. The press officer, Richard Reoch, was in his office catching up on some work. He took the call, since Amnesty, still beguilingly amateurish, has no duty officer for the week-end, not even an answering service. The call was from Buenos Aires. The caller identified himself. Reoch recognized his name because his brother was one of Amnesty's adopted prisoners whose case had been featured in an appeal for the Abolition of Torture campaign.

As Reoch took notes, the caller told him the police had arrested Dr José Westerkamp, who had toured Europe to raise support for the campaign on behalf of his son Gustavo, an adopted prisoner of conscience. Also arrested were Boris Pasik, Carmen Lapace, and Gabriela Iribarne who had lived in Canada for the past fifteen years and was only in Argentina on holiday. 'We don't know where they are. My mother is now at the central police headquarters trying to find out.' He went on to tell how plainclothes police had entered the offices of the Centre for Legal and Social Studies at 9.30 the evening before. They had presented an arrest warrant.

Reoch told the caller that he would contact the Amnesty researcher on Argentina and phone him back.

The researcher was traced at an Amnesty meeting outside the secretariat building. By noon, she had been briefed and was ringing Argentina for more details. She was told of new developments: the arrest of Emilio Mignone, a leading lawyer who often conducted the defence of political prisoners in Argentina, and of Augusto Conte MacDonell, the co-president of the Argentine Permanent Assembly for Human Rights. Two other lawyers working for El Centro de Estudios Legales y Sociales (CELS) had been arrested in their homes. Important files documenting abuses of human rights had been confiscated both from the CELS offices and the home of Mr Mignone. There was no news about which police station they were being held at

These arrests were the culmination of a long period of police harassment and intimidation of members of CELS. They had been threatened, their homes placed under surveillance, and their post and telephone communications often intercepted. Most of those detained had sons or daughters who had either been abducted by security forces and 'disappeared' or had been severely tortured.

In the course of the afternoon, Amnesty International received several calls from the USA and Canada, Europe and England from people active in human rights work, who were concerned about the situation in Argentina, and wanted more information from Amnesty. By chance, the former editor of *La Opinion* of Buenos Aires, Jacobo Timmerman, was in London, and he visited the Amnesty offices to discuss the situation with the researcher. He made suggestions about people it would be useful to contact in the USA to help raise the alarm. The Amnesty International representative to the United Nations was also in London and she came in to discuss moves that could be made to influence the UN machinery.

It was important to alert the world to what was happening. A news release was drafted as soon as it was realized that so far the wire services had carried no information. Reoch consulted Amnesty's secretary-general on the basic outline of a statement, which was then issued to the news agencies AP, UPI, AFP and Reuters. The news release drew attention to the fact that Emilio Mignone had testified on behalf of CELS to the UN working group on disappearances. The group's report, published only the week before, analysed thousands of cases of Argentinians who had been abducted by security forces and never seen again. It included extracts from Emilio Mignone's testimony.

A film on two prisoners of conscience, one of whom was

Gustavo Westerkamp, was due to be shown on British television the following evening, and included an interview with Dr José Westerkamp. Reoch phoned the BBC producers and arranged for a snap item on the arrests to be included at the end of the programme. The BBC also put him in touch with producers of a news programme being prepared for transmission in the morning.

Contact was made with Amnesty International's Toronto groups which alerted the Canadian media of the arrest of Gabriela Iribarne. The press officer in Toronto later told Amnesty that she had also spoken to Gabriela's father, who was living in Canada.

Meanwhile, on the advice of the researcher and the Amnesty representative at the UN, and with the agreement of the secretary-general, a telegram deploring the arrests was sent to the chairman of the UN Commission on Human Rights. A cable was also sent to General Videla, president of Argentina, urging that the reasons for the arrests be made clear and that the people be granted access to their families and lawyers.

The following day, Sunday, the press officer in Toronto told Amnesty International that Canada's major newspapers and networks had reported the events. The Amnesty International representative in Canada had also spoken by phone to the Canadian ambassador in Buenos Aires and, as a result, the Canadian government had asked for a representative to be allowed access to Gabriela Iribarne.

At about 8 o'clock on Sunday evening, the news was phoned through that she and two others had been released. Reoch asked if the charge against the leading figures had been clarified, but apparently Gabriela had said, on her release, that she had been unable to see the others; however police had told her they would be charged on Monday.

At 2 o'clock on Monday morning, the researcher received another call from Buenos Aires. She was informed that the Argentinian press had reported the case, stating that those arrested were being held incommunicado and would be charged under article 224 of the penal code for the possession of diagrams and plans of military establishments. (This carries a possible penalty of eight years' imprisonment.) The researcher surmised that the only plans of military establishments likely to be in the possession of the human rights activists would be diagrams of torture centres and secret detention camps drawn by former prisoners.

It seemed clear that those who remained under arrest would not be quickly released. Amnesty decided to issue an Urgent Action memo alerting its co-ordinators in a number of national sections to send telegrams to the Argentinian authorities urging that those detained be properly treated while in custody.

By the middle of the week, press coverage of the events was extensive. The Latin American correspondent of the *Guardian* wrote a major piece based on Amnesty information. A critical editorial appeared in the *Washington Post* and was reprinted in the *International Herald Tribune*. The *New York Times* carried a lengthy news item.

Exactly one week after the arrests, the phone rang again in the Amnesty researcher's office in London. The judge dealing with the case had called everyone into court for an announcement. At 11.45 that evening, a phone call from the American section of Amnesty brought the news that although the judge had said police investigations would be continued, he had issued an order for the prisoners' release, citing insufficient evidence.

On 15 May 1981 a court in Buenos Aires cleared the defendants of all charges against them and ordered the return of nearly all confiscated documents. The judge ruled that the seized material had no legal value as evidence (it had not been taken in the presence of the defendants). Nevertheless, he ordered that certain papers should be sent to the military authorities because they contained accusations against members of the security forces.

For Amnesty, this was a typical piece of Urgent Action, which also highlighted two interesting facts: that relatives increasingly trust Amnesty to take fast action and are careful to accumulate and pass on detailed information so that it can move into top gear; and that relatives and friends are prepared to take some personal risk in ringing directly Amnesty headquarters in London.

Amnesty International has many enemies – and lots of friends. Its membership, now more than a quarter of a million worldwide, is increasing. As recently as ten years ago, the secretariat employed nineteen people and had an annual budget of £35,000. Today, its staff is 150, there are 40 national sections, 2500 groups, and it has a budget of £2 million. It may still be small compared with most international organizations, but its impact on individual lives is greater than any of them.

Twenty years old in 1981, it was the product of the imagination of one man, Peter Benenson, a Catholic lawyer of Jewish descent, born of English and Russian parents, described by some who know him as a 'visionary', even a saint. A man, however, who, some people think, so lost faith in the creature he had created, that he later nearly succeeded in destroying it.

Benenson, aged forty when the idea of Amnesty came to him, had been active with the issue of human rights for a long time. He was defence counsel in a number of political trials, and in 1959 was a founder-member of Justice, an all-party organization of British lawyers which campaigned for the maintenance of the rule of law and the observation of the United Nations Universal Declaration on Human Rights.

Then, in November 1960, his imagination was fired by a newspaper report about two Portuguese students in Lisbon during the dark days of the Salazar dictatorship. They had been arrested and sentenced to seven years' imprisonment for raising their glasses in a toast to freedom.

How, Benenson wondered, could the Portuguese authorities be persuaded to release these victims of outrageous oppression? Somehow a way must be devised to bombard the Salazar regime with written protests. It was, as Martin Ennals, a future Amnesty secretary-general observed later, 'an amazing contention that prisoners of conscience could be released by writing letters to governments.'

As Benenson nurtured the idea, it grew roots and branches in his mind. He thought, why have just one campaign for one country, why not a one-year campaign to draw public attention to the plight of political and religious prisoners throughout the world? 1961 seemed a good year to launch his effort – it was the centenary of the freeing of the slaves in the United States and of the serfs in Russia.

Benenson approached two people in London whom he thought would be interested in the idea and whose reputations and contacts would help give it momentum: Eric Baker, a prominent Quaker, and Louis Blom-Cooper, the internationally-known lawyer who in 1980 defended Mr Edward Tekere, the Zimbabwean government minister charged with murdering a white farmer. The three men decided to call the campaign 'Appeal for Amnesty, 1961'. Their aims were limited but clear-cut – to work impartially for the release of those imprisoned for their opinion, to seek for them a fair trial, to enlarge the right of asylum, to help political refugees find work, and to urge the creation of effective international machinery to guarantee freedom of opinion.

At Benenson's office in London, they would collect and publish information on people whom Benenson was later to call 'Prisoners of Conscience'. The three men spoke to their friends and soon had a nucleus of supporters, principally lawyers, journalists, politicians and intellectuals.

Benenson sought the support of his friend David Astor, long-time editor of the influential liberal Sunday newspaper, the *Observer*, who agreed to provide space for the new group's opening shot. Benenson decided this should be published on 28 May, which was Trinity Sunday, the Christian feast day celebrating God the Father, Christ the Son, and the Holy Spirit. Benenson, always a man for symbolism, had conceived a method that was to last for many years – 'A Threes Network': each group of Amnesty supporters would adopt three prisoners and work for their release. One would be from a communist-bloc country, one from the West, and one from the Third World.

The article appeared in the *Observer* spread over a full page. *Le Monde* carried simultaneously its own piece, the next day other newspapers picked it up – the *New York Herald Tribune*,

Die Welt, the *Journal de Génève*, Denmark's *Berlingske Tidende* and Sweden's *Politiken*, as well as newspapers in Holland, Italy, South Africa, Belgium, Ireland and India. Even a Barcelona newspaper, taking a risk with the Franco regime, gave it a mention.

The *Observer* article focused on eight people whom Benenson called 'Forgotten Prisoners'. Among them was Dr Agostino Neto, an Angolan poet, later to become the first president of independent Angola. He was one of only five African doctors in Angola, but his efforts to improve Africans' health, combined with his political activities, had proved unacceptable to the authorities. He was flogged in front of his family, dragged away and imprisoned in the Cape Verde Isles without trial. Another 'Forgotten Prisoner' was Constantin Noica, a Romanian philosopher who had been sentenced to twenty-five years' imprisonment for 'conspiring against the security of the state' and 'spreading propaganda hostile to the regime'. The others were Antonio Amat, a Spanish lawyer imprisoned without trial for three years for trying to form a coalition of democratic groups; Ashton Jones, a sixty-five-year-old American minister, who had been repeatedly beaten up and imprisoned three times in Louisiana and Texas for demanding equal rights for blacks; Patrick Duncan, a white South African jailed for his opposition to apartheid; Tony Abiaticlos, a Greek communist and trade unionist jailed for his anti-regime activities; Cardinal Mindszenty of Hungary, who had first been imprisoned, then made a refugee in his own country, trapped in the US Embassy in Budapest; and the Archbishop of Prague, Josef Beran, also jailed because of opposition to his country's regime.

It was an effective piece of propaganda, which touched a wide range of political nerve centres. The reaction was overwhelming; a flood of letters and donations poured in, together with a great amount of information on thousands of other prisoners of conscience. In a piece of inspired improvisation, this concern was channelled by putting sympathizers in touch with others who lived nearby, and encouraging churches and schools to set up groups. Each group was to 'adopt' individual prisoners and then start pestering the life out of the governments responsible. They were to make contact with the prisoners' families, send them presents and raise money for them. Above all, they were to write to the prisoner, even if no reply was possible, in the hope that at least one letter would get through and a prisoner would know that someone somewhere cared about his or her plight. This idea, characteristically English – parochial, low-key, without much money, committed to working across ideological, religious and racial boundaries – was amazingly effective on the international scene.

Benenson asked a British artist, Diana Redhouse, to design an emblem for Amnesty based on a candle encircled by barbed wire. The image, which brilliantly illuminated the spirit of the movement, had come to him, Benenson said, when he recalled the ancient proverb, 'Better to light a candle than curse the darkness.'

The first Amnesty candle was lit on Human Rights Day, December 1961, on the steps of the beautiful Wren church, St Martin-in-the-Fields, on the corner of Trafalgar Square. Like the square itself, St Martin's has long been the home of great causes that have needed a meeting-room, a concert hall or a pulpit. Benenson asked Odette Churchill Halkern to light the first candle. Odette, as she is known far and wide, was the most famous British agent in occupied France; she was eventually captured by the Nazis and sent to a concentration camp but later successfully escaped.

Significantly, while Odette was lighting the first candle, a group which included Carola Stern, the head of a large publishing house, and a journalist, Gerd Ruge, was establishing the first Amnesty branch outside Britain, in West Germany. Their first three adopted prisoners were a Soviet poet, a Jehovah's Witness in Spain, and a communist writer in South Africa.

This was just a beginning: other national groups were springing up all over the place. It was important to bring the groups together, to exchange and co-ordinate views. Only eight weeks after the Trinity Sunday launching, delegates from Britain, France, Belgium, Ireland, Switzerland and the USA met in a café in Luxembourg. There was strong feeling on two counts. First, that Amnesty should not be a one-year flash in the pan; it must become a permanent movement. Second, it should change its name to Amnesty International. By the end of that year, there were Amnesty groups in Belgium, Greece, Australia, Sweden, Norway, Switzerland, France, West Germany, Ireland, the Netherlands, the UK and the USA.

One critically important person who had offered his services early on was Sean MacBride. Today, because of his role on a UNESCO committee attempting to draft 'A New Information Order', he has become almost an object of hatred by the West, particularly in the eyes of press commentators who see him as a stalking horse for totalitarian tendencies in the Third World and the Eastern bloc. MacBride, the only man ever to have won both the Lenin Peace Prize and the Nobel Peace Prize, has managed to straddle the great East/West ideological divide better than most political figures. He is the son of an Irish republican soldier who was executed by the British after the 1916 Easter Rising. He was, as a teenager, a political prisoner, along with his mother, the legendary Maud Gomme, the 'patron saint' of Ireland's oppressed. Later he became a lawyer, founded the Irish Republican Party and became a member of parliament. By 1948 he was foreign minister of Eire.

He worked with Benenson on much of the early planning of Amnesty, and helped establish high-level contacts. The first of what became regular missions to explore human rights abuses was initiated by MacBride. He and Benenson persuaded the weekly Catholic newspaper, the *Universe*, to put up the money for MacBride to take up the case of Josef Beran.

As a priest, Beran had been imprisoned by the Nazis in Dachau and Theresienstadt. After the communist coup in Czechoslovakia in 1948, he became the Archbishop of Prague, but he fell out with the new government. Preaching in St Vitus Cathedral, he delivered a defiant sermon. The police raided his home and carted him away, and nothing was heard of him for two years.

Benenson had put pressure on the Czech authorities through their embassy in London and Amnesty groups in other countries had followed it up. But nothing had happened.

MacBride was well enough placed to secure an interview with Jiri Hajeck, the Czech foreign minister, although the prime minister refused to see him. MacBride wrote in his report back to London: 'I pointed out that it was in the interest of Czechoslovakia to reassure the world that its new constitution of 1960 heralded a new era of freedom. I found this direct argument had some influence and I left feeling more hopeful about the future.'

Nothing on the surface, however, seemed to move. Amnesty stepped up its campaign with more letters, telegrams and embassy lobbies. Eighteen months later, the prison gates opened. Beran and four other bishops were freed – although they were put under house arrest and banned from religious activities.

Of course, there was no way of knowing if it was Amnesty pressure or other influences that had brought about the release. But Beran was clear. He wrote to thank Amnesty for help in gaining his freedom. 'I pray for Amnesty International,' he wrote, 'I pray for all who support Amnesty.' Two years later he was allowed to leave Prague for Rome. A year after that he came to London – to light a candle for Amnesty.

Another apparent success in these early days was Louis Blom-Cooper's mission to Ghana. In January 1962 he went to investigate the imprisonment of Nkrumah's opponents. Five months later, 152 detainees were released. The Amnesty membership began to feel that they had a machine that could fly. Built by the simple technique of letter upon letter, followed up by a personal visit to the country, it seemed a method that produced results.

The next mission was a visit by the Indian lawyer, Prem Kher, to the German Democratic Republic to investigate the case of Heinz Brandt, a trade unionist who had been spirited out of West Germany and was in jail in the East, awaiting trial. Kher procured an interview with the East German attorney-general who assured him that Amnesty would be allowed to send an observer to Brandt's trial. It was an empty promise. The trial was held in secret and Brandt was sentenced to thirteen years and six months' hard labour. In 1963 Brandt became

Amnesty's 'prisoner of the year' (an appellation used to produce added publicity but later abandoned because it was said to imply a competition). Two British clerics with contacts in East Germany, Paul Oestreicher and John Collins, visited the GDR to continue the pressure. The philosopher Bertrand Russell, probably the most powerful non-government voice then alive, also joined the campaign. He told the East Germans that unless Brandt was released, he would return the Ossretzky Medal which they had awarded him for his services to world peace. Brandt was released just two years after the Amnesty campaign began.

Altogether 1964 was a year that succeeded beyond expectation. Eire released thirty-seven prisoners on United Nations Human Rights Day. That summer Romania freed thousands of political prisoners. Greece, Egypt and Burma all took significant steps towards cutting down their prison population.

But 1964 also brought the fledgling organization its first internal controversy. It blew up around Nelson Mandela, held prisoner by the South Africans on the notorious Robben Island. He had been adopted as a prisoner of conscience in 1962 when he faced charges of trying to organize a strike of African workers and attempting to leave the country without a passport. He had been leading non-violent campaigns against the government's apartheid system for almost a decade. At various times, he had been banned from holding meetings and had restrictions imposed on his movement.

In 1964, he was convicted on a sabotage charge and sentenced to life imprisonment. The British group who had adopted him decided that his turn to violent opposition to the existing goverment meant they could no longer support him as a prisoner of conscience, although they kept up their campaign for him to be released one day. This triggered off a far-reaching debate that was only settled when Amnesty decided to poll all its members. The overwhelming majority decided in favour of maintaining the basic Amnesty rule that Amnesty should not adopt as prisoners of conscience those who used or advocated violence. But many Amnesty members were unhappy at abandoning Mandela just as he was being incarcerated with little hope of ever coming out alive.

In the end, a compromise was reached. Mandela would no longer be a prisoner of conscience, but Amnesty would make representations to the authorities if it thought the trial had been unfair, the prison conditions were severe or if torture was ever used. This kind of compromise, used many times later, has remained a source of controversy, not least when employed at the time of the imprisonment of the Baader-Meinhof gang (see Chapter 5).

Amnesty has been through long debates on the issue of violence, constantly reaffirming that it will argue for the right of a fair trial and humane treatment whatever the alleged offence of the prisoner. On the other hand, it will not ask for the release of a prisoner if it feels he has been objectively convicted for activities involving the personal use or advocacy of violence, however just the cause. In an explanatory note outlining their position, Amnesty states that many observers have thought wrongly that Amnesty is opposed to violence in any circumstances.

> This is not so. Amnesty International's position is entirely impartial. Amnesty International was not founded to work for general economic, social and political justice – however much its individual members may wish to do so – and are free to do so through other bodies – but to bring relief to individual victims of injustice . . . Amnesty International would be applying a double standard if it insisted that the police and prison authorities abstain from any act of violence or brutality yet maintained that those on the other side should be allowed to commit such acts and yet be unpunished.

Somehow this 'above the fray' position does not ring quite true in practice. If one reads through the Amnesty material on Central America, for example, Amnesty does seem to be preoccupied with the general state of injustice. The political violence in El Salvador or Guatemala has become so much a part of the political system that it's no longer easy to make such fine, clean-cut distinctions. The ambiguity will live on. Yet it is clear why Amnesty must at least have this norm. In an age where guerrilla activity is principally a left-wing phenomenon, Amnesty needs to maintain the credibility, support and influence of the right and centre if its work is to succeed.

The next great divisive issue in Amnesty – and the one that was to trigger a series of events that nearly led to its destruction – was the 1966 report on British army torture in its colony, Aden. A state of emergency had been declared by the colonial administration after a hand-grenade was thrown at the British High Commissioner. Mass arrests were ordered, and suspected terrorists were rounded up and detained indefinitely without being charged.

Amnesty handed the job of investigating the situation to its Swedish section, which in turn selected as its investigator Dr Selahaddin Rastgeldi, a Swedish national of Kurdish extraction. (One of Amnesty's early rules was that members should not investigate cases in their own country.) His report was extremely incriminating, alleging torture and violence by British soldiers against Arab prisoners and concluding that the state of emergency violated the UN Declaration of Human Rights. He also said the British Foreign Office had prevented him from visiting the internment camps so he had been unable to check first-hand the allegations. The high commissioner refused to see Rastgeldi and claimed that there were no political prisoners in Aden.

There is conflicting evidence about what Amnesty's London office did with the report. Robert Swann, by then the general secretary, said that everything possible was done to force the Foreign Office to take action by threatening to release the Rastgeldi report. Benenson, however, claimed that the matter was deliberately being suppressed by Amnesty under pressure from the Foreign Office. In September 1966, he decided to act himself. After a visit to Aden to check Rastgeldi's story, he took the report and had it published in Sweden.

The reaction in Britain was savage. A large section of the

British press accused Rastgeldi of bias, claiming that he could not be trusted because of his Turkish/Kurdish origins.

Benenson's suspicions about Amnesty's collusion with the Foreign Office continued to fester in his mind. Why had no action been taken until he personally intervened? Had somebody in the organization been persuaded to suppress the Rastgeldi report? If so, at whose request? Through his own high-level contacts in the Labour Party, he was able to arrange meetings with the foreign secretary, George Brown, the attorney general, Sir Elwyn Jones, and the Lord Chancellor, Lord Gardiner — the latter two former Amnesty colleagues. Their obvious embarrassment over the Aden issue deepened his suspicions that someone was working to keep the matter quiet. And top of his list of suspects was Robert Swann.

Swann, like Benenson, was an old Etonian and a Roman Catholic. Benenson had chosen him personally as somebody he could trust to carry on Amnesty's work while he devoted himself to his farming and to pioneering new ventures. Before joining Amnesty, Swann had worked for the British Foreign Office in Bangkok, and he admitted to Benenson that his work had involved 'para-diplomatic' activities. He was adamant, however, that his links with the Foreign Office had not made him susceptible to pressure.

Benenson was unconvinced. The atmosphere at Amnesty became supercharged. He began to suspect that Swann and many of his colleagues were part of a British intelligence conspiracy to subvert Amnesty. To his way of thinking, the only way the organization could survive was by moving its headquarters from Britain to a neutral country such as Sweden or Switzerland. But he could not convince anybody else at Amnesty.

In the end, he decided to resign as Amnesty International's president. He went off to the United States to explore the possibility of founding a new organization. Later he went into a Trappist monastery in France to try and think things out. He continued to write to Swann but the correspondence only seemed to add to Benenson's suspicions. Then, after much thought, he decided to withdraw his resignation and to fight it out with Swann and 'those behind him'.

Benenson contacted Sean MacBride, whom he regarded as a friend who would support him. After some discussion, they agreed to appoint an impartial investigator and chose Peter Calvocoressi, then reader in international law at Sussex University, whose findings and recommendations they would accept. Swann was asked by MacBride to take an indefinite leave of absence.

Before the Calvocoressi report was halfway completed, another bombshell exploded. An American source disclosed that CIA money was going to a US organization of jurists which in turn contributed funds to the International Commission of Jurists of which Sean MacBride was secretary. MacBride loudly disclaimed all knowledge of CIA funding, but Benenson became convinced that MacBride was tied up in a CIA network. His suspicions about a vast conspiracy ranged against Amnesty were intensified. The rift between Amnesty and Benenson deepened.

Shortly after this, the atmosphere was poisoned further by revelations in the British press about Benenson's own ambiguous relationship with the British government. They were made by Polly Toynbee, then nineteen years old, who had served as secretary to Sir Leary Constantine on an Amnesty mission which also included Lieutenant-Commander Michael Cunningham, to Nigeria and Rhodesia in 1966. In Nigeria, according to Miss Toynbee, 'We stayed in the Federal Colonial Hotel outside Lagos. We sat around doing nothing but drinking and entertaining the press. We must have spent an enormous amount but we never achieved anything. We never saw anyone important. We just got vague assurances that the prisoners were all right.'

The mission then went to Rhodesia. Following the white minority's Unilateral Declaration of Independence from Britain the year before, there had been mass arrests of the African political elite. The Amnesty group, however, seemed unclear as to what they were supposed to be doing. There was also a 'seemingly endless supply of money. I could go to the bank and draw out two hundred pounds a time. And there was no check on what I did with the money.'

When Benenson came out to Salisbury to join the team, Toynbee asked him about the money and the rumours then floating around Salisbury that it was coming from the British government. According to Toynbee, Benenson admitted it.

Later, Toynbee was expelled from Salisbury, but before she left she was handed a bunch of letters which had been abandoned in a safe. The letters were from Benenson, written in London in 1966 to the Amnesty representative in Salisbury. They were written in a thin code, some typed, some in Benenson's handwriting. Some were signed Margaret and some Peter. They contained frequent references to Harry, whom Polly Toynbee assumed was a code name for the British government. A few extracts:

12 January
The only news of any import comes from Harry. He's giving us the money we asked for.

20 January
Harry's present has arrived so all is well. Cunningham should reach you in about a week's time with part of the present.

1 February
According to my calculations you have £2000 at Jack Grant and the better part of £1000 from each of Bernard and Michael — total £4000. You can if you need have another £1000 on 15 Feb by the method to be explained.

2 February
Harry has developed a sudden enthusiasm for litigation. What with North Hull Harry wants a fair buzz of legal activity. Harry's financial problems apparently have been solved and he's in a generous mood.

Toynbee deduced that the last reference was to the Labour

government's new-found political strength. (On 27 January Labour had won the crucial Hull by-election, raising their paper-thin majority from three to four.) Her revelations caused a scandal. A parliamentary question was asked in the House of Commons. Harold Wilson, the prime minister, decided to answer it himself. He admitted that there had been an approach to the government for help, 'and we thought it right to suggest possible donors who might be willing to help.'

Amnesty headquarters denied all knowledge of any arrangement. The inference was that whatever approaches had been made had been on Benenson's own initiative.

Benenson did not deny that he had approached the government for money. In his view there was nothing wrong in taking British government money to help British subjects who were illegally imprisoned in Rhodesia by a rebel government. The money, he claimed, was for the prisoners and their families and not a gift to Amnesty. However, before agreeing to the arrangement, the British government, according to Benenson, had insisted for political reasons that it should be done secretly. Benenson had agreed, but very reluctantly, and the fact that Amnesty denied all knowledge of the arrangement only served to confirm his suspicions about British intelligence's infiltration of the organization's leadership.

By the end of 1966, Amnesty was in a state of severe crisis and in March 1967 its five-man executive held an emergency meeting at Elsinore in Denmark to try to resolve it. Benenson refused to attend. Sean MacBride said that the organization's crisis had been brought about by 'a number of erratic actions' by Peter Benenson, whom he blamed for 'wild and wide-ranging charges and some unilateral initiatives'.

The executive confirmed Benenson's resignation. The post of president was abolished and the new post of director-general (later changed to secretary-general) was created. One of Amnesty's founder members, Eric Baker, was provisionally appointed. The row surrounding Benenson's resignation had caused a major split between Amnesty's London office and many of the foreign sections. The Swedish section in particular had been very disturbed about the possibility that London had been bowing to British government pressure, and threatened to withdraw from Amnesty altogether. It was some time before their confidence was completely restored.

Peter Benenson retired to his farm near Aylesbury. His relations with Amnesty were understandably strained for some time, and for a while he seemed more or less to abandon the organization he had founded and nurtured. But he was not out of the public eye for long. In 1968, he founded the Coeliac Society, an international organization to help victims of this little-known digestive allergy from which Benenson himself suffers. He never lost his interest in humanitarian issues and is currently involved in another movement, called 'Nevermore', which has the ambitious aim of abolishing all war. It concentrates mainly on the problems of refugees and is particularly concerned with the situation in the Horn of Africa.

Benenson's relations with Amnesty are now restored and the bitterness of the 1960s is long forgotten. But he still fervently believes that Amnesty should be based in a neutral country. The fact that the headquarters are in London, he says, seriously inhibits the organization's ability to investigate the problems of Northern Ireland, which he considers to be Amnesty's biggest failure to date.

For Amnesty in 1967, the loss of Benenson was a bitter blow. He had been the heart and soul of the movement. An incredibly charismatic figure by all accounts, he could inspire other people with his enthusiasm and energy. In the early days of Amnesty, he was able to accomplish a great deal through his personal contacts on his own initiative. He was answerable to nobody and missions and initiatives in the early days were often undertaken just on his say-so. There was little in the way of organization or administration – budgets were so small they were often worked out on the back of a cigarette packet in the pub. Everything hinged on Benenson's own personality and he inspired deep affection and loyalty in those who worked with him.

The loyalty he engendered was difficult to break. Even the people Benenson attacked for being involved with the British secret service were unwilling to criticize him. They were concerned about his state of health and felt powerless to help him. Many of them still look back on it all with pain. They resented what they saw as efforts by the press to exploit his vulnerability. Many of Benenson's friends and colleagues believe that he suffered terrible disappointment and personal disillusionment over the Labour government's handling of the Aden torture report. He expected better of a Socialist government and especially of his friends in the Labour movement.

Early 1967 was the nadir of Amnesty's fortunes. Its leadership had been divided, financial disaster loomed. It was simultaneously unpopular with the British Foreign Office and accused of being in the government's pocket. Morale was at rock-bottom.

But Baker's level-headed industriousness did much to save Amnesty International from the early death widely predicted at that time. Between June 1967 and June 1968, the number of groups grew from 410 to 550; 293 of the 2000 prisoners adopted were released. By the end of 1967 Amnesty was going from strength to strength.

In July 1968 Martin Ennals was appointed secretary-general of Amnesty International. He was to remain in the job for twelve years. A dogged, persistent administrator was one part of him; the other was a man of strong political motivations that lent a certain cutting edge to Amnesty. He had won his initial reputation when he'd worked as general-secretary of the National Council for Civil Liberties. He was regarded as a man of left-wing sympathies, but one who had a broad perspective on life and by no means saw all virtue on one side of the political fence. Amnesty at this stage in its life needed a careful but wily backroom boy who could accept that he was accountable to the movement. A more obviously dynamic and high-profile character would have been an added tension at a time when the organization needed to recuperate and steady its nerves.

Under Ennals's careful supervision, the organization grew and expanded. The mood of disillusionment in the West as the Vietnam war progressed helped it in its recruitment. The right-wing coup in Chile in 1973, overthrowing a democratically elected government, also encouraged people to join. Amnesty became recognized in the public mind as the source of accurate information on human rights. Its capacities changed. Its purpose did not. It maintained its narrow focus on the prisoners of conscience, but it is a measure of Amnesty's achievement during Ennals's secretary-generalship that human rights, instead of being generally regarded as a problem marginal to the real affairs of state, became the issue which determined governments' images in the eyes of the world. When in 1980 President Marcos of the Philippines abruptly cancelled the planned state visit of Chile's President Pinochet because of Chile's human rights abuses, it was an indication that the world of the 1980s was very different from the one Amnesty had looked out on in 1961.

Not all the credit can go to Amnesty. The International Commission of Jurists, Freedom House (the New York-based human rights organization), the churches and the unions had all been active. But Amnesty symbolized the concern, provided much of the raw data on which other organizations based their efforts, and was a constant inspiration to groups of individuals around the world, in countries where persecution was an everyday occurrence, to set up their own human rights watchdogs.

Jimmy Carter's decision to make human rights the focus of his presidency was also a major milestone. Martin Ennals rightly foresaw that it would be impossible for the US government to sustain its commitment untainted. It was bound to become intertwined with other aspects of foreign policy and in so doing be devalued. But it also did help raise human rights to a new level of political potency. Certainly in Latin America, Washington's new concern emboldened church, labour and liberal groups to be more openly critical of their regimes. And it provided a yardstick against which the foreign policy of Western nations had to be judged, even when Carter began to turn his back on his earlier commitment. Amnesty, the atmosphere it created, the people it inspired, must take much of the credit for this. Certainly these were some of the factors that weighed with the committee which awarded the Nobel Peace Prize to Amnesty in 1977, for its contribution' to 'securing the ground for freedom, for justice, and thereby also for peace in the world'.

Characteristically, Ennals did not go to Oslo to receive the prize himself. He already had another commitment – a conference in Stockholm to mobilize support for Amnesty's opposition to the death penalty. This was a cause close to Ennals's heart. He wanted Amnesty to replace its rather half-hearted concern with a fully-fledged commitment. The International Executive Committee instead sent to Oslo a small delegation headed by the committee's chairman, Sweden's Thomas Hammarberg – the man who took over from Ennals as secretary-general in July 1980.

Now thirty-nine years old, Hammarberg is by background a journalist, a former foreign editor of *Expressen* and correspondent for Swedish Radio. Politically a social democrat, he is probably nearer to the centre of the political spectrum than Martin Ennals. He has an intimate feel for the organization, a detailed and practical knowledge of the issues that concern it, and a well-developed political sense. Diffident in manner, his appointment suggests that Amnesty consciously wants a low profile for their leadership. The issues it handles are difficult and sensitive. A man with an ego, even a 'presence', might complicate the already difficult job of making Amnesty's criticisms palatable.

One story told about him recalls a visit to Hanoi in December 1979 to discuss the issue of political prisoners with the Vietnamese authorities. Just as official talks were about to begin, a messenger came in and whispered in the ear of the senior Vietnamese hosting the mission. A BBC news bulletin had just announced that Amnesty had accused Vietnam of holding more political prisoners than any other country.

Amnesty's diplomacy looked as if it was skewered. The Vietnamese were irate. Hammarberg set to work to assure them that the BBC had got it wrong. It was Amnesty policy, he told them, never to make comparisons. The rough edges soothed by Hammarberg's gentle but purposeful arguments, tempers cooled and the Amnesty team was allowed to stay and continue its work. In June 1981, after exchanges of memoranda with the Vietnamese, Amnesty published a report calling for the abolition of re-education camps, officially said to hold some 20,000 people who have not been charged or tried.

Hammarberg now presides over an organization that hopes to double its membership and level of financial support over the next two years. An ambitious target — half a million members worldwide and a budget of £4 million. Will the organization acquire twice the vigour, or will it become more careful, cautious and weighty, chewing out its decisions among more staff, losing its present straightforward effectiveness?

The great strength of Amnesty today is its lack of pretension or cultivated sophistication and its ability to react quickly to turbulent events.

Hammarberg, with his cardigan and sandals, easy smile and soft-spoken manner, suggests that it will stay on its present course. But it will take all the muscle he has to stop it going the other way. Dealing with the Vietnamese could be easier than confronting the cold logic of bureaucratic growth in which caution replaces spontaneity and Amnesty becomes itself a prisoner, hemmed in by the inertia of size and the immobility of responsibility.

2. The Amnesty Machinery at Work

No. 10 Southampton St. The address means many
things to Londoners: it is the centre of the capital and
it is not far from the lively and charming old market-
area of Covent Garden.

But when you pass through the gloomy portals of
the block that houses Amnesty, or, to be more precise,
the organization's International Secretariat and its
British Section, then you quickly forget the casual,
even slightly frivolous atmosphere that prevails in the
street. The receptionist peers through the glass, and
scrutinizing each visitor very carefully, presses the
button to open the automatic door only when he has
had permission to do so from someone in the office.
One can't help wondering why they have to take such
precautions. Do not the organizers proclaim that
Amnesty is kept going by the enthusiasm of public-
spirited people, that the organization's work is carried
out in the open, perfectly legally, and that there would
be no point in working in secret? [from a recent article
in *Izvestia*]

A trade union leader, seized in one of the big police swoops
made in the Dominican Republic in 1975, was being held naked
in an underground cell. Amnesty International learned of the
case and, after investigation, issued a worldwide appeal on his
behalf. Letters were mailed addressed to him in prison and that
Christmas members in many countries sent cards. The
following January he was released by order of President
Joaquin Balaguer.

The prisoner, Julio de Pena Valdez, later recalled the effect of
the hundreds of letters and cards he received:

When the first two hundred letters came the guards gave me back my clothes. Then the next two hundred letters came and the prison director came to see me. When the next pile of letters arrived, the director got in touch with his superior. The letters kept coming and coming: three thousand of them. The President was informed. The letters still kept arriving and the President called the prison and told them to let me go.

After I was released the President called me to his office for a man to man talk. He said: 'How is it that a trade union leader like you has so many friends all over the world?' He showed me an enormous box full of letters he had received and, when we parted, he gave them to me. I still have them.

In 1979, Amnesty International's regional liaison officer for Latin America met Julio de Pena in the Dominican Republic and showed him the case sheet prepared by Amnesty International's research department after his arrest. De Pena read it carefully and slowly. There wasn't a single error in it, he said. He was astonished by how much personal information Amnesty had dug out about him.

Among those working for his release was a former refugee from Nazi aggression, Hannah Grunwald, living in New York. She had regularly phoned President Balaguer to protest about the treatment of Julio de Pena, who has now started to call her 'mi mama gringa' (my Yankee mother).

The Dominican Republic is only one of numerous countries holding political prisoners. From 60 nations, there have been allegations of torture in the last five years. In more than 50 countries, citizens can be detained by administrative order without charge or trial. In 134 countries, the death penalty is in force, in many for politically related offences.

The adoption group is the central cog in the machinery Amnesty uses in its struggle to combat all this. The adoption group might be based in a factory, in a church or a neighbourhood. A small group of people, often with not very much politically in common, but sharing a commitment to free speech, free thought and free association, take it upon themselves to write carefully worded letters to a prisoner, his jailer, the political authorities and anybody who might be able to help get their prisoner released. Amazingly there are instances, some well-documented like Julio de Pena's, but most less so, where it seems to produce results.

Most of the letters are unanswered. Groups can work for years on behalf of a prisoner and never know whether or not their work has achieved anything. Even if he is actually released, it is hard to know if they were responsible for his freedom. Amnesty is always reluctant to claim credit in such circumstances. So keeping up morale is a major problem. In the end the work depends on the sheer dedication of the group members. But it helps if new ways can be found of bringing pressure to bear apart from the standard letter-writing rota. Publicity is one of Amnesty's most powerful weapons, and some local groups have devised some interesting ways of attracting it.

One group in Islington, North London, has been working for more than two years on behalf of two political prisoners – one in the Soviet Union and one in Uruguay. The group noticed that both prisoners had a birthday in May. Why not have a joint birthday party? It seemed a good idea. They hired a local hall and invited the press, local politicians, trade union leaders, local businessmen and church leaders – anybody, in fact, who might be able to use their influence to help. The group provided food (including a birthday cake), drink and entertainment, all paid for out of group funds raised from membership. In return, the guests were asked to contribute to a birthday appeal on behalf of the prisoners and their families, and to take what other action they could to help get them released.

Another of their ideas was a 'soup kitchen'. They provided people with a lunch one day of bread and soup in order to draw attention to the meagreness of a prisoner's diet.

But apart from what might be called 'publicity stunts', the group has tried to find more ways of bringing direct pressure on the Soviet and Uruguayan authorities. They discovered that their Russian prisoner had been a construction worker before his arrest, so they wrote to twenty-five construction companies asking them to appeal to the Soviets on his behalf. They did the same with the relevant trade unions in the belief that unions might get a more sympathetic hearing from the Russians. They had postcards printed and distributed with the prisoner's photograph and a short text in both English and Russian explaining who he was and why he had been adopted by Amnesty as a prisoner of conscience.

All these things take time and money and, most important of all, information about the prisoner. So each prisoner is allocated a caseworker in the local group whose job it is to find out as much as possible about his or her background – family, occupation, hobbies, interests, political causes and so on. Getting information from the Soviet Union is relatively easy, thanks to the chain of informants who are now expert at getting messages out. Consequently, the North London group found they were devoting more time and energy to their Russian prisoner and less to the Uruguayan, about whom they knew little other than his name and where he was being held. At one time, the level of interest was so low that they even considered abandoning him and asking the International Secretariat to allocate another case. But consciences were pricked and instead they appointed two new caseworkers and redoubled their efforts on his behalf.

At the core of Amnesty is 'the mandate', a set of rules which determine the scope and limitations of Amnesty's action, and which has been likened to an onion. The fundamental concern (the heart of the onion) is to seek the immediate and unconditional release of *Prisoners of Conscience*. These are people detained anywhere for their beliefs, colour, sex, ethnic origin, language or religious creed, provided they have not used or advocated violence. Secondly (the middle layer of the onion), Amnesty works for fair and prompt trials for *all political prisoners*, and works on behalf of such people detained without charge or trial. The third point (the all-embracing, outer skin of the onion) covers *all prisoners without reservation*, for whom Amnesty opposes the death penalty and torture or other cruel, inhuman or degrading treatment.

No Amnesty group works for prisoners in its own country. Nor are Amnesty workers expected to provide information on their own country, and they have no responsibility for action taken by other groups or by the international headquarters about their own country.

Every prisoner of conscience whose case is taken up by Amnesty International becomes the object of a world campaign. The relevant government and prison officials are faced with persistent, continuous and informed appeals from a number of adoption groups urging a reconsideration of the case. Letters are dispatched to government ministers, embassies, leading newspapers and international organizations. Public meetings and vigils are arranged. Influential people are asked to add their names to petitions and protests. In emergencies, distinguished lawyers and jurists are sent to controversial trials or to plead for the life of a sentenced victim.

Individual Amnesty International members and adoption groups have a handbook which tells them what to do and lays down the rules of the organization. Amnesty International's monthly *Newsletter* keeps them in touch with new developments and presents to them the cases of three 'Prisoners of the Month' selected by the Research Department of the International Secretariat (more about this later). These are prisoners of conscience who are in urgent need of help because they may be facing imminent execution or they may be very ill or have been detained in bad conditions for a long time. An estimated twenty thousand members participate in each monthly campaign.

Originally, Amnesty International had a 'Prisoner of the Year' scheme which for a time proved fairly successful. Heinz Brandt of East Germany, who was Prisoner of the Year in 1963, was released in 1964. In 1964, Julieta Gandra of Portugal, imprisoned since 1959 for 'plotting against the internal security of the state', was adopted as Prisoner of the Year. Early in 1965 she, too, was released. However, the following year, a teacher in Guinea, Madou Ray-Autra Traore, sentenced to five years for opposing the nationalization of education, was Prisoner of the Year. His selection had hardly been publicized when news came that he had already been released. Amnesty International had to apologize for its activities on his behalf, and that year the Prisoner of the Year scheme, already criticized by some members, was dropped.

There are now more than 2500 adoption groups, distributed among the 140 countries where Amnesty has supporters. Each group has a minimum of two prisoners for which it is responsible. Individual subscriptions and fund-raising efforts organized by the national sections give Amnesty its income. The strongest groups are still in Europe. Amnesty has always had big groups in Scandinavia, and groups have been very successfully established in Holland and West Germany. (The German group has 10,000 active members and is known for its vitality.) Surprisingly, the United States was slow to take off, and even today, despite all the interest in human rights and the constant recourse of US journalists and congressmen to Amnesty for information, it remains a small national section. Partly this is because when Amnesty International was getting off the ground twenty years ago, potential American Amnesty supporters were preoccupied opposing the Vietnam war and working for civil rights. Today, perhaps, it reflects the gathering mood of nationalism in the United States. Maybe, as President Reagan continues with his policy of 'rolling back communism' in the Third World, even if it means backing rigid, near-totalitarian regimes like those in Chile, Guatemala and El Salvador, this will spark off a new awareness of Amnesty's role.

In France, although *Le Monde* carried a big story on the day Amnesty was launched, support was slow in developing. Today, however, it is the fastest growing national section in the world and the most meticulously respectful of the mandate. The French traditionally have not had much room or time for political groups outside the main established parties and movements. Recently, though, with the birth of the ecology movement and the rise of Amnesty, it seems the French are being drawn to new forms of political expression.

Surprisingly, the homeland of Amnesty, Britain, did not immediately produce a large national section. Partly this was because many of the keenest people were involved in Amnesty International, the parent body, but it was also partly due to the British tradition of trying to run an organization with voluntary unpaid workers. In 1974 this changed when it hired a full-time staff of salaried campaign workers under the imaginative leadership of David Simpson. Within three years, membership more than trebled. Radio, TV and the press are now often quick to respond to its activities. Even so, its appeal tends to be concentrated in the so-called 'quality press'. The British Section is, for no good reason, a middle-class movement. In the spring of 1981, it received a major setback when, after a complicated, prolonged and bitter dispute, the director of the British section, Cosmas Desmond, was dismissed.

Cosmas Desmond, an ex-priest and himself once a prisoner of conscience while under arrest in South Africa, had been responsible for dynamic and controversial campaigning on issues such as arms trade to Chile. In the two years that he was director, membership in Britain grew from some 10,000 to over 17,000, a growth which placed severe internal strains on the section. It was against this background that a proposed office reorganization sparked off a dispute which cut across both professional and volunteer staff. The tension which had been brewing came to a head when two members of staff objected to the appointment of a new superior, on the grounds that their responsibilities would be diminished. They were so adamant that they took their case to the union. Desmond reacted by proposing their suspension on full pay. He was overruled by the standing committee of the British Section's council. But then, as an act of support for their director, some members of staff walked out on strike. The staff and volunteers who remained behind drew up a contingency plan to take over the office work. Desmond interpreted this as a 'coup' and posted a notice on the door condemning it. The chairman of the British Section's council then ordered the office to be closed for three days for tempers to cool. A commission of enquiry which was set up reported that there had been no 'coup'. Desmond was given the option of resigning, which he refused. By a narrow margin, the council voted to dismiss him. The following week, an AGM motion to reinstate him was narrowly defeated. He had no choice but to leave.

Amnesty International and its various national sections are still very much rooted in the wealthy northern countries with tentacles only slowly reaching out to the south. In his farewell message in 1980, Martin Ennals was critical of Amnesty's effectiveness in building groups in the Third World: 'It was a point of principle to have sections in Asia, Latin America and Africa, but the differences of culture, finance, attitudes towards non-governmental organizations and means of expression, were not always appreciated in either practical or conceptual terms.' Nevertheless, Mexico, Peru, Venezuela, Ecuador and Costa Rica, all have local Amnesty groups. One of Amnesty's chief concerns in the 1980s must be to find ways of enlarging and strengthening them.

Each year around two hundred delegates from the national sections (and other bodies such as the UN and the Red Cross) attend the International Council, which is Amnesty's main, democratically elected governing body. It decides on long-term policy for the movement, discusses priorities for the coming year and reviews the activities of the national sections, International Secretariat and the International Executive Committee.

The nine-member International Executive Committee is elected by the International Council to implement policy. It meets as often as necessary – usually four or five times a year – to discuss and approve missions, publications and other important initiatives; it gives general guidance to the International Secretariat, and appoints its senior staff. Its chairmen have been in turn an Irishman (Sean MacBride), a German (Dirk Börner), a Swede (Thomas Hammarberg), and today a Chilean (José Zalaguette).

London HQ, although leaving much of the agitation work to the local groups, still makes many of the critical decisions. It is the Research Department in London which examines who can be named as prisoners of conscience. It then passes on to the local groups the dossier containing information on the country and instructions for coordinated action, a case sheet giving personal details of the prisoner, information about the arrest, trial and health, and news of the family.

Each dossier is compiled by, or under the supervision of, one of the researchers using information collected from press reports – not least from the local press which, even if censored, may carry a line or two on an arrest – government statements, interviews with lawyers, refugees and, often most important, the news provided by recently released prisoners. The researchers have built up links with local human rights organizations and exile groups. In certain parts of the world the church is a particularly valuable ally. Often, yesterday's adopted prisoner can be today's government minister, perhaps part of a government that is engaged in its own repression. Nicaragua is one example. The problem then is keeping good relations while maintaining vigilance.

Amnesty reckons that approximately a third of a researcher's time is spent on investigating individual casework. The rest is spent studying legislative and political changes and preparing missions, reports, campaigns and policy proposals.

The case of Norma A. gives an insight into how Amnesty works.

In October 1979, Amnesty's London office received a letter from an Argentinian exile living in France asking them to take up the case of Norma A. He claimed she was still in jail in Argentina although she had a year ago completed her three-year sentence for possession of subversive literature.

The letter was filed pending further investigation. By chance, Norma's name cropped up again in April 1980. An Argentinian refugee now living in Sweden, Juan V., wrote to Amnesty about the 'disappearance' of his brother. He also asked Amnesty to take up the case of Norma A. who, he claimed, was being held under PEN (*poder ejecutivo nacional*: national executive power), a notorious legal weapon widely used in Argentina whereby prisoners are held in preventive detention by presidential decree. With two sources of information now available, Amnesty decided to act. It wrote back to Juan V. requesting more information concerning Norma A., the circumstances of her arrest, where she was being held, whether she was a member of any revolutionary group committed to violence.

In reply Juan V. provided extensive details about Norma. She had been arrested along with himself, his wife Marta and another man, Adolfo, in 1975, and charged with possession of subversive literature. Her only political connection was her membership of the Metalworkers Union. The lawyer appointed by the relatives of the accused was forced to leave the country after threats against his life. All four had been convicted and given sentences ranging from five to seven years. Norma was sentenced to five years which, on appeal, was reduced to three years plus PEN. All the others had now been released but Norma was still being held in Villa Devoto jail. She had also been refused 'the right of option' which is enshrined in the constitution and entitles people detained under PEN to go into exile as an alternative to imprisonment. The other woman imprisoned with her, Marta, had been given permission to leave the country and was now living in Sweden. According to Juan V., Norma had visas for England, Sweden and France.

Amnesty then contacted the other two ex-prisoners, Adolfo and Marta, and they confirmed Juan's story. Amnesty also tried to find out if there was any reason why Norma was the only one of the original four who had not been released. Juan suggested that it might have something to do with her behaviour while in prison. He said that Norma had mixed a lot with members of guerrilla groups like the Montoneros and the PRT (*partido revolucionario de los trabajadores*: Workers' Revolutionary Party) during prison recreation periods. The authorities held this against her.

Amnesty then checked the story with sources on the ground in Argentina. Satisfied she could not be accused of belonging to a guerrilla group, Norma was formally adopted as a prisoner of conscience in October 1980. A French Amnesty group was asked to take up her case.

The cost of working on a case? On average, taking into account staff time, telecommunication costs, it comes out at about £200 a prisoner. This figure does not take into account the ongoing work of monitoring a country's legal and political system.

It is difficult to imagine just what emotions a prisoner feels when he suddenly learns out of the blue that far away in London or Mexico City or Tokyo, someone is actually aware of his existence and has written him a letter.

Friday, 9 June 1978 remains etched into the memory of thirty-two-year-old Shahid Nadeem, a Pakistani television producer and trade unionist imprisoned four times for his union work and student political activities. It was a day of searing heat. One of his fellow prisoners died of heat-stroke. Eight others collapsed in the factory at the notorious Mianwali maximum security prison in the semi-desert region of the Punjab. It was also the day a letter arrived.

In 1978 Shahid Nadeem had been sentenced to one year's imprisonment and fifteen lashes. His crime: organizing a staff occupation of four television stations in Pakistan. The occupation was completely peaceful and followed a refusal by management to abide by a pay and conditions agreement. The security forces had moved in and more than a hundred arrests followed. Shahid Nadeem and thirty others were held in a cell measuring 10 by 15 feet. The next day they were tried in a military court. Within hours of sentence being passed, they were on their way to Lahore central prison. Two months later they were sent to Mianwali. There the prisoners worked in temperatures of up to 45°C. Shahid Nadeem's cell was next to an open toilet used by seventy prisoners, and the stench often made sleep impossible. Mianwali houses 1200 inmates. There was no doctor.

Shahid Nadeem describes how at about 6 p.m. on 9 June 1978 a fellow prisoner arrived in his cell just before locking-up time with a piece of paper which he called 'your letter from the USA'. It was a copy he had made of a letter in the possession of the prison superintendent, who was studying it, suspecting it contained a secret coded message. Addressed to Shahid Nadeem, the letter said: 'You are not alone; don't lose heart. We pray for you. If there is anything you need, don't hesitate to ask.'

Nadeem later recalled that moment: 'Suddenly I felt as if the sweat drops all over my body were drops from a cool, comforting shower . . . The cell was no longer dark and suffocating.' Soon the whole prison knew about his letter from an Amnesty International adoption group member in San Antonio, Texas. 'My colleagues were overjoyed and their morale was suddenly high.'

That evening the deputy-superintendent summoned him. 'He was so friendly and respectful I was shocked . . . He explained his dilemma as a God-fearing jailer who had to obey orders and follow the rules . . .' The head warden also began to 'behave himself'. Taking their cue, the junior staff changed as well.

After a week, the original letter was handed over to Shahid Nadeem.

Nadeem was later released. He often muses on how 'a woman in San Antonio had written some kind and comforting words which proved to be a bombshell for the prison authorities and significantly changed the prisoners' conditions for the better.'

Writing from prison in 1976, a martial law detainee in the Philippines sent this message to an Amnesty International group: 'I have just been adopted as a prisoner of conscience by your organization. Political prisoners in the Philippines have always regarded your organization as their beacon of hope and sentinel of human rights . . .'

His words were echoed in dozens of letters that came out of camps and prisons in the Philippines during the long period of martial law, imposed by President Ferdinand Marcos, that only ended in early 1981.

Amnesty International sent a mission to the Philippines in 1975 and reported evidence of systematic torture. Case after case was taken up by the organization, and international appeals were made in an effort to halt the torture of prisoners.

In early 1977 came a letter with more news. It read:

I was released from detention last December 14, 1976 — thanks to the efforts of your organization. Immediately after my release I was summoned to the office of Undersecretary Carmelo Barbero where they showed me the folders of letters from Amnesty International pressing for the release of political prisoners . . . I do hope your organization will continue to exert pressure . . . There are still hundreds of political detainees. And the dictatorship continues to arrest and incarcerate political dissenters.

Critically important though they are, the adoption groups and their letter-writing and lobbying campaigns are not the only weapons in Amnesty's hands. The special mission is another important tool. In its twenty years Amnesty has sent over 350 missions to different countries. They have ranged from visits to re-education camps in Vietnam, and interceding on behalf of a death penalty case in the United States, to observing a trial in Poland and investigating torture allegations in Spain.

Proposals for missions and suggested delegates are always submitted to the International Executive Committee, which makes the final decision. Delegates are selected according to their specific experience. For example, the mission sent to India to collect evidence on what had happened during the emergency and to look at safeguards to prevent cruelty was led by James Fawcett, president of the European Commission of Human Rights. He was chosen because of his experience of high-level talks with officials of governments and Supreme Courts. In other cases, lawyers familiar with the legal traditions of a particular country have been chosen. Since the late 1970s, missions have often included a medical expert. Mission members, apart from Amnesty staff, are unpaid.

Missions are subject to a strict set of rules. For example, no mission is allowed to enter a country clandestinely. No statement must be made to the press while the mission is in the country. (This avoids undue pressure for a statement on their findings.) A report is made on return to the International Executive Committee. A memorandum is then sent to the government with the findings and recommendations. In some cases, there will be follow-up exchanges with the government about the interpretation of the law, more detailed information on prisoners, and so on.

Not all missions publish the full results. Some are not sent for the purpose of enquiry but rather to present Amnesty's point of view, as in the case of an execution, or to witness a trial to make sure it conforms to international standards.

Sometimes missions are refused entry into a country. In other cases, missions are harassed. For example, in July 1966, Nils Groth, a Danish lawyer sent to Guinea to enquire about prisoners of conscience, was arrested shortly after his arrival. He was detained without trial until September when he was sentenced to ten years' hard labour for alleged espionage. Fortunately, he was released twenty-two hours after sentencing under a special amnesty declared by President Seko Touré. In October 1970 in Iran, Hossein Rezai was arrested while accompanying a German lawyer sent by Amnesty International on a mission to investigate allegations of torture. The lawyer was expelled from the country but in October 1971 Mr Rezai was sentenced to ten years' imprisonment after trial by a secret military court in Teheran. A mission to Argentina in November 1976, consisting of Lord Avebury (a member of the British House of Lords), Father Robert Drinan, (a member of the House of Representatives of the US Congress) and a member of the International Secretariat, was followed everywhere by twenty plainclothes policemen who questioned, intimidated and even detained a number of people whom they met. On one official visit to two refugee hostels, the delegates were accompanied by four Ford Falcons containing sixteen armed men, whose presence did little to reassure the refugees and encourage communication. The most serious harassment occurred when several people meeting the delegates were openly threatened by plainclothes policemen, and two women were detained.

Often, traditional adoption and mission methods have proved insufficient or even harmful in certain situations, and Amnesty has had to develop new techniques to cope. In Guatemala, where there are 'no political prisoners, only political killings', the adoption system has been virtually discarded. A mission would not be welcomed. The country was taken on in a more direct way with a public report sharply denouncing its practices. In some countries, such as the Shah's Iran, the adoption system was abandoned for a different reason: Amnesty intervention on behalf of a prisoner was seen by the regime as proof of the prisoner's links with Western subversive organizations, and conditions sharply worsened as a result. In Malawi, Dr Hastings Banda announced that he would be happy to punish individually every prisoner named by Amnesty. In both cases, Amnesty switched attention from individual cases to the country's regime: special reports and press releases were issued in an effort to make sure the spotlight stayed on the general problem even though specific, personal lobbying efforts had to be quietened.

Amnesty groups are encouraged to develop their own new techniques. One group discovered the Russian respect for telephone calls: having had no response from their letters, they made a call direct to the mental hospital where their prisoner was being held and had a remarkably frank conversation with the doctor in charge. It did not lead to a release, but at least the group was aware that it had registered its protest. Another group asked for a reversed-charge call to their prisoner in Greece and, although they couldn't speak to him, the director of the prison was in such confusion that he agreed to pay for the call. For the first time, the man on the spot became aware of international concern for the prisoners in his charge.

Only rarely does Amnesty get feedback from governments. No government likes to admit that the release of a prisoner or the slow-down in executions or killings is due to pressure rather than clemency. But there are the occasional stories, such as this one mentioned by Sean MacBride: unofficially and very much off the record, a high official of an East European country told MacBride that it was the cumulative effect, the infuriating load of Amnesty-inspired letters, which led his government to review the imprisonment of thousands of social democrats, priests and members of the old order who had been locked away for fourteen years. In 1965 the country released 12,000 political prisoners.

Another, less well known, part of Amnesty's work is the financial assistance that Amnesty sometimes gives.

In the twelve months from May 1979 to April 1980, the International Secretariat received donations for relief totalling £175,133. In the same period, drawing on relief funds already in hand, it sent £202,172 to prisoners and their families in Africa, the Americas, Asia, Europe and the Middle East. It also sends, whenever it can, medical supplies and books and funds for food and clothing. On occasion, too, it will pick up the legal bills. Relief often goes to the families of prisoners who are suffering hardship and deprivation because of the imprisonment of a close relative. Here are a few examples:

£75 to a mother of ten children whose son, the family's sole breadwinner, is held as a prisoner of conscience in Argentina;

£100 to enable a refugee to travel out of a country from which he faced probable deportation to Ethiopia where he might be threatened with arrest and possible torture;

£286 to cover medical costs for a former political prisoner requiring surgery as a result of having been repeatedly beaten on the soles of the feet with an iron bar while in detention in Iran;

£2000 to a rehabilitation programme for individual surviving victims of political terror under the regime of President Idi Amin of Uganda;

£2000 to a local organization that provides food, legal aid and medical attention to martial law detainees and their families in the Philippines.

Archana Guha, now 38 years old, was completely paralysed from the waist down as a result of torture during police interrogation in Calcutta, India. At the time of her arrest she was headmistress of a girls' school and, as far as Amnesty International is aware, was not involved in politics. She is believed to have been detained because the police suspected some of her relatives were involved in a violent left-wing political movement, the Naxalites.

Archana Guha was arrested at about 1.30 a.m. on 18 July 1974 and taken to Calcutta's notorious Lal Bazar Police Station. Her hands and feet were tied to a pole placed behind her knees. The pole was placed across two chairs, so that she hung with her head down. She was hit on the soles of her feet by one inspector while another stubbed out burning cigarettes on her soles and elbows. The nails of her toes and fingers were also burned.

Later that day she was again hung from a pole while drops of water were dripped on to her forehead.

The next day the interrogation continued. Archana Guha was beaten on the head and forced to sign a paper she could not read. She was threatened with execution if she did not 'confess'. She was thrown to the floor. She was pulled up by the hair and, while hanging in that position, was kicked and burned.

The same methods were applied the next day. She was also threatened with rape and beaten on the head with a rope.

At this point she was unable to walk back to her cell. But she continued to be interrogated almost every day for ten days and was then transferred to prison as an 'under trial prisoner'.

Her physical condition deteriorated rapidly; she often fell unconscious. She received no medical treatment. She could no longer walk.

On the insistence of other women prisoners a specialist was eventually called in. But it was not until 22 December 1975, four months after her transfer to prison, that Archana Guha, by then paralysed from the waist down, was taken to hospital for a minor operation on a gland.

She was returned to prison on a stretcher on 24 January 1976.

On 9 February the prison authorities arranged for her transfer to Medical College, Calcutta, as a 'life-saving case'. She remained in hospital for nine months until she was released on parole.

She could not walk.

Archana Guha was suffering from a lesion of the lower part of the spinal cord. After unsuccessful attempts to treat her in Calcutta lasting more than a year, her case came to the attention of an Amnesty International mission visiting India. The mission interviewed her and described her plight in its report.

Amnesty International's Danish Medical Group arranged for her to be taken to Copenhagen in January 1980 for intensive diagnosis and treatment.

After two months of care she was able to rise from bed, steady herself and walk short distances without assistance.

On 1 May 1980 she wrote from Calcutta: 'My friends and relatives are simply astonished to see me walk again! . . . now I can walk and move! . . . The secretary and colleagues of my school are waiting eagerly (for the day) when I'll be able to join the school. I have improved much in walking and climbing the staircase . . . You have given me a new life – you have caused rebirth to me!'

A question often thrown at Amnesty is how does it maintain its impartiality? How does it stop itself becoming an anti-establishment lobby? More than that, how does it make sure it doesn't become a left-wing lobby, since a social-conscience organization is bound to attract in its staff a disproportionate number of ideologically committed people? That it does remain impartial is evidenced by the abuse it receives equally from, say, the columns of *Izvestia* and the South African regime of Piet Botha. Amnesty's brief reply to this constant refrain of abuse is to quote its own motto, the words of Voltaire: 'I may detest your ideas, but I am prepared to die for your right to express them.' More precisely, Amnesty International officials point to Article 2a of their statute which requires the organization 'at all times [to] maintain an overall balance between its activity in relation to countries adhering to the different world political ideologies and groupings.'

In practice, Amnesty has a method of work that goes a long way to protect them from partiality.

Adoption groups must work simultaneously for at least two

prisoners of different ideological, political or religious back-
grounds. Groups are not allowed to work for prisoners arrested
by their own governments.

The selection of a prisoner to be adopted is carefully
controlled. Before a researcher makes a final decision, he must
check his judgment with a researcher working on a different
country. If any doubt then arises, the choice can be referred to
the Borderline Committee, which is made up of three people
from different countries, appointed by the International
Executive Committee.

The organization is careful, too, that it does not get drawn
into campaigns that support the beliefs of prisoners. It does not
co-operate with exile groups in their lobbying or other
activities.

Whenever possible, major reports are sent to the government involved well before they are published. Comments are
invited. Amnesty insists it will always publicly correct its
errors.

Fund-raising has to be carefully watched. Ever since the
Rhodesia scandal in 1966 it has been a sensitive issue. No
money is accepted for use for a specific purpose, unless it be a
very broad programme like the medical programme or refugee
support fund. Any donor who would want to give more than 5
per cent of Amnesty's income at any level of the movement
must be vetted by the International Executive Committee.
Amnesty takes great pride in the fact that it is independently
funded, and receives no government's funds except a European
Economic Community grant for their work on the relief of
prisoners. It is answerable only to its individual membership.

Membership fees vary from 25 dollars in Canada, to 20 rupees
(£1) in India. In Britain the fee is £6 (£3 for students), which
includes the Amnesty *Newsletter*. Each national section pledges
to raise a certain amount each year. This can come from
donations, bequests, sales of publications, street collections or
any other fund-raising event. Sometimes an artist will donate a
painting for auction, or a concert will be given, as in the case of
Leonard Bernstein and Claudio Arau. Amnesty supporters in

Barbados cut sugar cane for a day and donated their wages to
Amnesty. One of the more novel events was an advertisement
by the British section in the *Guardian* saying, 'If you believe in
justice, why isn't your name here?' All those who donated
more than £5 had their name put down – the page was filled and
£7000 raised.

3. Four Special Efforts

From time to time Amnesty has decided to conduct a special effort to put a major theme of its work across to the public. Some of these efforts are continuous, such as the campaign against torture. Others have been one-off affairs, like the effort to highlight the issue of children and human rights. All of them have been remarkably successful in dramatizing a number of issues basic to human rights.

To single them out, as I have done with the principal four, is to risk distortion. The normal work of dealing with individuals and countries goes on while the intensity of particular campaigns wax and wane. The fact that the children campaign has not been repeated certainly does not mean the problem of children being tortured has been dealt with and overcome. Not at all. Only very recently in El Salvador there was a particularly nasty case of an eleven-year-old girl being tortured in front of her parents. The fact is, it's difficult to sustain for more than a year or two the cause of a single-issue campaign. But they have their uses. They dramatize certain essential issues that are at the heart of Amnesty's concerns. If progress could be made on these four problems – capital punishment, torture, the persecution of children and the arms trade – the standard of human rights would be raised beyond measure.

Against capital punishment

Amnesty International opposition to the death penalty was for a long time a source of controversy among its membership. Some members said it took up valuable time and resources for dealing with the cases of people often convicted of crimes of violence, when that time could better be devoted to prisoners of conscience, who are non-violent.

In a column written in January 1978, the distinguished American newspaper columnist, William Buckley Jr, wrote that he'd just heard of the anti-capital punishment campaign. 'Why is it the business of Amnesty to insert itself in quarrels over appropriate forms of punishment?' he asked, then promptly resigned from the Advisory Board of Amnesty's USA Section.

Buckley is a superb writer, but a poor reader. If he had looked up the founding statutes of Amnesty he would have found that the capital punishment campaign was no new departure – it is part of the original mandate. Indeed, in Peter Benenson's *Observer* article in 1961, the abolition of executions is singled out as an objective in paragraph one.

As early as 1964, at the annual Amnesty conference in Canterbury, members decided to appeal to governments not to carry out death sentences for political offences until six months after sentence or until appeal to a higher court had been heard. In 1965, Amnesty International circulated a resolution at the UN for the suspension and eventual abolition of the death penalty for peacetime political offences.

Nevertheless, it is true that there was a period, between 1965 and 1973, when the death penalty cause took a back seat to other campaigns. Many members were unhappy with it and for the sake of unity, it was shunted temporarily on one side. But in 1973 at the Vienna meeting of the council of Amnesty International, it was decided that the death penalty 'must now be seen as a violation of the human right not to be subjected to torture and cruel, inhuman or degrading treatment.'

In December 1977, Amnesty convened in Stockholm an international conference on the death penalty. Delegates from fifty countries issued a declaration condemning executions committed or condoned by governments.

In 1979, a report, *The Death Penalty*, was issued. It had been compiled by the research department, the legal office and a young British barrister, Brian Wrobel. Wrobel had begun his work with Amnesty International when he was sent to observe the trial in South Korea of eight members of the People's Revolutionary Party. They were sentenced to death for 'anti-state' activities and allowed no time to appeal nor to petition President Park. They were hanged immediately. The experience confirmed Wrobel as an abolitionist. And it was similar events all over the world that made it impossible for Amnesty to refuse to give priority to the issue.

But should Amnesty's growing concern about the use of the death penalty come as a surprise? After all, an organization that is involved with prisoners of conscience and political prisoners must be concerned with a form of punishment which, once implemented, is final. The question of whether the person executed has been judged guilty of a violent crime or not becomes irrelevant. The issue is the inability to bring back the life of a man or woman from the grave. The arguments for abolition are overpowering once one accepts that all courts are fallible and even the best judicial systems now admit that in the recent past innocent people have been sent to the gallows.

This line of reasoning is argued not just by the more left-wing members of Amnesty. Andre Sakharov, the outspoken Soviet supporter of human rights, has thrown his weight behind the death penalty campaign. Five years ago he wrote to Amnesty:

> The abolition of the death penalty is especially important in such a country as ours, with its unrestricted dominance of state power and uncontrollable bureaucracy and its widespread contempt for law and moral values. You know of the decades of mass executions of innocent people which were carried out without any semblance of justice (while still more innocent people perished without any court judgment at all). We are still living in the moral atmosphere created in that era.

There is in many people's minds one powerful argument in favour of capital punishment – when it is used to punish terrorists. The morality or immorality of killing terrorists is difficult to distinguish from the morality or immorality of killing enemy soldiers in a war. The distinctions between innocent and guilty of normal judicial practice become blurred. The question then becomes one of political wisdom. Is it sensible to engage the terrorist in this way? Is it not likely that capital punishment for terrorists would lead to further terrorist outrages? The terrorist could be expected to apply the doctrine of an eye for an eye. More and more innocent people would be killed. The inevitable impact of the death sentence, the drawn-out appeals that often follow, and the execution itself play into the hands of the terrorist groups. The condemned terrorists become martyrs, even heroes in the eyes of many. The demarcation lines between supporters and opponents of terrorism begin to fade as liberal abolitionists become drawn into supporting the campaign for their reprieve.

There is also, perhaps, another argument. It was used by Victor Gollancz in 1961 in an attempt to stop the execution of Adolf Eichmann, the Nazi official in charge of the concentration camps. It is an argument of emotion and passion, and ultimately of faith:

> For a court of three mortal judges to award death to such a man, on the ground of compensatory justice, is to trivialize, in a manner most grievous, the crucifixion of a whole people. One man's death, carried out with at any rate a pretence of decency, against the bestially contrived deaths of a million! There is a Roman word — *sacer* — which means at once sacred and accursed: touchable, as one might translate it, only by God. Cain, in the old legend, was *sacer*: a mark was put upon him by God, precisely so that he might go forth among men and not be killed. Well, if the need for compensatory justice and the total guilt of Adolf Eichmann are both accepted, he, perhaps above all living men, is — *sacer*.
>
> He belongs to God: God alone can repay.

Against torture

Torture, the systematized use of violence to inflict the maximum amount of pain in order to extract information, to break resistance or simply to intimidate, is a product of civilization. Primitive man, like other animals, followed his instincts and killed his enemy as swiftly as the job could be done. Archaeologists, who have dug up prehistoric skeletons, have found no evidence of torture. Even human sacrifices were made without prolonged suffering.

Man for several hundred thousand years existed without using torture; only in the last few thousand has it become a weapon of state. According to Egon Larsen, who has made a special study of the subject the great Roman and Greek civilizations have left detailed records of the use of torture Both of them prohibited torture for a citizen, but for others it was permitted. In ancient Athens a slave's testimony was not considered reliable unless he had been tortured. Rome tortured the early Christians and sent them into the arena to fight with lions. As Rome became increasingly despotic in its later years, even the free man could be tortured for a wide range of offences.

The Christian Church, repelled by the torture of Christians in the hands of Rome, for a thousand years used its great strength in Europe to abolish torture, and until the time of Pope Innocent IV in the thirteenth century it was practically unknown in the Western world.

The Inquisition brought it back. Heretics were forced to undergo a very systematic use of torture, while a magistrate sat close by logging carefully the instruments used, the length of the torture and the confessions extracted.

The use of torture in Europe slowly began to die out in the seventeenth century. In 1640 it was abolished in England by law, although the torture of suspected 'witches' continued for some time. After the 1789 revolution, France made the use of torture a capital offence. Most German states and Russia abolished it early in the nineteenth century. Indeed the European imperial powers did much to dampen down its use in the many parts of the world where they had their empires.

Torture, however, returned with a vengeance during the twentieth century. It has reached a scale that dwarfs even the darkest Middle Ages. In the civil war that followed the Russian revolution, torture was used sporadically and unsystematically. It was Mussolini's fascists that were the first government in the twentieth century to make torture an official policy of state. The blackshirts invented their own particular technique – pumping a prisoner full of castor oil to 'purge him of the will to exist.'

The German Nazis not only developed the concentration camp for mass extermination; they regularly used torture with their political prisoners. Spain, under Franco, continued using torture right through into the 1970s. Indeed, a particularly horrifying use of torture was revealed as late as 1981, six years after the death of Franco. Spanish police, still staffed by many who had received their training in the days of Franco, were discovered to have been using it against Basque dissidents. The resentment caused by the sacking of senior police officers in the wake of the revelations was said by commentators to have been one of the elements that led to the attempted coup in late February that year.

Much torture these days, to the casual newspaper reader, seems to have bizarre sexual ingredients – electrodes in the testicles and bottles pushed into the anus.

It was the Marquis de Sade two centuries ago who gave his name to sadism, the sexual enjoyment of cruelty.

Sade recognized that it was a perversion and suspected that many other people besides himself derived great pleasure from it. He wrote plays and novels about it and even tried to develop a philosophy to explain it.

More recently, a hundred years ago, the Austrian novelist, Leopold von Sacher-Masoch took Sade's insights even further. He described the sexual abnormality of those who found pleasure in themselves being tortured, hence the term sado-masochistic.

It appears that when torture becomes part of the police apparatus of a state, sadists are attracted to it, or, the latent sadism that exists in many humans is brought to the fore and given licence. On the other hand, even when it has become a well-developed part of police practice, a tough government can bring it to an end, as proven by post-Franco Spain or post-Geisel Brazil where surprisingly few cases now surface.

Torture is already prohibited under the International Covenant on Civil and Political Rights, and under the European Convention and Inter-American Convention on Human Rights. The UN General Assembly has unanimously adopted a declaration against torture. However, there is nothing in the world statute book which *imposes* specific legally binding obligations on states, apart from the European convention which is limited in its geographic application. And this is why Amnesty has lent its support to various efforts to get it formally banned.

Amnesty's campaign, launched in December 1972, to arouse public awareness of the fact that torture not only continued but was actually on the increase, has now become an essential part of its whole programme. Sean MacBride launched the campaign with these words:

> The growth of torture has been described as epidemic. To control dissent and maintain power, governments have submitted torture to intellectual analyses and produced progressively more sophisticated methods of torture, including mind-shattering audio-visual techniques that make the medieval thumb-screw and rack look like children's toys.

The main function of the campaign is to investigate and publicize both individual cases of torture and the methods by which it is inflicted, and to encourage a popular demand internationally for effective action. A petition was circulated in thirty languages calling upon the General Assembly of the UN 'to outlaw immediately the torture of prisoners throughout the world'. By the end of 1973, over one million people had signed. Recognizing that popular pressure, to be effective, must rest on accurate knowledge, Amnesty organized a series of regional conferences to consider the medical, legal, socio-economic and political dimensions of torture. To document the problem, a 224-page report was published, as a prelude to the first international conference convened by Amnesty in Paris in December 1973, attended by over 250 participants and observers from forty countries. This most revealing document, *Report on Torture*, opens with the horrifying testimony of Ayse Semra Eker, born in Turkey in 1949, arrested on 18 May 1972:

> On 18 April 1972, I was attacked by several people in the street. My eyes were covered by a special black band and I was forced into a minibus. The vehicle did not move for a few minutes. During this time I noticed that the people around me were addressing each other with expressions like 'my colonel', 'my major'. They started asking me questions from the first moment they put me into the minibus. When I did not answer, they started threatening me in the following manner. 'You don't talk now,' they would say; 'in a few minutes, when our hands will start roaming in between your legs, you will be singing like a nightingale.' The vehicle travelled for quite a long time before it stopped before a building I could not recognize. When I got off the minibus, I realized that I was in a relatively high open space. I was then taken into the basement of the building before which we had stopped, and then into a rather spacious room. I was surrounded by people whom I guessed to be military officers from the ways they addressed each other. They asked me questions and kept on saying that unless I spoke it would be quite bad for me and that we would have to do 'collective training' together. After a short while they forced me to take off my skirt and stockings and laid me down on the ground and tied my hands and feet to pegs. A person by the name of Umit Erdal beat the soles of my feet for about half an hour. As he beat my soles he kept on saying, 'We

made everybody talk here, you think we shall not succeed with you?' and insulting me. Later, they attached wires to my fingers and toes and passed electric current through my body. At the same time they kept beating my naked thighs with truncheons. Many people were assisting Umit Erdal in this. One was a rather large man, tall, with curly hair and a relatively dark skin. A second was a small man with a relatively dark skin, black hair and a moustache. The third was a young man with a fair skin, dark hair and a moustache. The fourth was rather elderly, of middle stature, and of a dark complexion. He constantly wore dark glasses. The fifth was rather old, fat, of middle stature and with blue eyes and grey hair. At the same time, during the tortures, a grey-haired, stout and elderly colonel, and a grey-haired, blue-eyed, tall and well-built officer would frequently come in and give directives. After a while, they disconnected the wire from my finger and connected it to my ear. They immediately gave a high dose of electricity. My whole body and head shook in a terrible way. My front teeth started breaking. At the same time my torturers would hold a mirror to my face and say: 'Look what is happening to your lovely green eyes. Soon you will not be able to see at all. You will lose your mind. You see, you have already started bleeding in your mouth.' When they finished with electric shocks, they lifted me up to my feet and several of those I mentioned above started beating me with truncheons. After a while I felt dizzy and could not see very well. Then I fainted. When I came to myself, I found out I was lying half-naked in a pool of dirty water. They tried to force me to stand up and run. At the same time they kept beating me with truncheons, kicking me and pushing me against the walls. They then held my hand and hit me with truncheons in my palms and on my hands, each one taking turns. After all this my whole body was swollen and red and I could not stand on my feet. As if all this was not enough, Umit Erdal attacked me and forced me to the ground. I fell on my face. He stood on my back and with the assistance of somebody else forced a truncheon into my anus. As I struggled to stand he kept on saying 'You whore! See what else we will do to you. First tell us how many people did you go to bed with? You won't be able to do it any more. We shall next destroy your womanhood.' They next made me lie on my back and tied my arms and legs to pegs. They attached an electric wire to the small toe of my right foot and another to the end of a truncheon. They tried to penetrate my feminine organ with the end of a truncheon. As I resisted they hit my body and legs with a large axe handle. They soon succeeded in penetrating my sexual organ with the truncheon with the electric wire on, and passed current. I fainted. A little later, the soldiers outside brought in a machine used for pumping air into people and said they would kill me. Then they untied me, brought me to my feet and took me out of the room. With a leather strap, they hanged me from my wrists on to a pipe in the corridor. As I hung half-naked, several people beat me with truncheons. I fainted again. When I woke, I found myself in the same room on a bed. They brought in a doctor to examine me. They tried to force me to take medicines and eat. I was bleeding a dark, thick blood. Some time later they brought in Nuri Colakoglu, who was in the same building as myself, to put more pressure on me. They wanted to show me into what state they had put him. I saw that the nails of his right hand were covered with pus. I realized that they had burned him with cigarette butts. They themselves later confirmed this. The sole of one of his feet was completely black and badly broken. The same night we were transferred to Istanbul together with Nuri Colakoglu. The next morning, the colonel I have already described came into my cell (I do not know where the cell was). He beat me and threatened me. 'Tonight I shall take you where your dead are. I shall have the corpses of all of you burnt. I will have you hanging from the ceiling and apply salt to your cut soles.' When he did not like the answers I gave him, he beat me again; then he had my eyes tied and sent me to another building. I was brought into a small room with my eyes tied. I was tied on the ground to pegs from my arms and ankles and electricity was passed through my right hand and foot.

They then administered falanga. During the whole time I was in Istanbul, my hands were tied to chains. Because of this and because my tongue was split, I could not eat. A doctor would occasionally come to look at me and suggest first aid. One night I heard the sound of a gun and the sound of a man fall and die on the ground very close to me. I cried out: 'Whom have you killed?' They answered: 'It is none of your business. We kill whomever we want and bury him into a hole in the ground. Who would know if we did the same to you?' As I knew already, there was no security for my life.

During the ten days I stayed at MIT (the Turkish Secret Service) the same torture, insults, threats and pressure continued. On 28 April I was sent to the house of detention. Despite the fact that I went to the doctor at the house of detention and explained that I was badly tortured, that my right hand did not hold and that I had other physical complaints including the fact that I had no menstruation for four months in the following period, I was given no treatment. Some of my physical complaints still continue.

[Signed here and at every page]
Semra

In 1974, the campaign involved further individual members and supporters by setting up its Urgent Action system to send appeals on behalf of prisoners feared to be suffering torture and whose cause needs immediate worldwide action. In 1975, Amnesty made a direct appeal to those whose professional work put them in contact with torture. Its 1976 publication, *Professional Codes of Ethics*, points out that 'torture is often furthered and supported through the complicity of doctors, lawyers, judges and other professional groups.' Amnesty elaborated a draft code of conduct for law enforcement, which it submitted to the Council of Europe. Amnesty also set up a Medical Programme, which involved research into torture, in an attempt to enlarge understanding of its effects and to improve the treatment of victims.

The many publications produced for the Campaign Against

Torture include a monthly bulletin, which appears as part of the Amnesty International *Newsletter*.

In 1981, the Swedish government and the International Association of Penal Law, presented drafts for a convention against torture, for discussion by the United Nations Commission on Human Rights. It would provide the authority for bypassing Article 2 of the Charter of the UN, which prohibits nations from interfering in 'matters which are essentially within the domestic jurisdiction' of other states. And, perhaps most important of all, it would give human-rights activists in a state which practises torture some point of reference to which they could work. It would extend the jurisdiction to try a torture offence to countries other than where the crime was committed. So if, for example, an Iraqi police official involved in torture went to London on holiday or business, he could be arrested and tried there and then.

But who will sign a document that would allow international bureaucrats such latitude to pry and interfere in the internal affairs of sovereign nations? What kinds of court would try torturers? How would defence lawyers be appointed? Who would be the judges? Reservations and objections have come from various quarters. Some Western countries objected to instituting criminal proceedings against foreign guests. The main argument, however, was that they would have insufficient evidence to try someone outside his own territory.

In fact, there are already a number of useful working models that the UN could adapt, of which the most recent is the UN convention on the taking of hostages.

For the first time since the working group was set up three years ago, suggestions for implementation, included in the Swedish version, were finally discussed in the March 1981 session of the Human Rights Commission. Proposals included the establishment of a monitoring body to supervise states' behaviour, where necessary by on-the-spot visits. This produced uneasiness in various quarters, particularly European countries, which tend to be sensitive about their prisons.

Eastern Europe, led by their honorary member, Cuba, did not reject the idea, but was anxious to clarify what kind of people would be appointed to the visiting groups. They suggested they should be selected by governments. A new Dutch draft, introduced at the last minute, proposed that visits should only be obligatory where there had been specific complaints of ill-treatment. This let Europe off the hook, but was objected to by other countries, including Brazil, which demanded an optional system with nothing compulsory. At one point, the whole discussion was thrown into disarray by a cable from the legal counsel of the UN in New York. The proposals entrusted the task of international supervision to the Human Rights Committee, established under the International Covenant on Civil and Political Rights. The Dutch amendment provided for the establishment of a committee which would be composed of the members of the already existing Human Rights Committee. The legal counsel's view was that this would not be possible without first amending the original convention, which set up the covenant.

No particular country was guilty of blocking progress, but no consensus was reached. It will not be fully discussed again until the spring of 1982 when the Human Rights Commission has its next annual meeting. There is little sense of government urgency, little press publicity, and an important issue is being left to the slow machinations of faceless diplomats.

To persuade all the countries of the world to turn their back on torture will be a long, tough haul. But Amnesty says we should remember the Red Cross convention, which began with only 11 signatories and now has 140. We should observe the recent changes in China, where the government, once so secretive, is now prepared to admit openly that it has done wrong.

And we should note, too, the rapid changes that have taken place in Europe in the last few decades. Torture was used in recent times in Greece, Spain, Portugal and certain Eastern European countries. It is now fair to say that European countries no longer use systematic physical torture – although psychiatric hospitals in the Soviet Union and the interrogation techniques used by the British Army in Ulster (abandoned as recently as 1972) come near to it.

Amnesty has shown that some governments can be embarrassed by the constantly-drawn attention to their practices. This is why its campaign against torture is so important.

Governments react in different ways to the glare of public opinion. Amnesty analysed the various responses of governments in a document they published in 1973. It found the Greek government at first sensitive to the adverse publicity created by Amnesty accusations of torture. But once Amnesty's findings on torture had been accepted by the European Human Rights Commission, Greece simply denounced the convention and withdrew their co-operation from the Amnesty investigation.

In Britain, however, domestic and international newspaper allegations of brutality and torture in Northern Ireland persuaded the government to initiate an investigation of its own, the findings of which were made public.

Internment without trial was introduced in Northern Ireland on 9 August 1971. That day, 342 arrests were made, and large numbers of arrests continued for several days. By the end of the week, the first reports of brutality on the part of the British Army found their way into Irish newspapers. By mid-October, they had reached the British press, taken up by the *Sunday Times*, forcing the government into action. On 31 August 1971, the Home Secretary appointed a three-man committee of enquiry, chaired by Sir Edmund Compton, to investigate allegations of brutality. Amnesty, however, considered the enquiry hampered from the start by procedures which effectively, if not intentionally, prevented the complainants from testifying before the committee.

The committee did conclude that certain techniques, such as hooding, loud noise, and sleep deprivation had been employed by the security forces in an attempt to extract information from detainees. However, while the critics accused the security forces of physical brutality and torture, the committee's conclusions spoke only of 'physical ill-treatment'. It did not make a finding of brutality because, 'We consider that brutality is an inhuman or savage form of cruelty, and that cruelty implies a disposition to inflict suffering, coupled with indifference to, or pleasure in, the victim's pain.' Amnesty, in a comment on the report, noted: 'According to this definition, the regretted use of electric shock to obtain information would be neither cruel nor brutal.'

About two weeks before the Compton Report was published in early November, Amnesty International set up an International Commission of Enquiry into allegations of torture in Northern Ireland. Unlike the official government enquiry, Amnesty heard evidence given by and on behalf of internees, ex-detainees and ex-internees. However, the UK authorities refused to co-operate and grant facilities to the commission. Members of the security forces were not permitted to testify.

Amnesty's findings concluded that 'it is a form of torture to force a man to stand at the wall in the posture described for many hours in succession, in some cases for days on end, progressively exhausted and driven literally out of his mind by being subjected to continuing noise, and being deprived of food, sleep and even of light.' The report presented medical and psychiatric evidence of the long-term damaging physical and mental after-effects suffered by the victims.

On 16 November, the day on which Compton handed in his findings, another government enquiry was launched – the Parker Commission – with the specific purpose of investigating the interrogation techniques. Although the majority report justified the methods used (provided there were safeguards against excessive use), Lord Gardiner produced a minority report. He refuted his colleagues' conclusions and leant stongly towards the Amnesty position. He described the interrogation methods in Ulster as 'secret, illegal, not morally justifiable and alien to the traditions of what I believe to be the greatest democracy in the world.'

Lord Gardiner's words were heeded. The Conservative government announced that the five techniques – hooding, subjecting to high-pitched noise, forcing to stand for long periods against a wall, and deprivation of sleep and diet – would no longer be used. In June 1972, the Palace Barracks, where these methods had been used, was closed down, interrogation decentralized and new regulations brought into force.

Nevertheless, the government of Ireland decided to bring a case against the UK before the European Commission on Human Rights. The investigation was exhaustive and dragged on for four years. Only in 1976 did the Commission in Strasbourg reach a verdict: guilty of 'torture, inhuman and degrading treatment'. Moreover, it found that this had constituted an administrative practice, condoned by the authorities. Two years later, after an appeal by the UK, the verdict was modified. The 'torture' count was dropped. Amnesty reacted to the Strasbourg court modification with a sharp press release announcing that it would continue to denounce as 'torture' the use by any government anywhere of the interrogation practices used by the UK in Ireland in 1971.

To save the children

In 1978 Amnesty ran a special campaign to highlight the cruelty that is on occasion meted out to children, usually as part of an effort to intimidate, silence or punish their parents. Amnesty's casebook is full of children who have been separated from parents, who have been imprisoned or who have become political refugees. Some children have been orphaned after their parents have been killed or abducted. Some governments have registered the orphans under false names and birth dates to prevent them being traced by next-of-kin. There are instances where women prisoners give birth in prison and the babies are immediately removed and never seen again.

In many of these cases Amnesty has checked, double-checked and triple-checked their authenticity. An Indonesian boy named Narto is one of these:

Mrs S. had been under detention for several years because of her associations with the left-wing women's organization, Gerwani. Her husband had been murdered in Jakarta shortly after the coup attempt and, ironically for her, had been buried at the heroes' cemetery in Jakarta because his death was thought to have been the result of an attack by communist youths. When she was arrested she took one small child with her to prison and left her other children with relatives. The relatives never visited her and she had no news of her children.

One day some years after her arrest she, together with several other women prisoners, was carrying garbage out of the prison where she was being held in Jakarta when, glancing towards the crowded streets, she suddenly began to scream: 'Narto! Narto!' The prison commander who was guarding the women prisoners on garbage duty asked her why she was shouting.

'That's my son,' she cried.

The Commander saw the boy and began to run after him. The boy, seeing a soldier running after him, took to his heels and fled. Many startled bystanders joined in the chase; the boy was soon caught and the commander took him back to the prison. Only then did the child realize that his own mother had been calling him.

She embraced him and carried him into the prison. She was torn between joy at finding her child after years of separation and anger at seeing him in such a wretched condition. Nothing could more poignantly have depicted the tragedy of so many families torn asunder by political events for which they are not responsible.

After bathing and dressing her son in her own clothes, the mother discovered that he had been staying with an uncle who had found the responsibility of looking after him too burdensome and had made his life a misery. The boy had run away and had been living on the streets for weeks, begging and sleeping under railway carriages in sidings.

For some months he remained in prison with his mother until a visiting priest found a place for him with another family and he was able to start going to school again.

Children not only have been separated from their parents when the parents were arrested but they have themselves been imprisoned, often in another jail where they have no contact with their family. A child of eleven, Veneque Duclairon, was among the crowd of peasants who were arrested in Haiti in 1967, following protests about the deteriorating economic conditions. Veneque was isolated from the outside world and given no chance – or even knowledge – of obtaining a lawyer. If he is still alive, he would be twenty-three. But those who have desperately tried to obtain information about him now fear that he may have died in prison.

In South Africa, since the schoolboy protests that triggered off the Soweto riots in which 400 died in 1976, there have been an increasing number of cases of children being locked up. They are often detained without trial under the Terrorism Act. There are well-confirmed reports that they have been interrogated and brutally treated by the police. Some have been kept in solitary confinement.

The South African authorities are not obliged, under the terms of the law, to give information to the parents of children detained incommunicado. On 21 February 1979 the minister of justice stated in parliament that 252 young people under the age of eighteen were detained under the Act. Twenty-five of these were girls. He refused to give details about their ages. However, years before he had admitted that six children, one of fourteen and five of fifteen years of age were imprisoned in the notorious isolated maximum security prison, Robben Island.

The brutality meted out to these children is often severe. Kwezi Kadalie, who was imprisoned in a Johannesburg prison cellar with 150 other children and young people, gave Amnesty this account:

> We squatted on the ground in front of a concrete wall with hands at the back of our necks, while twelve policemen guarded us with automatic pistols ready to fire. Interrogations lasted from nine to twenty-four hours, without a pause, while the prisoners, who had to kneel, were punched with clenched fists in the face and were also

kicked. I was witness to some prisoners having to kneel for six days without sleep and food. One prisoner had to stand up under interrogation, which lasted twenty-four days, with only six hours' pause during the day. We were also threatened with 'You could easily disappear – you could be so unlucky as to fall downstairs and break your neck.'

Amnesty has published side by side two photographs of the seventeen-year-old son of the Paraguayan doctor, painter and philanthropist, Dr Joel Holden Filartiga, who is well known for the help he gives the rural poor and his constant opposition to the Stroesner dictatorship in Paraguay. The photographs tell the gruesome story. On the left is young Joel, a bright, intelligent, attractive boy. On the right is the picture taken during his autopsy. On the night of 30 March 1976, in an effort to intimidate his father, the boy was abducted from his home and tortured to death by the police. The evidence that he died from torture includes medical certificates indicating that the wounds and burns on his body are similar to those resulting from severe beating and torture with electric shock treatment.

One of Amnesty's most terrible stories is told by the mother of Tamara (who wishes to keep her identity secret). Tamara was three when she was carted off to prison, there to be tortured in full view of her mother. 'They undressed my little daughter, and whipped her with a leather whip. The put her in a barrel with ice water and held her head under the water until she almost drowned. They threatened to rape her and whipped her again. This was repeated four times a day for four days.'

The Soviet Union has raised almost to a science the process of separating children from their parents in a carefully calibrated campaign of bringing pressure to bear. This has happened particularly to families who belong to religious communities. The government decree 'On Religious Associations' permits religious activities only by congregations which have been officially registered. Many congregations, however, refuse to register under the conditions laid down or alternatively have had their requests refused. Even if registered, the decree is restricting: it is forbidden 'to organize special gatherings of children, young people or women for prayer.' Numerous cases have been reported to Amnesty International of Baptists, Pentecostalists and Adventists who have had some of their children taken into state care for ignoring the decree.

In East Germany, too, children are used as a tool for punishing their parents. Prisoners of conscience in the German Democratic Republic have the opportunity of emigrating to West Germany once they have served their sentences. This is because of a special scheme operated by the two governments. The children of the prisoners are usually allowed to leave too, to follow their parents, but often only after months of anxious waiting. Amnesty has evidence of ten children whom the authorities have refused to allow to leave. The children were placed in state homes or with foster families.

In one particular instance, an architect and his wife tried to escape with their two children from East Germany to Austria via Czechoslovakia. They were caught and sentenced to three years in prison. The children were taken away and their parents were not allowed to keep in touch with them. In 1975 the parents were allowed to leave for West Berlin. All their efforts to have the children join them have been rebuffed. The children have been adopted by another couple.

The killing of a hundred children in the Central African Empire, on the authority and probably with the active connivance of Emperor Bokassa, is the subject of Chapter 7. Less is known about the students and children who have been arrested, tortured and killed in Ethiopia. In 1974 Emperor Haile Selassie was overthrown by a left-wing coup. His regime was feudal and oppressive. However, nothing he did can quite compare with what has happened since.

One of the worst incidents known to Amnesty occurred in April 1977 when soldiers and paramilitary guards in Addis Ababa attacked a gathering of students and other young people on suspicion that they were preparing an anti-government demonstration. Amnesty estimate that 500 young people were killed that night. The secretary-general of the Swedish Save the

Children Fund, Hakan Landelius, reported: 'A thousand children have been massacred in Addis Ababa and their bodies, lying in the streets, are ravaged by roving hyenas . . . The bodies of murdered children, mostly aged from eleven to thirteen years, can be seen heaped by the roadside.'

Later that year, the Ethiopian chief of state, Colonel Mengistu Haile Mariam, ordered what he called 'Red Terror' to be inflicted on 'counter-revolutionaries' in response to a wave of assassinations that had taken the lives of many government officers.

The Red Terror campaign lasted six months. There were mass arrests of students and young people and it is estimated that five thousand of them, between the ages of twelve and twenty-five, were killed. During the peak period, a hundred or more were killed each night. Summary executions often took place in public places and the bodies displayed with placards warning 'This was a counter-revolutionary. The Red Terror will flourish.' Parents on occasion were allowed to buy the bodies for burial – 'paying for the bullet' the revolutionaries called it.

Since 1976, a team of volunteer doctors working on behalf of Amnesty International has been studying the problem of children who have been exposed to imprisonment and torture. They have concentrated on examining fifty-eight Chilean children now living in Denmark. A significant number of them show serious psychosomatic symptoms. Many are nervous: noises such as cars braking or people speaking loudly make them cry. Some have difficulty falling asleep and have recurring nightmares full of images of police, soldiers, murder and death. Others are introverted and depressed, finding it difficult to make contact and friendship with other children. A few are aggressive and rough.

The doctors sadly conclude that many of them will have serious social and physical problems for years to come, maybe for the rest of their lives.

Against the terror trade

Without doubt, the most controversial of Amnesty's recent decisions on its future development is the one made to work against sales of repressive technology.

In 1979, after years of painful debate, the International Executive Council elaborated a carefully nuanced position. It is by no means a blanket condemnation on the issue of selling arms. Nevertheless, its implications are clear – and have been made plain in El Salvador and Guatemala: Amnesty is going to use its muscle to try and stop governments sending military and police equipment and the advisers to go with them when they will be used by governments to detain prisoners of conscience, to carry out torture and executions, or to repress innocent and defenceless people.

The total value of the international arms trade is now estimated at £10 billion a year. Even the most sophisticated weapons can be purchased on the open arms market – sometimes before they enter the arsenals of the producer countries.

The Third World is taking an increasing share of world military expenditure, up from 3 per cent of the total in 1955 to 14 per cent today.

The Third World is spending three times more on the military than it receives in official development aid.

The Third World, no one needs to be told, is the new battleground, where besides solving its own multi-faceted disputes, it stages and fights the proxy wars of East and West. Since 1945 nearly all the wars fought have been in the Third World. Around three-quarters of the current international arms trade is now with the Third World and is still on the increase. The number of aircraft, missiles, armoured vehicles and warships supplied to the Third World in the last half-dozen years is equal to that sent in the previous twenty.

Arms sales are increasing at 12 per cent a year, far above the rate of economic growth of even the fastest-growing developing countries. Africa is increasing its purchases at 20 per cent a year.

Since the Third World patterns its armies on the industrialized states, these costs will continue to escalate. Weapon systems are becoming more intricate and more expensive and obsolescence sets in quicker as every year goes by. Long-range surface to air missiles went to one developing nation in 1958 and to twenty-seven in 1975. Supersonic aircraft went to one developing nation in 1957 and to forty-three in 1975.

The newspapers periodically highlight arms racketeers and their illegal traffic. The truth is that the illegal trade is no more than 4 per cent of total arms transfers. The arms trade is £10 billion a year of officially sanctioned business. Its motivation is a mixture of profit and politics – and it's not always easy to see where one begins and the other leaves off.

Take, for example, the Middle East, where 70 per cent of US arms exports go. The vast sales of new weapons to Iran and Saudi Arabia, begun by President Nixon and continued by his successors, have been justified not only by the imperatives of national security but by the need for the United States to regain some of its lost petrodollars.

Who is to blame? The Third World countries themselves have a lot to answer for. It is they who too often invite in outside powers to help settle their disputes. It is they who have grandiose ideas of what being a modern state implies. Libya, through whose territory Rommel and Montgomery fought their great desert campaigns in the Second World War, has today twice as many tanks as those two generals had together.

The major culprit is the superpowers. Selling guns is a crude way of winning friends and influencing people. It is quicker and easier to administer an arms programme than economic aid. It is also more profitable in the short term. In fact, the Russians especially seem to prefer it. In Africa, the Soviet Union spends about three times more on guns than butter.

The third culprit is the competition between the Western nations themselves. At one time the United States was in the arms trade business almost alone. These days both Britain and France are seriously at the game of outselling the Americans.

The United States is still the Third World's largest arms salesman, providing, according to the Stockholm International Peace Research Institute, 38 per cent of the world's totals. Britain and France, however, are providing another 18 per cent. Indeed, adding all the Western sales together, one gets the figure of 61 per cent of the total arms sales to the Third World. The Soviet Union and its allies in contrast provide only 35 per cent. The balance is made up by China, 2 per cent, and the Third World's own domestic production, 2 per cent.

Amnesty's search through this thicket of arms traffic to find a legitimate role for itself has not been easy. Many of its members feel instinctively that the arms trade is bad. Yet this is a moral judgment that only has any validity if it can be shown that the arms trade is a direct instrument repressing human rights. Many Amnesty supporters and staff members have argued that it is extremely difficult to draw lines. If one starts talking about arms, then it will not be long before Amnesty is asked to condemn the economic system of the country. Some will say capitalism or socialism is repressive. Amnesty will lose the directness and simplicity that gives it such a wide measure of support. Moreover, sovereign countries, they say, have a legitimate right to buy in modern weapons, and repression, if the government is determined to carry it out, can be done with First World War rifles and riding-whips.

In the end, with countries such as El Salvador and Guatemala erupting into civil war, where equipment supplied from abroad has been used so obviously as the weaponry of a repressive regime, the more conservative forces in Amnesty have had to go along with a new role for Amnesty.

Amnesty have since 1979 initiated three campaigns against the transfer of repressive technology. All had to be approved by the International Executive Committee. The first was the West German section's campaign to stop its government sending pistols and ammunition to Guatemala. The second was an Amnesty International decision to campaign against the United States making military transfers to El Salvador (see Chapter 4). The third was a broad campaign launched by the

British Section and built around a pamphlet published in early 1981, 'The Repression Trade'. The writing of this had been triggered by press revelations that Idi Amin's secret police in Uganda were using British equipment.

The British Section wrote to government ministers suggesting that they should undertake a review of the system for licensing the export of military equipment. It told the government that Pye Telecommunications, a well-known electronics firm, was supplying materials to the 'State Research Centre' which, Amnesty estimated, had killed between 100,000 and 500,000 people in the eight years of Amin's rule.

Pye and other firms involved took the position that the morals of the case were not their responsibility. If the government wanted to forbid it, then they should legislate. Until then, they were free to sell to whom they wanted. The firms persisted in their competitive sales efforts, although Amin's regime was often in default of payment and despite the fact that one salesman was hammered to death by State Research Centre agents, apparently on account of deficiencies in the supply of equipment by his firm.

British Amnesty, during the latter half of 1979, kept up a continuous lobbying effort. In the end, Prime Minister Margaret Thatcher replied herself. Resisting Amnesty's call for tighter surveillance and restrictions of trade in technology that could be used for repressive purposes, she said that widening 'the scope of the existing controls would present us with very considerable implications for our trade and our relations with other countries.'

The British Section of Amnesty felt that it had a particularly strong case for continuing their dialogue with the government when Lord Carrington, the foreign secretary, made the decision in the summer of 1980 to resume arms sales to Chile and then a month later announced that it was going to ban arms sales to the government of Grenada. A small island in the Caribbean, Grenada had been taken over after a left-wing revolution. A few people had been put in prison but it was small beer compared with the tens of thousands incarcerated and thousands tortured in Chile. Nevertheless, Carrington had been brutally frank: '. . . our policy is to sell arms to our friends and those whom we wish to encourage to defend themselves.'

Amnesty so far has not caused the government to change its mind. But it has clearly been embarrassed by the powerful critics who have joined Amnesty's cause, including Cardinal Basil Hume of Westminster. He wrote to the government: 'I most seriously question the wisdom of lifting the embargo on arms sales [to Chile] imposed by the British government in 1974 . . . I understand that in July 1980 alone, over 1000 people have been arrested . . . I am also told that prolonged and sophisticated methods of torture have been introduced once again.'

The government's answer to Amnesty is to say the line is difficult to draw. Anything, including a skipping rope, can be used for repression. And they use this argument to duck the hard issues. British Amnesty in a sense give the government ammunition for this defence when they write in their pamphlet:

> Given the contemporary development of military and security technology, much of it with internal application, it is hardly surprising that regimes that use repression in order to contain and defeat dissent should look to Britain and to other world leaders in this technology to provide them with what they need. The range of these technologies is a wide one. The consequence is that the suppression of dissent in far distant countries frequently becomes operationally dependent upon sources of supply in the advanced industrial countries. This may happen without even the suppliers knowing what is happening (e.g., the reported use of Western computer technology by the Soviet KGB).

Restraint in the export of repressive technology is a difficult cause for Amnesty to push. One can see why it has provoked so much debate and dissent within the organization and why, in this case, the British government, aware of the divisions, tries to frame its response in the way it does.

But it is an issue that will remain alive. However difficult it is to draw lines, it is clear, as in El Salvador today, that US arms supplies are a major factor in undermining human rights. Amnesty International kept up its pressure on the US government all through 1981 and one can safely assume, given the pressures from national groups, particularly in Britain, West Germany and the United States, that Amnesty will get more involved in this cause, not less.

4. Central America: Guatemala, El Salvador, Nicaragua

The little slice of land that links the great continents of North and South America is now the place where human rights are most violated. Proportional to its population, more people are being tortured and killed for their beliefs here than anywhere else on the globe.

For decades, the Central American countries were part of a global backwater where life ran its painful course in societies long used to the writ of the local strong man. Now, rather suddenly, they have become the focus of superpower interests. The United States, long the passive supporter of the local strong-men, has become an activist participant, not 100 per cent on the side of the dictators, but often so. On the other side are the guerrillas, supported, it is said, by the Cubans and, through them, by Moscow.

It is a simple view of life and the analysis that follows attempts to explain its complexities. One thing is clear, however; the suffering is of a magnitude scarcely comprehensible. Too many brave, dedicated and honourable people have lost their lives.

Amnesty's work here is vital. It has not been able to do enough. But the work persists, day by day, attempting to roll back the holocaust. All one can say is that without Amnesty it would probably be worse.

The three countries discussed are all tightly linked, the history of each overlapping with the others. Nicaragua is where the revolution has just been, El Salvador is where it is happening and Guatemala is where it is to come. These countries are so small, so cheek by jowl, that what happens in one produces tidal waves in the others. To describe one without the other two would have been to paint only a corner of the picture.

Guatemala: Amnesty's front burner

Guatemala is no longer a banana republic. The days are long gone when the United Fruit Company, furious at being deprived of its banana estates by a reforming government in the 1950s, could expect the CIA to help overthrow the president. Neither is Guatemala a political fiefdom of one man, as its neighbour Nicaragua used to be in Somoza's day. Nor is it ruled by an oligarchy as in El Salvador. Until recently, to judge by outward appearances, it was a successfully developing country, still with much poverty, to be sure, but also with high annual rates of growth, industrializing fast, discovering rich deposits of oil and nickel, and building up a broad-based middle class.

Yet behind this façade of economic well-being lies the most ruthless oppressive regime in Latin America. This is a view shared by Amnesty International. According to an Amnesty report published in February 1981, over three thousand people have been killed and another six hundred have simply disappeared since 1978, most of them victims of government-sponsored death squads. The report, in an indictment unusually strong even by Amnesty International standards, concludes that 'the selection of targets for detention and murder, and the deployment of official forces for extra-legal operations can be pinpointed to secret offices in an annexe to Guatemala's National Palace, under the direct control of the President of the Republic.'

Thomas Hammarberg, Amnesty's Secretary-General, told me that in 1981 Guatemala was Amnesty's top priority. I therefore decided, as Amnesty entered its twenty-first year, to visit Guatemala to see at first hand the kind of problems Amnesty has to deal with. Before I left, Hammarberg cautioned me: 'Guatemala is not a typical Amnesty country – there are no political prisoners, only political killings.' Amnesty's usual practice of dealing with human rights violations – the adoption of prisoners – was fruitless in the Guatemalan case, he explained. Most of the time, news of an arrest arrives after the prisoner is dead. On some occasions, when the notification has been immediate and Amnesty has been able to intervene within hours of the arrest, there have been a handful of successes. But, he added, no more than ten or fifteen in the whole of the last ten years.

Guatemala, I found, is a country in the grip of fear. Government critics, with very rare exceptions, will not be seen talking to a foreign reporter inside Guatemala. To do so is to court assassination.

Surprisingly, to enter Guatemala was no great effort. Passport control was lax and it was easy to disappear into the airport throng with only a tourist visa. Downtown the atmosphere, superficially at least, was easy-going. There were a few soldiers lazing in the sunshine. Even a visit to the press spokesman for the army, Major Francisco Djalma Dominguez, whose predecessor was murdered by guerrillas a year before, was made without inspection of papers and with only a pleasant middle-aged secretary to question one's purpose. The single soldier on the doorstep was day-dreaming.

All this was deceptive. The violence comes and goes like the seismic eruptions that periodically spill out from Guatemala's breath-taking chain of bubbling volcanoes. On occasion they reach tragic proportions.

Every day the morning newspapers have more of the same: ten or a dozen bodies discovered, another wave of killing. Since 1966 there have been 30,000 deaths. The bodies of the victims have been found piled up in ravines, dumped at roadsides or buried in mass graves.

Guatemala has the worst human rights record of any Latin-American country. The violence has not reached the crescendo it has in El Salvador today, nor have as many people 'disappeared' in as short a time as after the coup in Chile in 1973, but no country can be compared with Guatemala for long-term, systematic assassinations and torture.

Guatemala has a long tradition of political violence. The

Guatemalan Nobel prize-winning novelist, Miguel Angel Asturias, wrote about it in 1920 in his novel, *El Senor Presidente*.

Since 1944 the Guatemala ruling class has been living in fear of a left-wing revolution. In that year a military rebellion broke the grip of fourteen years' rule by Jorge Ubico. A university don, Juan Jose Arevalo, was given the job of sorting out the long legacy of misrule, social deprivation and economic inequality. He stepped down in 1951 and in free and fair elections his defence minister, Colonel Jacobo Arbenz Guzman, took over the reigns of government.

Guatemala at that time was a classic 'banana republic'. Arbenz, a determined reformer, decided to end once and for all the United Fruit Company's control of vast estates and its near monopoly of banana production. The first beneficiaries were to be the Indian population. Despite their spectacular cultural heritage – their direct ancestors, the Mayans, were the great civilization that built mammoth temples and houses and pioneered major breakthroughs in astronomy and mathematics – the Indians were a people who had experienced worsening poverty. They made up half of the population – though most of them did not speak Spanish, the majority language – and they were becoming increasingly overcrowded on their traditional territory, the mountainside fields. Their infant mortality rate was high, their diet was deteriorating annually, and younger sons were reduced to scraping a living on precipitous slopes that barely held the soil to the mountainside.

Arbenz issued a decree expropriating the large estates. In doing so, he took on imperial capitalism at its crudest. The United Fruit Company for decades had had its way throughout Central America, much of the Caribbean and parts of South America. By the 1950s United Fruit's investment in Guatemala accounted for almost two-thirds of the country's total foreign capital. It owned 2,500,000 square kilometres of territory, the country's single railway line, and had great influence in many of Guatemala's most important institutions.

Arbenz's experiments not only threatened United Fruit, they aroused Washington's fears. At the height of the Cold War, the

US government was afraid of anything that smacked of communist influence. No matter that Arbenz himself was clearly not a communist and that only four out of fifty-six Guatemalan congressmen were self-confessed communists at that time. The Central Intelligence Agency was asked by President Eisenhower to help overthrow Arbenz, using as a cover a group of mercenaries and exiles.

The deed was done. United Fruit retrieved its estates, Arbenz and his sympathizers were hunted down and killed. Arbenz's successors ruled largely by decree. Occasionally there were street demonstrations led by students and trade unionists. But nothing really disturbed the status quo until 1960. Then a small group of nationalist army officers attempted an uprising. It came to nothing in itself. It was the start, however, of a guerrilla campaign which has waxed and waned ever since.

By 1966 the guerrillas' strongholds in the mountain ranges of Sierra de Las Minas and Sierra de Santa Cruz seemed a genuine threat to the government which, with the aid of paramilitary civilian groups, moved ruthlessly to suppress them. Colonel John Webber, United States military attaché, was reported by *Time* magazine (26 January 1968) to have acknowledged that 'It was his idea' to mobilize these groups, which were the precursors of the 'independent' civilian death squads that still exist today. In June 1966, the first leaflets of the Mano Blanco (White Hand) appeared. (Mano was the acronym for the Movimiento Anti-Communista Nacional Organizado [National Organized Anti-Communist Movement].) The guerrilla movement did not re-emerge until the mid-1970s, when a group surfaced calling itself, disarmingly, the Guerrilla Army of the Poor. By 1981, there were another three groups at work in different parts of the country, concentrated in the highlands and mountains of the north – the People's Armed Organization, the Revolutionary Armed Forces and a breakaway branch of Guatemala's communist trade union.

Their members are few – the army says only two hundred, sympathizers say one or two thousand. But they are multiplying fast and, to the surprise of observers of the Latin American scene, are winning a great deal of support and membership from the Indians. (When Che Guevara was hunted down and killed by the Bolivian army in 1967, it was widely observed by both left and right that he made the mistake of thinking the Latin American Indians and mestizos would be willing supporters of the guerrillas. In fact they were too apathetic and fearful and he was quickly isolated.) Guatemala is the first country where significant numbers of Indians have been politically active to the point of lending their support in measurable terms to the guerrilla effort to overthrow the government.

While the guerrilla movement's activities have been sporadic, the right-wing pro-government death squads have maintained their murderous march. Executions without trial began in 1966, reached a peak in 1971, diminished briefly in the prelude to the 1974 elections and have become more and more numerous ever since.

Amnesty International has always maintained that the association of the death-squads with important key government and political figures was close enough to cause serious concern. In its 1981 annual report, it talked of the 'political murder' encouraged by the Guatemalan government. But it stopped short of saying that the killings were directed by the government: Amnesty at that time was still awaiting irrefutable evidence to confirm their suspicions.

This nuanced approach was discarded on 18 February 1981, when, in one of the most outspoken reports ever issued by Amnesty, it stated unequivocally: 'People who oppose or are imagined to oppose the government are systematically seized without warrant, tortured and murdered . . . these tortures and murders are part of a deliberate and long-standing programme of the Guatemalan government.'

The government for its part denies having made a single political arrest or holding a single political prisoner. The 'disappearances', senior government officials told me, are brought about by right-wing and left-wing death squads.

The Amnesty report is an accumulation of horrors that point a firm finger at the government. My own conversations with exiles in Costa Rica and with the vice-president of Guatemala who fled the country in late 1980, back it up.

Nearly 3000 Guatemalans have been seized without warrant and killed since General Lucas Garcia became president of Guatemala in 1978. Many of them have been tortured. Death for some had been quick and clean, a bullet in the head. Others had died slowly and painfully, suffocated in a rubber hood or strangled with a garrotte. One letter received by Amnesty International described a secret grave in a gorge, used by army units who had seized and murdered the leaders of a village earthquake reconstruction committee (Guatemala was rocked by an earthquake in 1976; 20,000 people died):

> More than thirty bodies were pulled out of the 120-foot gorge . . . but farmers who live near the site told me there were more bodies, many more, but that the authorities didn't want to admit as much or go to the trouble of dragging them out. They said vehicles have been arriving at the edge of the gorge at night, turning out their lights, engaging in some mysterious activities.
>
> We went down to the bottom of the ravine the next day . . . About halfway down the ravine the stench became unbearable. Barely visible in the dim light were piles of bodies. Most were in extremely advanced states of decomposition, but still with remnants of tattered clothing.

The people killed are often, like these villagers, simple peasant folk, but who have shown some initiative like running an earthquake reconstruction committee that badgers the government for help, or a co-operative or church leadership training group. Overwhelmingly, it is the incipient peasant leadership that has suffered the most. The next sizeable group to have been penalized are students and labour leaders. After that, a whole range of professional people have disappeared – journalists, clergy, doctors and educators and the cream of the Social Democratic and Christian Democratic parties.

Anyone who speaks out and complains, much less organizes a formal opposition grouping, is the target for assassination.

How did Amnesty arrive at its conviction that the government were in charge of the killings? A series of violent events, observed and recorded by reliable witnesses, all suggest government involvement.

The most widely reported mass killing by regular army forces took place on 29 May 1978. One hundred Indians, including five children, were shot dead in the town square of Panzos. The Indians had been protesting about land rights. They were cold-bloodedly shot down by soldiers positioned on rooftops and inside buildings. Townspeople have told Amnesty that mass graves were dug two days before the killings. In January 1980 a group of Indians occupied the Spanish embassy to protest against this and other abuses carried out by the army in El Quiche province. The government, outraged by the protest, ordered the army to attack the embassy. One peasant, Gregorio Yuja Xona, and the Spanish ambassador were the only survivors. Yuja Xona was held under police guard in a hospital, then, without explanation, the police allowed him to be removed. His body was later found, mutilated.

There have been a number of occasions when prisoners officially acknowledged to be in police custody have been found dead – for example, thirty-seven killed by garrotte in 1979 and dumped in a ravine. Or the twenty-six labour unionists, who in June 1980 were arrested by plainclothesmen while the street was closed to traffic by uniformed police, and have not been seen since. The government denies holding them.

There is evidence from one of the very few who have escaped after being picked up. Amnesty International has published a taped interview with the former prisoner. He describes how he was held in Huehuetenango Military Base and tortured by being pulled up by his testicles and hooded with a rubber inner tube of a tyre lined with quicklime. His testimony is terrifying in its simple directness.

Before my very eyes they killed three people; they strangled them. The way they killed them was with a piece of rope, a kind of noose, which they put round the neck and then used a stick to tighten it like a tourniquet from behind – handcuffed, and with their heads held down in the trough. When they came out, their eyes were open; they'd already turned purple. It took at most three minutes in the water. I also saw that one of these three, a boy, when they threw him down on the floor with his clothes wet, was still moving and one of the officers ordered them to put the tourniquet on him again until he stopped moving.

They just showed me the other six bodies and said the same thing would happen to me if I tried to lie to them.

On other occasions, plainclothesmen have been over-powered and found to possess identification papers associating them with the intelligence services. One such event occurred when Victor Manuel Valverth Morales, student representative on the executive committee of the Universidad de San Carlos, was seized at gunpoint on 10 June 1980 by two men in plainclothes inside the university school of engineering in Guatemala City. His assailants did not identify themselves as law enforcement officers or produce a warrant for his arrest; when he tried to escape they shot him several times. Other students then came to his assistance and overpowered the attackers, one of whom, Adan de Jesus Melgar Solares, was murdered by students when a force of uniformed army troops attacked his student captors inside the university precincts.

Students took the dead man's identification card, which showed him to be a military intelligence agent from the 'General Aguilar Santa Maria' army base in Jutiapa Province. The second man, who was not harmed, carried an identification card issued by the Guardia de Hacienda (Treasury police) for 'Servicio Especial' (Special Service), in the name of Baldomero Mendoza. The government denied that either of the two men who attacked Victor Valverth were members of the security services, but the dead man's widow later confirmed his identity to the press.

I spent four hours in Mexico City with the researcher for Amnesty International, cross-examining him on how Amnesty garnered such a wealth of information and established its truth. It is clearly an exhaustive process. External organizations – church, union and political – who have live networks inside Guatemala feed him with information all the time. He and other members of the small Amnesty team have to evaluate carefully, learning over time who can be trusted, who has a propensity to exaggerate and who they can ask to double – and even triple-check. When it came to the crucial indictment – that these killings were organized from an annexe to the central palace, Amnesty's method of verification and double-checking indicated to me, an outside investigator, the difficulties and complexities that confront Amnesty.

Amnesty research on the matter required a visit to Washington in 1979 to look at the records and files of United States government agencies. With access granted under the Freedom of Information Act, they were able to pinpoint key developments in the Guatemalan security apparatus.

A 1974 document described the Centro Regional de Telecommunicaciones as Guatemala's principal presidential-level security agency working with a 'high-level security/administrative network' linking 'the principal officials of the National Police, Treasury Police, Detective Corps, the Presidential House and the Military Communications Centre'. This organization has built up a sophisticated filing system listing anyone who might be a potential leader of anti-government movements or a critic of the government.

Amnesty also knew from reliable sources that the agency is directed by the joint head of the presidential general staff and military intelligence, Major Hector Montalvan.

How can Amnesty confirm, however, that the organization is something more than a records agency? The research team answers by pointing to the lines of command under Major Montalvan, which lead direct to some of the killings described above, the capture by dissidents of papers on agents they have overpowered, and denunciations from people who are well known and trusted and who have friends and relatives who work in the Presidential Palace.

Montalvan's headquarters are situated in the presidential

guard annexe to the National Palace, adjoining the presidential house. I walked around it. Next door, innocently sandwiched into the same blocks, is the office of the Obras Pontificias Misionales. For a moment I assumed I was at the wrong building, but only yards further on a soldier peered over a balcony and caught my eye; and to his right a television camera monitored the street. On top of the roof were three large telecommunications masts and around the side of the building was the main entrance. In this sidestreet, which on the other side had the door to the president's house, heavily armed soldiers stared at passers-by. Cars with foreign plates or without licence plates at all were parked alongside.

A slip of the tongue in a later conversation confirmed that this was indeed the centre of intelligence operations. I was interviewing the head of press information of the army, Major Dominguez. In an aside he told me he knew that a distinguished social democratic politician had been bumped off by a rival. I asked him how he knew. 'You see, I used to be military intelligence. But don't tell anyone or the guerrillas will kill me.' Casually as I could, I said, 'Oh yes, you had your office in the presidential annexe.' Surprised, he nodded: 'Yes, but remember, don't tell anyone what I've told you.'

My loyalty to secrecy in such a situation is, I regret, thin. The only task left to do was to confirm the Amnesty investigators' conviction that the intelligence operation did do the killings.

Since in Guatemala it is impossible to talk to anyone about politics frankly, I flew to Costa Rica and met some of the Guatemalan exiles who live there. In the relaxed atmosphere of this green and pleasant land – Costa Rica has been democratic for all but a year since it gained its independence from Spain in 1821 – it was possible to talk to people who underlined Amnesty's findings. Frustratingly, they were still secondary sources. They insisted that they knew soldiers or officials who had links with the intelligence agency. But only one person I met said he had sources right within the heart of the operations centre.

Some of them knew Elias Barohona y Barahona who had been the press spokesman of the minister of the interior until he resigned in September 1980. He had told them (and Amnesty has his statement) that blank letter-head stationery of the alleged 'death squads', Ejercita Secreto Anticomunista and Escuadron de la Muerte, was stored in the office of the minister of the interior. According to him, the lists of people to be eliminated were prepared from the records of military intelligence and the national police. They included the names of 'trade union leaders and peasants provided by the Department of Trade Unions of the Ministry of Labour and by a sector of private enterprise.' He also said that an officer in military intelligence had told him that the 'definitive lists' of those to be killed were 'approved at meetings attended by the ministers of defence and the interior and the chief of the general staff of the army.'

Again, it could be argued that this is still a secondary source. Neither Amnesty nor I have been able to talk directly to people involved in the command structure of the intelligence agency. A visit to Washington DC, however, brought me close to doing so. I called on General Lucas's former vice-president, Francisco Villagran Kramer now living in exile in the USA. He had just finished reading the Amnesty report and although it had been written without any consultation with him, he said it was 'absolutely accurate'. While he was in power, he said, he learned how the system worked and is in no doubt that the overwhelming majority of killings are decided in the presidential palace. Nevertheless, he argues that the independent death squads do play a role, a point which Amnesty in its report seems to play down.

Whenever he wanted to intercede on behalf of a person who had 'disappeared' he went to one of three persons – Montalvan, the chief of the president's staff and of intelligence; the army chief; or the minister of the interior. These were the three, working through Montalvan, who were responsible for deciding who should be picked up and killed. The fact that Villagran was successful half a dozen times proved to him that those arrested were in hands under their command. There was also the telling fact that others who had been picked up in the same swoops never reappeared.

His conclusion was reinforced by the scores of army officers who came up to him privately and said, 'Mr Vice-President, you're a friend of so-and-so. Do your best to get him out,' or 'Let him know they're after him.' Only if the army was intimately involved in the assassinations would this happen.

There was even a man known to him personally, Villagran told me, who was phoned by President Lucas himself and told to get out while the going was good. Although ideological opponents, they were old school buddies and the President was moved to short-cut the normal process of his governmental machine.

The final piece of evidence presented by Villagran was the information given to him by a military officer. According to Villagran, he was senior enough in the military hierarchy to know how the system functioned. The senior army officers were a clique with an *esprit de corps* developed over the years of intimate contact. Villagran, who says he became convinced against his will that the government was responsible for the killings, had no reason to doubt what he was told in confidence by this man.

After a series of conversations in Guatemala about who has killed whom, why and where, it becomes difficult to keep a sense of perspective and to remember that the deaths are not simply a total to be compared with, say, deaths in neighbouring El Salvador. Moreover, conversations with senior army officers and government officials lull one quickly into false feelings of security. Their hospitality and bonhomie is disarming. Often enough, probing questions are turned aside graciously and without rancour. Of course, they do not have much to do with the soldiers and intelligence officials who actually carry out the tortures and killings. They give the orders and the lower ranks implement them. Blood never touches their hands: it is an antiseptic world that allows them to make their decisions with the required single-mindedness and ruthlessness.

After a morning of such meetings, I decided to drive the 140 kilometres from Guatemala City to Lake Atilan, a silver sheen of water lying below three cloud-covered volcanoes. The boat takes eighty minutes to reach the village of Santiago. Described by one tourist I had talked to as a 'Shangri-la', it certainly gives that first impression. Small houses, inhabited by Indians, rise up the hillside from the water's edge. The men are dressed in broad-striped white pants cut off just below the knees, the hems full of coloured birds laboriously embroidered by their womenfolk. All the women have skirts, blouses and shawls of an intricate weave, combining deep reds, browns and yellows, so that when, as I arrived, they poured out of the village Catholic church after mass there was a riot of colour.

I found the American missionary father, an elderly man who told me he was standing in for the young parish priest who had returned to the United States after the governor of the province had warned him that his life was in danger. Six months earlier, twenty-five Indians had been murdered. Four of them ran a little radio station established by the parish; the others were active in the agricultural co-op. 'Anyone who shows any leadership potential gets wiped out,' the priest told me — an opinion that echoed the Amnesty report.

Set against the alleged government-inspired murders, killings by the guerrilla forces are still on a small scale. Although it is difficult to get firm figures — with the army claiming they lost only sixty-two men in 1980 — a reasonably well-informed estimate would be that about three hundred army, police and government officials have been killed in the last twelve months. The conflict at the moment is over-whelmingly one-sided.

Full-scale guerrilla warfare is still some time away, although assessments on its imminence vary widely. Army spokesmen believe they have the situation contained, and point to the relaxed atmosphere in Guatemala City. It is true that, compared with Belfast, for example, the army presence is relatively unobtrusive. Western diplomats say that the build-up of the guerrillas has accelerated in the last twelve months. The resentment bred by the wanton killings has fuelled their cause more than anything else. Exiled sources say that the country is becoming politicized and polarized very fast. Many of the student, church, labour and peasants' organizations, together with the Social Democrats and some Christian Democrats, have joined the Frente Democratico Contra La Represion (Democratic Front Against Repression) – a loose but firm coalition based in Costa Rica. Although distanced from the guerrillas, their clandestine educational work inside Guatemala helps produce sympathy for them.

However, the changes necessary to avert an attempted revolution are not impossible to contemplate. Diplomats and many dissidents agree that if the government-inspired violence were brought to a halt, if fair elections were allowed and the moderate left and the centre 'allowed room to breathe', if the Indians were protected from land-grabs and given effective agricultural and medical aid, the guerrillas would soon be isolated, enough of their objectives achieved.

These reforms are less drastic than those put into effect in Nicaragua or those expected by the opposition forces in El Salvador – largely because, unlike their neighbours, the majority of Guatemalan peasants own their own land, however poor and tiny are the plots, and, although many are landless and there is the added problem of 'land-grabbing' by local planters who encroach on Indian land, land distribution is not the vital issue. For all that, the will to change course does not seem to exist. Rule by violence has become embedded in the fabric of the Guatemalan government. And the government has the overwhelming support of the middle class. The few senior businessmen who have tried to warn the government of the need for change have been intimidated by the assassination of some of their colleagues.

Does Amnesty itself have any influence? Superficially, one could say, quite the reverse. The killings have escalated since Amnesty sent a mission to Guatemala in 1979. Francisco Villagran, for one, feels that Amnesty's pressure in the short-run might have been counterproductive. Government officials are obsessed about Amnesty, hardly letting a week go by without denouncing it, just as they made President Carter's human rights policy an object to be scorned and repudiated.

Yet over the long run Amnesty may have been more effective than Carter. For many years, because of pressure on Washington from Britain, worried about Guatemalan threats to Belize, there had been a gradual reduction of arms sales to Guatemala. By the time Carter and his arms sales policy came on the scene, Guatemala, not having much left to lose, itself decided it would be better off without US arms. Apart, then, from resisting suggestions from the US embassy to try and woo the Guatemalans to better behaviour by dangling the possibility of renewed arms sales and counter-insurgency training, Carter's pressure didn't add up to very much. The occasional critical speech and an attempt, which Guatemala resisted, to send them a liberal ambassador was the sum of it.

Amnesty, on the other hand, has succeeded in alerting a wide constituency to the violence and horror of Guatemala. To take one example, on the basis of Amnesty reports, church, liberal and union groups in Europe mounted a boycott of Coca-Cola (though Amnesty itself refrains from boycott action). In the United States, the threat of such a boycott was much evident, US labour, liberal and other groups holding talks with Coke management, and eventually putting sufficient pressure on Coca-Cola to buy out its franchise holder on human rights grounds. The manager, apparently, was a personal friend of Army Colonel German Chupina, director of the national police, and allegedly would simply ring him up if he had a labour problem, and the security forces would be sent in to eliminate the leadership of the local union. (Several union secretary-generals are said to have been killed in this way.) The publicity produced by the Coke affair in Europe and the United States, together with other reporting, often Amnesty-inspired or at least containing a hard core of Amnesty facts and figures, created an atmosphere that hurt Guatemala economically.

The press reactions to the Amnesty report on Guatemala, following its publication in February 1981, make one understand why the Guatemalan government feels it is the victim of a co-ordinated and widespread attack. The report received blanket coverage: two articles on the editorial page of the *International Herald Tribune*, one in the *New York Times*, extensive coverage by the BBC, a long news report in the *New York Times*, a front-page report in the London *Times* and Mexico's *Excelsior*, and detailed reporting by publications as varied as *Le Figaro* and the *Economist*. One can perhaps forgive the outburst of the Secretary for Public Relations of the Presidency who told the Guatemalan City daily, *El Imparcial*, that Amnesty 'had set out to undermine the prestige of Guatemala's institutions and headed up an orchestrated campaign to damage the image of Guatemala for the simple reason that its government is not disposed to permit the activity of international communism.'

The consequence of this kind of bad publicity is that the bottom has fallen out of the tourist market, once the third largest export earner. For the last year or so, there has been no significant foreign investment. A number of US banks have closed down their Guatemalan offices, although publicly they have given non-political reasons for doing so. None of this, it must be admitted, has yet had any discernible impact on the government's thinking, so single-minded and determined is the regime.

However, Amnesty's human rights initiatives give a great deal of succour and support to the opposition. All of the exiles I talked to gain an enormous psychological boost from the Amnesty campaigns. Here they are, citizens of a small country, vulnerable and expendable, being given international attention. Although, unlike other countries where the governments hold people prisoner rather than kill them, it is impossible to mount campaigns to release people, the Amnesty publicity does give a sense of assurance to those who are determined to bring about a major change in government policies.

Inevitably, Amnesty's psychological underpinning extends beyond the non-violent opposition to the guerrillas, particularly since many of the activists in the Frente have a degree of sympathy for the guerrilla cause, increasingly despairing of any other solution. This support is intangible and immeasurable. But it exists and is important.

Is there anything left for Amnesty to do? It certainly has to make sure that Western governments continue their restrictions on military aid. The Reagan administration in Washington is sympathetic to those who argue that arms and counter-insurgency training would give Washington some access to the government and increased leverage on its leadership. But there are no grounds for thinking such an intransigent government would be moved by such blandishments. The additional arms now offered will merely make the government's oppressive machinery more thorough.

The pressures within the Reagan administration to supply more lethal arms will mount as the guerrillas become successful and the Cubans become more involved in supplying arms. (At the moment Cuban aid is minor, but events are pushing the guerrillas towards Cuba.) Amnesty's position is neutral on such political developments. Nevertheless, if it keeps the spotlight turned on Guatemala, matters will become more difficult for Reagan and easier for the Cubans.

Amnesty, when confronted with such dilemmas, points to how critical it has been of Cuba's human rights record and how it has long kept the pressure on other communist regimes such as East Germany and the Soviet Union.

I would add another point. When the West cannot be consistent about its own democratic values, when it refuses to support, even with non-violent help, an oppressed people in situations of such hopelessness, then it has only itself to blame if the revolutionaries, driven to their position out of desperation, cast around for support from elsewhere. Besides, the Cuban threat is grossly overstated. The Cubans helped the blacks come to power in Zimbabwe, yet the government of Robert Mugabe gives them scant recognition and, indeed, for a while refused the Soviet Union an embassy in Salisbury. Increasingly, liberated Third World countries realize that to survive in the tough economic climate of the 1980s they need Western technical and material help and Western financial discipline.

Given the right support, Central American countries would, once they have overthrown their tyrants, look Westward.

Moreover, there is no good evidence, even if they kept their Cuban sympathies, that the Russians would erect missile-launchers or take other provocative steps to tilt the balance of power in their favour. This is not 1962. The Russians are altogether more cautious and careful.

This may or may not be an accurate reading of the political situation. Whichever is the case, Amnesty will keep battering away at the excesses of Guatemala. Human rights, their defence and encouragement, is their *raison d'être*. It is now an independent political force which the superpowers can neither ignore nor shunt aside.

El Salvador: Amnesty in the eye of the revolution

The only country presumptuous enough to name itself after Jesus Christ, El Salvador, must today have one of the world's most God-forsaken governments. In the last two years, the rate of killing carried out by the government armed forces has exceeded that of anywhere else in the world, and the victims, if not innocent of opposition to the government, are usually defenceless and unarmed.

During the last five years Amnesty have devoted an increasing proportion of their attention to this tiny country.

The major problem of El Salvador is land. This is what has brought the country to civil war and this is what intermittently for the last half a century has been the cause of strife.

El Salvador, beautifully well-ordered from the air, with its lush green fields and backbone of smoking volcanoes, has the densest population of any country in Latin America. Just over 4 million people live there. 200,000 of its peasant families are landless, compelled to work for minimal wages on the great coffee and cotton estates. Half of the nation's productive land is in the hands of 1800 property owners while 100,000 small farmers live on less than one hectare each. Many of those who do have land own only a pocket-handkerchief. In some cases, desperation forces them to cultivate up the slopes of active volcanoes. El Salvador has the lowest per capita calorie intake of any Latin American country. A government study in 1973 recorded that 73 per cent of Salvadorean children under the age of five were suffering from malnutrition and that 63 out of 1000 children die before the age of one.

It is part of the folk-lore that El Salvador is ruled by 'Los Catorce' – a tight group of fourteen families. In truth, rather more than fourteen families make up the country's oligarchy, linking by marriage and by personal interest the higher echelons of the army, government and landowners. There is not the well-developed middle class such as exists in Guatemala.

The military has ruled El Salvador since 1931 – longer than any other Latin American country. Its tradition of ruthlessness goes back at least to the suppression of the peasant revolt of 1932 when 30,000 peasants were killed: three out of every one hundred inhabitants, the equivalent of six million people being killed in the United States today. The revolt was a terrifying, bloody affair triggered by the collapse of the coffee market, which left the peasants bereft of even the meagre seasonal wages they usually earned on the plantations.

It was the first uprising in the Western hemisphere in which communists played an active part, although the evidence suggests that their influence was not central. The uprising has left its scars on both sides. Members of the upper class and the military officers have ever since equated communism with peasant agitation. Even moderate opposition raises the spectre of 1932. Electoral politics since then have been a charade. Although there were occasional strong opposition movements, the army always controlled the elections, counted the ballots and made sure that their candidates retained office. The country seemed passive.

The situation began to change in the early 1970s. A new electoral law allowed the opposition parties to build up strength in congress. The presidential elections in 1972 were won by the Christian Democrat, José Napoleon Duarte, but his accession to power was prevented by a military coup. It is indicative of the ambiguous (is he a democrat or a dictator?) role later played by Duarte that when the coup seemed successful, Duarte declared his support for it on a radio broadcast.

By the 1977 elections, a change in the electoral council had reduced the opposition in congress to only one person. It was considered the crowning insult when the army General Romero claimed he had won a victory over the coalition of Christian Democrats, Social Democrats and Communists. Disillusioned young Roman Catholic activists such as Ana Guadulupe Martinez, who became a guerrilla commander, drifted into the People's Revolutionary Army, led by Joaquin Villalobos. They began to kidnap, and kill, members of the fourteen families. They also kidnapped business executives and demanded huge ransoms in return for their lives. With the money they bought weapons.

The reaction of the government was to turn up the heat of repression 'to save the country from communism'. The government organized a right-wing paramilitary organization to harass and kill peasant leaders. From then on, the guerrillas went from strength to strength with branches that reached deep into the peasant, union and student organizations. Communist influence in the early 1970s had been marginal: all opposition hopes were sunk in the Christian Democrats. But the government determination to break the Christian Democratic leadership destroyed the party. Most of the leaders were driven into exile and the rank and file had nowhere to go but to the left. The country entered a period of rapid polarization that has continued until today.

The 1977 election in El Salvador came soon after the accession to power in the United States of Jimmy Carter. Although human rights was a leading preoccupation of the new president, El Salvador, with its small population and 'banana republic' image, was not given much attention, despite continual pressure and publicity generated by Amnesty. A routine critical human rights report issued by the State Department, and Congressional hearings on human rights, had provoked the El Salvadoreans to decide to renounce US arms aid. Apart from that, contact was desultory.

Only in the summer of 1977 did El Salvador catch the eye of senior Washington officials. One of the government-financed death squads, the White Warriors' Union, threatened to kill all the Jesuits in El Salvador, who, they claimed, were a communist-front organization. A number of socially engaged priests had already been assassinated so the threat had to be taken seriously. Church groups in the United States lobbied strenuously in Washington and, as a result, the Carter administration engaged in a major effort to convince General Romero, the President of El Salvador, that such a massacre would lead to a diplomatic estrangement between the two countries. To underline its point, Washington postponed a vote on a $90 million Inter-American Development Bank loan to El Salvador.

Temporarily, the activities of the death squads subsided. But a few months later Washington reversed its position on the loan, apparently feeling that carrots as well as sticks were necessary to lead El Salvador on to the path of virtue. The Romero government interpreted the easing up differently. It assumed that it could now continue much as before. It passed a series of draconian laws – which introduced press censorship, banned public meetings, outlawed strikes, made it a crime to disseminate information that 'tends to destroy the social order' – and suspended normal judicial proceedings. Washington seemed acquiescent. The US ambassador told the El Salvadorean Chamber of Commerce that governments had the right to monitor public order, and Terence Todman, the assistant secretary of state for inter-American affairs, made a speech saying 'terrorism and subversion are the major problems confronting the people of Latin America'.

As General Romero interpreted it, the United States was signalling for him to take his gloves off. The Catholic Archbishop of San Salvador, Oscar Arnulfo Romero, dismayed by US policy, said, 'I feel greatly disappointed because we had hoped US policy on human rights would be more sincere.' Amnesty began to intensify its activity, lobbying the United Nations and The Organization of American States. The radical left in El Salvador reacted against the new laws using what they called 'destabilizing tactics' – strikes, 'invasion' of private farms, church and embassy occupations and street protests.

The government in turn escalated its repression. Following a street demonstration in March 1978, the largest of the paramilitary groups, ORDEN, was let off the leash. Hundreds of peasants were murdered in cold blood.

Washington began to worry. Policy was again reviewed. It was important, it was decided, that reform should be pushed in El Salvador, though revolution must be avoided.

Early in 1979 Washington began to pressure General Romero to agree to electoral reform. By agreeing to listen to Washington, however, Romero began to lose his hold on the right, who increasingly took 'law and order' into their own hands. El Salvador started to fall apart.

Then, in October 1979, a group of young army reformists, including two colonels, overthrew Romero. It was a totally unexpected move which engendered a spirit of hope throughout the country. The officers brought politicians from the opposition into the government and announced a bold programme of reform. The guerrillas were split, and momentarily it seemed that a way out through the centre could be found. Washington was delighted. The centre was stronger than in neighbouring Nicaragua. The business community was less alienated and the guerrillas more ruthless and Marxist. The centre must be made to hold.

The junta, however, did not deliver. The coup leaders did not have the power, or perhaps the will, to rein in their fellow-officers. They were not prepared to contemplate a split in the army and the rump of the army and its paramilitary friends continued their old practices of cold-blooded murder. By January 1980, the government had collapsed. The civilian members had resigned in disgust and the education minister announced he was joining the guerrillas.

A new junta was formed, also publicly committed to reform. Cautiously leaned on by the Americans, the Christian Democrats agreed to be part of it. They were working uphill. The population was increasingly cynical, was more aware of the continuing repression by the army and paramilitary groups than of the reforms which included the nationalization of the banks and the appropriation and redistribution of several hundred of the largest estates. Even when Washington increased its enormous pressure on the junta, hoping that the pace of reform would win the sympathy a viable government needed, every progressive step was obviated by killings and torture. For example, peasants who claimed the land that they had been formally given, were promptly executed by local members of the security forces.

Efforts to legitimize the regime by giving the presidency in March 1980 to José Napoleon Duarte, whose election had been stolen eight years previously, made little difference to the level of violence. The right was still untamed. Prisoners were not taken and guerrillas, said to have been killed in the heat of the battle, were found tortured, raped and burned. The land reform was being implemented unevenly. Large uncultivated estates were being redistributed, but the peasants found they could not get bank credits to buy seeds and fertilizer. The more serious reform – the redistribution of medium-sized farms to sharecroppers and tenant farmers – was paralysed by the government's refusal to distribute titles to the land. Few of the prosperous coffee farms were touched.

During 1980, Washington, more and more scared of Marxist domination of the left, substantially increased economic and military aid, although the State Department made efforts to describe the latter as 'non-lethal'. Yet at least while Carter was President, Washington's influence was directed equally towards containing the excesses of the right.

Then, in yet another lurch in policy, after four US nuns were murdered in December 1980, economic and military aid was suspended. Economic aid was renewed twelve days later on the grounds that the Salvadorean economy was about to collapse. But military aid remained suspended while the El Salvadorean government conducted a proper investigation into the nuns' deaths.

That policy, too, was soon laid aside. The guerrillas mounted a major offensive and, with reports of Cuban arms flowing in, the dying administration of Jimmy Carter decided not only to restore military aid but to sell the El Salvadorean government lethal weapons and to second counter-insurgency advisers. The Reagan administration quickly built on this, increasing the number of arms and military advisers, and at the same time easing the pressure on El Salvador to pursue its investigation into the nuns' deaths. Not since the 1960s has the United States been so involved in trying to defeat a Marxist-led insurgency in Latin America, albeit an insurgency that, unlike its predecessors, has much sympathy from the church, the democratic left and even the centre.

Amnesty International did not get intimately involved in El Salvador until 1976, when a mission was sent to discuss the situation with the government. Its role has not been seen as prominent as in Guatemala, mainly because the Catholic Church has taken such an active part. Under the leadership of Archbishop Romero, who was assassinated by a right-wing gunman in 1980, the church took the lead in monitoring violations of human rights and relaying, through its own network, the information to the outside world. The large and vocal liberal wing of the Catholic Church in the United States has efficiently amplified all the messages it has received.

Nevertheless, Amnesty's role has been significant. When journalists, church spokesmen or even members of government want to make their case about El Salvador, it is usually the Amnesty facts and figures that they quote. Amnesty is considered dispassionate and objective. Their thorough monitoring of the situation has established beyond doubt – even by conservative observers in the West – that the violence has been overwhelmingly one-sided. As Amnesty states in a report to the Organization of American States:

> While human rights abuses have to be placed in the context of open conflict between governmental forces and several violent guerrilla organizations (themselves guilty of serious abuses), the victims of torture and death at the hands of security forces have not generally been shown to have any direct involvement in armed insurrection. Most of the deaths have occurred after the victims had been seized from their homes or work places and were defenceless.

Amnesty's interest in El Salvador has been critically important at two main periods. The first was in the early days of Carter's presidency when his announced policy of putting human rights ahead of more traditional foreign policy concerns made it easier for Amnesty to get world attention for the abuses of a regime that was considered to be in the United States' backyard. The casebook reporting of Amnesty, relayed to a worldwide audience that had been alerted to the new purity of purpose in Washington, inevitably had a needling effect upon Jimmy Carter. In 1932, 30,000 peasants could be massacred and it all seemed rather far away – anyway, that was the tough way these countries had to be run. In 1977 the world was rather more interested. Every month Amnesty had new cases of atrocities to report. The files contain a tragic list of torture and death. One case, as reported in the Amnesty International *Newsletter*, reads:

A political prisoner in El Salvador who was fed only twice a week for ten months eventually lost so much weight that he was able to squeeze through the bars of his tiny prison cell and escape.

Reynaldo Cruz Menjivar, a peasant organizer for the Salvadorean Christian Democratic Party, who escaped from incommunicado detention in late September 1978, has now told his story after being given asylum by the Venezuelan embassy in the capital, San Salvador.

Until his escape from prison on 29 September 1978, Reynaldo Cruz Menjivar had 'disappeared'. He had been arrested on 21 December 1977 at the home of his brother by members of the Policia de Hacienda (Treasury Police) – one of El Salvador's main security forces. Although his brother was a witness to the arrest, the government refused to acknowledge it.

After ten months in incommunicado detention, Reynaldo Cruz escaped into a tropical rainstorm after squeezing through the bars of his prison cell. His weight had dropped to 31.5 kilograms. He escaped wearing only his underpants, his body scarred by torture.

He said he had been tortured after his arrest and then held continuously in a dark and filthy cell which was so small that he was unable to stand up in it. Most of the time he was kept in manacles.

He was able to communicate with two other prisoners, one of whom was seriously ill and who he believes may have died in his cell a few days before the escape.

The other prisoner, Cecilio Ramirez, is reportedly still detained in the San Salvador headquarters of the Policia de Hacienda, possibly in secret underground cells below the outdoor basketball court in the Treasury Police complex.

The second period when Amnesty's role was crucial began in December 1980 with a series of incidents. First, the Archbishopric of San Salvador reported that it had been forced to close its legal aid office because it had been raided seventeen times in the previous week by the police.

Then two members of the El Salvador Human Rights Commission were killed: its young press secretary, Maria Magdalena Enriquez, was found dead in a shallow grave about twenty miles from the capital. Witnesses confirm that she was abducted while shopping by uniformed police. Another commission worker was shot while driving his car. A month later, a leading member of the commission was abducted from his home by plainclothes policemen. Typically, the authorities denied holding him, and it was assumed he had been assassinated. The commission's offices were destroyed by bombing three times in the course of 1980 and the 'liberal' president of El Salvador, José Napoleon Duarte, publicly accused it of being unpatriotic. The commission was forced to close down. Nevertheless, the persecution of those associated with it continues.

On 28 January 1981 at 9.40 p.m., uniformed members of the security forces and the army burst into the house of Marianella Garcia Villas, president of the Human Rights Commission. She was not at home, but staying at her house were seven friends, including three of their children aged five, seven and thirteen. They were questioned about the whereabouts of Marianella

Garcia Villas. They said they did not know. The soldiers began to beat and torture the adults in front of the children who cried and begged them to stop. Then the children were beaten in front of their parents. The soldiers, unable to extract the information they required, took them all off to the National Police Station. Amnesty have been unable to discover where the adults are now detained, although they traced the three children to a juvenile reform centre.

With the church and the Human Rights Commission out of action, Amnesty's responsibility becomes graver. No organization remains to monitor effectively human rights abuses. Moreover, the US embassy, now reporting to President Reagan's secretary of state, Al Haig, is less concerned with publicizing human rights abuses than it was in Carter's day. Amnesty is increasingly alone in having both the channels of access and the means of communication to keep the world alert to what is happening in El Salvador.

Events in El Salvador have led Amnesty to take on issues that even many friends and members of Amnesty regard as 'hot potatoes'. In particular, it has waged a campaign against the decision taken by the Carter administration to provide security assistance to the junta. On 16 July 1980 Amnesty issued an international news release saying that 'The proposed US security assistance to El Salvador could be expected to worsen the widespread murder and torture.' This was the first time Amnesty had made such a move. It had been preceded five months before by a letter on the same lines from Martin Ennals to the US deputy secretary of state, Warren Christopher. The letter was hushed up and no reply ever sent.

The position of the State Department was that the military equipment was merely to improve the mobility and operational capability of the security forces. However, it also included such items as helicopters, jeeps, communications equipment, patrol boats, aircraft engines and parachutes. Similar equipment, specifically the helicopters, was used by the security forces in a well-documented killing of civilians in the Honduran border area in May 1980. In addition, licences were issued for the export by private US commercial companies for carbines, handguns and rifles.

Amnesty was careful when marshalling its arguments against the arms deal to avoid being drawn into the political debate of whether they supported a left- or right-wing victory in the civil war. Amnesty's point was that the violence used by the El Salvadorean security forces and the paramilitary groups far exceeded the normal needs for self-defence. They reaffirmed the point they had made time and time again, that in all the long lists of cases of violent deaths that Amnesty had presented to the world, there was not the slightest evidence that the victims had attacked or violently resisted security forces or participated in armed confrontation. Few victims were killed in battle. They were usually 'executed' by being stood up against a wall and shot. Amnesty was convinced, it said, that this military assistance, by improving the communications and mobility of the security forces, would improve the technical capability of the army, police and paramilitary groups, and lead to more torture and more execution-style killings of the non-violent opposition.

This was a new venture into more controversial political territory. Amnesty was now throwing itself into the middle of the political maelstrom. Yet in a situation of such ferocity, it seemed inevitable that Amnesty should expand its concern in this direction.

Is Amnesty effectively one-sided in its approach to El Salvador? It may, because of the one-sidedness of the killings, look that way, and undoubtedly there is not much sympathy within Amnesty's staff for the junta. Nevertheless, whenever the occasion has offered, Amnesty has criticized the left. For example, when guerrillas kidnapped the foreign minister in 1977, Martin Ennals cabled the President expressing concern for the minister's well-being and reiterating Amnesty's long-standing policy of condemnation of executions, whether it be done by governments or by revolutionary forces.

Again, in February 1980, Amnesty sent cables to the government and to Archbishop Romero protesting against the kidnappings carried out by left-wing guerrillas. The hostages had been threatened with execution. The cables pointed out that Amnesty 'condemns every case of execution of prisoners, kidnap victims or hostages by governments or other organizations of whatever political orientation.' The text of the cable was read from the pulpit the next day by Archbishop Romero. His sermon was broadcast on nationwide radio.

The war continues its messy course in El Salvador. The guerrillas, while adding to their strength, appear unable to match the government's firepower. The Duarte government remains on top, the penchant of the security forces for brutality and savagery only marginally tamed by the political leadership. Every week more cases arrive on Amnesty's doorstep. The US government, however, gives the impression of being disinterested in what Amnesty reports. The only good news is that the Western European governments are embarrassed by Washington's stand. They, while never having been so enthusiastic about Human Rights as an instrument of foreign policy as President Carter, are today not as cold about it as President Reagan. Amnesty's concerns appear to find a resonance in Bonn, in Stockholm, in Paris, and even in London. Yet, so far, European pressure, while inhibiting the United States from stepping up its military commitment to Mr Duarte, is unable to ameliorate the situation within the country.

Nevertheless, the continued reporting by Amnesty is percolating through to a wide strata of opinion in the United States, Western Europe, and in Latin America too. The Duarte government is widely considered as an international pariah. Without substantial reform of its practices, it is not going to find it easy to attract the long-term support it needs to survive. Too small a country to go it alone, it at least needs the tolerance of the international community of diplomats, bankers, and investors. While Amnesty maintains its vigilance, it is not going to get it.

Nicaragua: overthrow of a tyrant

It was an act of God in the great tradition of the Old Testament that began the movement which brought down the Somoza Dynasty in Nicaragua. On 23 December 1972, the earth began to move in Nicaragua, destroying much of the capital city of Managua and killing thousands of people. Anastasio Somoza Debayle, whose family had ruled Nicaragua for nearly fifty years, shamelessly used the international aid sent for relief, reconstruction and the victims of earthquake to enrich his own fortune. In a practice long established, the aid was channelled through Somoza-owned banks, Somoza-owned construction companies and, often enough, straight into Somoza coffers. This final act of audacity, coming after decades of exploitation and self-enrichment, not only fuelled the animosity of the working class and the peasants, who erupted into a wave of strikes, demonstrations and land seizures, it also alienated large sections of the middle and upper classes. From then on, a bloody, torment-strewn path led inevitably to the fall of Somoza in June 1979 – an event which spurred on the revolts in El Salvador and Guatemala.

Seldom has a single earthquake so disturbed the political landscape! It seemed to galvanize the resentment beneath. Two lines of opposition quickly emerged. One coalesced around Pedro Joaquin Chamorro, the editor of the main newspaper, *La Prensa*. The other centred upon the Frente Sandinista de Liberacion Nacional, popularly known as the Sandinistas, named after Augusto Cesar Sandino, who led the guerrilla campaign against the occupying US marines in the 1920s, and whose assassination was arranged by Somoza's father. Although it had been in existence for a decade, it was only in 1974 that Sandinistas attracted real attention. Sandinista guerrillas invaded a Christmas party held in honour of the American ambassador and took prisoner twelve of Nicaragua's most prominent business and political leaders. They ransomed them for one million dollars and the release of political prisoners.

Somoza, furious, declared a state of siege. He obtained nearly a doubling in US military aid and set about hunting out the guerrillas. Yet so broad was his campaign of repression, it was more often the innocent who suffered. Torture and mass execution became widespread.

This roused the church, which articulated clearly its concern. In 1977 the Roman Catholic Bishop accused Somoza's National Guard of 'humiliating and inhuman treatment ranging from torture and rape to summary execution'. Amnesty International relayed these criticisms to a wide audience. Until Amnesty took an interest in Nicaragua, the news media had, by and large, ignored the human rights problem, focusing on the corruption rather than the cruelty of Somoza. His image was of 'jovial dictator'.

Amnesty had been monitoring events from a distance since before 1974. Correspondence with bishops, priests, students and trade unionists was regularly received and Amnesty used the information in its usual diligent way. In May 1976, Amnesty sent a special mission consisting of Dr Kurt Madlener, director of the department of Hispaneamerican penal law of the Max Planck Institute, West Germany, and Amnesty's Latin American department's researcher. Their intention was to interview Somoza, the minister of the interior and justice, the minister of defence, and the president of the Supreme Court of Justice, as well as prisoners held in the Model Prison of Tipitapa. All requests for interviews were refused, except for one with the minister of the interior and justice. The authorities made no effort to restrict the Amnesty team's movements nor hinder meetings with lawyers, churchmen, and local activists, although they were constantly followed, photographed, and, on occasion, harassed. For example, whenever the team needed to use their hotel's Telex machine, they were informed that it was out of order. They were pushed to the extreme of having to lurk behind a pillar and wait for a businessman to come along and use it, then suddenly pounce and explain how lucky that it was now working! Most of their interviews were with relatives of prisoners, in their private homes. In the five years since the mission left Nicaragua, half the people it interviewed have been found dead.

Amnesty, in the mission's report, did not seek to question the right of the government to introduce martial law and suspend constitutional guarantees after the event of the great kidnapping. But it seriously questioned whether, two years later, martial law should still be in force, and it sharply criticized the government for using the emergency as a cover for dictatorial repression. 'The armed attack of December 1974 was an isolated event, not followed by other grave disturbances of public order in the capital city area.'

In a long legal document contained in the report, Amnesty argued that the existing military codes were illegitimate instruments, and that the maintenance of martial law was not in accordance with the constitution.

The Amnesty mission had tried to make a rough count of the political prisoner population. In the end it proved too difficult – prisoners who were not acknowledged by the authorities to be in custody vastly outnumbered those who are. Nevertheless, Amnesty did reach some firm conclusions, in particular that the prisoners who openly stated that they had been members and activists in the Sandinistas were in a minority. And that the killings were extensive and ruthless. The report talked of the 'wholesale killing of peasant farmers' and 'the populations of entire peasant villages have been reported exterminated or taken away as prisoners'.

Amnesty also concluded that few of these campesinos had directly participated in guerrilla operations. Indeed, there seemed to be little direct relationship between guerrilla activity in a given area and military operations of the National Guard.

Torture, Amnesty found, was extensive. The report listed the following methods which, it concluded, were used on prisoners held in the Model Prison of Tipitapa:

Beatings with fists, sticks, rifle butts, the edge of rulers, rubber hoses and kicks: inflicted to varying degrees on most prisoners, affecting all parts of the body.
Striking of the ears with cupped hands, referred to by guards as 'the telephone' (*el telefono*) or 'ringing the bell' (*golpes de campana*): suffered by most prisoners, some of whom have

serious ear trouble as a result. Indicted prisoners Vicente Godoy Bustamante and Alejandro Lopez Guillen are said to have suffered burst ear drums.

Electric shocks: inflicted on most indicted prisoners, affecting the most sensitive parts of the body, especially the genitals, tongue and chest. The shocks are apparently applied with electric cattle prods, or with wires connected to ordinary household current.

Near drowning: used against prisoners Orlando Castillo Estrada and Liana Benavides Grütter, involving repeated submergence of the head in filthy water.

Hanging by the arms or feet; simulated execution by hanging: reported hung by arms – Orlando Castillo Estrada, Rodolfo Amador Gallegos; reported hung by feet – Francisco Maldonado Lovo; simulated execution by hanging – Pedro Joaquin Rivera Torres.

Burning by cigarettes: Francisco Maldonado Lovo, Xavier Carrion.

Threatened castration: reported by several prisoners; tying a cord round the testicles while prisoners lie on their backs, then pulling, thereby forcing them to arch their backs.

Hooding: the placing of a hood of heavy black cloth over the head, causing disorientation and difficulty in breathing. Most political prisoners were reported to be hooded during initial interrogations. Prisoners charged with the greatest degree of responsibility for actions of the Sandinistas were apparently kept hooded and incommunicado for long periods: Luis Armando Guzman Luna, ninety-five days; Juan Jose Ubeda, two months and four days; Herberto Incer, four months. Some prisoners were reportedly taken to the military court for initial testimony while still disorientated from the effects of the hooding.

Cold room: prisoners were stripped naked and placed in a bare room made extremely cold by air conditions; when interrogation is not in progress, they are kept handcuffed to a chair; treatment can be prolonged, and other techniques simultaneously applied, such as deprivation of food and water. Prisoners reported confined in the cold room: Luis

Armando Guzman Luna, nine days; Herberto Incer, five days; Orlando Castillo Estrada, five days.

In the absence of a credible government challenge to the validity of detailed and consistent testimony from church, family and legal sources, Amnesty concluded that it was highly probable that the majority of prisoners in the custody of the military had been tortured. More than that, Amnesty found an absence of concern about the accusations when it attempted to discuss them with the authorities. No accusation of torture had been investigated. No orders to halt it were given.

The Amnesty team had asked the minister of the interior and justice, who was a personal friend of Somoza, what he did when he found out that security officials had been involved in torturing. He had replied that there had never been any such case. They had then asked how he reacted when prisoners themselves claimed to have been tortured. Straight-faced, he said that no prisoner had ever made such a claim.

In the Amnesty team's long report, most moving of all was a letter they reproduced, written by two Franciscan priests to the Commander of the National Guard in the Northern Zone. Dated 1 January 1977, it read in part:

As lovers of peace and order, as this is the essence of Christian life, we permit ourselves to express to you our concern at tragic events which have profoundly affected the communities along the River Tuma and the area that lies between Las Bocanas de Muy Muy Viejo and Bilampi.

1. On 9 December, the Minco-Chavelo patrol, without warning, destroyed the home of Gloria Chavarria in Bilampi and killed her, her three grown-up daughters and two children. All these people were completely defenceless. Four small children were left and they are being cared for by relatives. Afterwards, another patrol arrived. The soldiers . . . continued the massacre in the surrounding area.

2. Santos Martinez and family: the house in the Ronda de

Cuscawas near Bilampi was set on fire and all the members of the family, that is, the mother, father and two youths (reserve members of the National Guard) were beheaded for no reason at all. The two small children fled.

3. Marcelino Lopez was killed by the National Guard a few months ago. Then, the so-called 'Black Patrol' (*Patrulla Negra*) came and set fire to the house nearby and murdered his wife and four members of the family [Chilo and Dario were reserve members of the National Guard]. Only two small children escaped.

4. Around Marcelino Lopez's house, that is, in the area of the Chapel of San Jose de Cuscawas, the National Guard had established a colony of eight families. The people, seeing how the 'Black Patrol' were acting, all managed to escape and the patrol could only set fire to the houses.

5. Nearby was the house of Santiago Arauz. The same 'Black Patrol' went and killed the eldest children, Arnoldo and Antonio. The rest of the family fled, leaving behind them everything they possessed: their cattle and their land.

6. Near Ermita de San Antonio, still in Cuscawas, the same 'Black Patrol' recently destroyed practically the whole colony of eighteen houses, which the National Guard had established in the previous months, murdering several peasants. A large number of the inhabitants of the colony fled.

7. Near Capilla de San Antonio was the house of Santos Blandon. The 'Black Patrol' killed him, his wife and a grown-up son, and set fire to the house.

8. At the same time, the '*Patrulla de Reynaldo*' went into action, going to the home of Bonifacio Martinez, killing him and three grown-up sons, although they had shown identity papers given them by other National Guard patrols. The women ran away.

9. Juan Arteta's family fled in the same way.

The flight of these people and their children through the

areas of El Cacao Rosario and Cuabo has spread fear among the communities through the telling of these tragic events. Prominent members of the communities and others have even voiced their fears before the Colonel Commander of the General Headquarters, Northern Area, saying that if things continue like this they will have to abandon their homes and leave the area. The Cuscawas and Bilampi areas, which have suffered greatly in past months, have now been completely devastated. His Excellency President Somoza a short time ago gave his assurance that the National Guard would work in the defence of public order in the mountain areas and guarantee the safety and livelihood of the peasants. If this wave of terror and fear which currently holds sway in the mountains is not stopped, we shall see a massive exodus to the cities. The expanses of desolate uncultivated lands and of abandoned lands in the mountain region will grow even larger, corn and other crops will become even more scarce in the cities to which these destitute women and children will take only their sorrow and misery.

> [Signed by two priests and stamped with the seal of the diocese of Matagalpa]

Amnesty's reporting, which became more intense once its mission was home, and much of which was backed up by the US State Department's own observations (which itself draws extensively on Amnesty),* persuaded Jimmy Carter to make an example out of Nicaragua. His human rights policy was fresh on the table and it was decided that here was a reasonably straightforward case, not too big, not too strategically important, that could be suitably punished. US military assistance was reduced.

There is no doubt that in the early months of his term of office, Carter's human rights policy was meant to leave an impression. It had not yet been tarnished by the compromises that came later in El Salvador and Guatemala. In this instance it

---

* Amnesty, fearing they might be used in some way they would not approve, approached the State Department and asked them if they would refrain from quoting Amnesty International.

provided a galvanizing impact on political and social forces within Nicaragua. Liberal and church elements felt that at last they had a friend in Washington – previous Presidents had ignored the needs and problems of the region, as long as the communists and other anti-American agitators were kept at bay. Little did they realize that as they became more powerful and Somoza more vulnerable, Carter would swing back to a more traditional US posture.

In October 1977 the Sandinistas, having laid low for nearly three years, launched a series of small-scale attacks on National Guard garrisons. They were easily driven off; nevertheless, Somoza was being challenged once more.

Around the same time, twelve influential Nicaraguan professionals who were in exile in Costa Rica issued a statement sharply criticizing Somoza and asserting that Sandinistas would have to play a role in any permanent solution to Nicaragua's problems. This band of twelve – el Grupo de los Doce – was to become an increasingly important voice for the more moderate opposition.

Despite the upsurge in guerrilla attacks, Somoza appeared invulnerable. His National Guard dealt out its medicine with unashamed ruthlessness. Then, on 10 January 1978, they miscalculated. The editor of *La Prensa*, Pedro Joaquin Chamorro, was assassinated.

The nation erupted. There were two weeks of riots in Managua. The business leaders, long alienated from Somoza, joined the protest. They called a general strike, demanding Somoza's resignation. This was not class warfare – it was a nation against a man.

The next six months were punctuated by a series of violent acts. The guerrillas gathered strength; the moderates lost theirs. They had expected Carter to support the effort to dislodge Somoza. Instead Washington prevaricated, hoping that somehow Somoza could keep order *and* reform his government. Six months after Chamorro's death, Carter sent Somoza a letter congratulating him on his improved human rights record.

This simply fuelled the anger of the opposition. The moderates began joining with the guerrillas. A coalition front was formed – the Broad Opposition Front – uniting the moderates and radicals.

In August 1978 the guerrillas seized the National Palace and took a thousand hostages. There were mass insurrections in the cities. The National Guard took to the air, bombing guerrilla centres, but often laying waste the homes of the innocent, and destroying large sections of Nicaragua's cities in the process.

The United States, still desperate for a middle course, tried to isolate the guerrillas by organizing a political rescue effort in which the Front was linked with Somoza's political party. All this did, however, was weaken the influence of the moderate elements within the Front. Washington's actions had the effect of pushing the polarization it was seeking to avert. Part of the cause was bad intelligence. The CIA had reported that Somoza's fire power would keep him on top. The guerrillas' strength was discounted.

In June 1979, the Sandinistas launched the 'final offensive'. The United States tried to persuade the Organization of American States to send in a peacekeeping force, but the Latin American members vetoed it. By July, even the conservatives in Nicaragua were urging Somoza to go. Finally, with the Sandinistas poised to take over, the United States bowed to the inevitable and worked to edge Somoza out. On 17 July, Somoza went into exile in Miami. The National Guard collapsed and a Sandinista-supported junta took power.

Jimmy Carter had, with his convoluted policies, almost lost sight of his human rights goal. As William LeoGrande put it in an article in *Foreign Affairs*:

As events unfolded in Nicaragua, the United States consistently tried to fit a square peg of policy into the round hole of reality. By failing to assess accurately the dynamics of Somoza's decline, the United States produced proposals which were invariably six months out of date. When the political initiative lay with the moderate opposition, the United States acted as if it still lay with Somoza. When the initiative shifted to the radicals, the United States acted as if it lay with the moderates. And when, at the last moment, the

United States recognized that the radicals held the initiative, it seemed to think it could cajole them into returning it to the moderates.

The mistakes made by the United States in Nicaragua are being repeated in El Salvador, and the ground laid for them to be repeated in Guatemala. It is one of the enduring mysteries of the Carter presidency, how the man who raised the issue of human rights to the pinnacle of state-craft should find himself unable to face its consequences.

Amnesty International's Central American exposés would never have achieved such potency had not Jimmy Carter supported them. Yet by the end of his presidency, Carter had become a drag on Amnesty's efforts. His goodwill and ambitions for a better world were still apparent, even as he struggled in the last hours of his presidency with the decision whether or not to renew arms sales to the El Salvadorean junta, but he was racked, as all his predecessors had been, and as his successor was to be, by the fear of Cuban expansionism. No matter that the Cuban support was tardy, small and relatively marginal to the strength of all the guerrilla movements, its contribution was enough to set Washington's alarm bells ringing. All other concerns and priorities appeared to be vaporized by the almost paranoid fear of Cuban potency, and the conviction that Cuba was a stalking horse for Soviet imperialism in the Western hemisphere.

While Jimmy Carter was picking up the political pieces from his débâcle in Nicaragua and trying to cope with the complexities of El Salvador, Amnesty was turning its attention to the new Sandinista-backed regime.

Amnesty, which had fought valiantly to save who could be saved and expose all that had to be exposed in Somoza's time, was finding that the new regime also had its human rights defects.

The new junta had stated categorically that it wanted to wipe the slate clean. It released all the junta's prisoners and, on the first day in office of the Government of National

Reconstruction, issued its Estatuto Fundamental. This dissolved the National Guard, the secret police and the military intelligence service. It also gave full recognition to the Universal Declaration of Human Rights. The death penalty was outlawed, and torture, and cruel, inhuman and degrading treatment forbidden. Freedom of conscience and religion were enshrined in the law in such a way that even for 'reasons of public order or state security', they could not be withdrawn. However, habeas corpus was suspended.

The government argued that it had no alternative but to suspend habeas corpus while it was dealing with 'those individuals who are under investigation for crimes included in the penal code and the International Covenant during the Somozo regime.' In the weeks after Somoza's defeat, an estimated seven to nine thousand people were detained. Most of them were former members of the hated National Guard, local police officials, members of the political police and former members of the Somoza government or members of his family enterprises.

In the first months of the new government there were also reports of some executions of National Guardsmen who had surrendered. Nevertheless, the government did move to stop the rash of illegal executions – its own figure was one hundred – getting out of hand. It arrested several hundred of its own supporters. Also, in April 1980, it ended the state of emergency and theoretically the full panoply of constitutional and legal rights were now in force.

Amnesty had been concerned about the way things had been going. In January 1980 it sent a team to attend as observers a number of the trials. Besides meeting with senior government ministers, it also met with the re-established, independently and privately run Permanent Commission for Human Rights.

The mission tried to assess the procedural aspects of the trials and raised with the authorities points of law relevant to the new court structure. It also, at the invitation of the government, visited the principal prisons. Overcrowding, it concluded, was a major problem.

A second mission, in August 1980, continued the monitoring of the trials of former members of the security services, observing the proceedings and examining the documentation of hundreds of individual cases.

Amnesty now estimates that there are around five thousand people imprisoned for crimes said to have been committed by the *ancien regime*. On a number of occasions Amnesty has written to the successive governments to enquire into individual cases of imprisonment. Generally, the governments have replied promptly and acted favourably, releasing the prisoner concerned.

At the end of March 1980, Amnesty was particularly concerned about the fate of four people connected with the left-wing newspaper, *Pueblo*. The government had closed it down, after it had been highly critical of the political course taken by the revolutionary government. The four were to be punished under a law that appears to contradict many of the constitutional commitments. The law establishes a sentence of up to two years for those who publish 'proclamations or manifestos that seek to injure the popular interests and abolish the victories achieved by the people'.

Although no Nicaraguan prisoners of conscience were adopted by Amnesty in 1980, Amnesty quietly indicated to the authorities that if these people were convicted, Amnesty would have no recourse but to put them on its list. Soon after, the government dropped its case and they were released.

Press freedom in Nicaragua has become an increasingly charged issue. In January 1981, the International Press Institute published a long article about the problems faced by *La Prensa*. Now edited by Pedro Joaquin Chamorro Barrios, the son of the editor murdered by Somoza, it regards itself as having to fight some of the same battles as in Somoza's day. The son, to make the point, has been re-running the articles written more than forty years ago by his father.

There have been a number of difficult moments. In early October 1980, *La Prensa* ran a report about a peaceful demonstration, in the town of Bluefields, against Cuban teachers and advisers. The protesters carried placards saying

'Cubans go home'. The Sandinista press and radio immediately launched a biting attack on the newspaper. Junta members appeared to encourage the attack. One was quoted as saying that the newspaper 'is using the media in a completely unpatriotic way and they are helping create the climate of destabilization that the enemies of our revolution here and abroad want to see.' Other members of the junta, however, have defended *La Prensa*'s right to report the news and to speak out. Nevertheless, it is a fraught situation. It seems tragic that the newspaper whose spark helped light the revolutionary fire should now be threatened by its flames.

Even more worrying at first sight was the decision by the government in February 1981 to close down the Human Rights Commission and arrest its founder, Jose Esteban Gonzalez. Its office was occupied by the armed forces and its documents confiscated. Amnesty fired off a cable to the junta asking for the decision to be annulled. The cable said it was 'an untimely and tragic decision both for the people and the good of Nicaragua and for the global work of Human Rights, particularly considering the Central American context in which other Human Rights Commissions have recently been attacked, their documents confiscated and their members arrested or assassinated.'

The answer came back the next day, saying that Gonzalez was being well treated and would be given full legal guarantees. A few days later, Gonzalez was released and the Commission allowed to reopen. However, Amnesty, while in no way exonerating the junta's action, concluded that Gonzalez had misrepresented the facts. The summary executions of National Guardsmen in rural areas, which he had highlighted, had not been done on government order, but by angry peasants.

Amnesty therefore appears to be playing a crucial role in shaping the human rights performance of the revolutionary government and in preventing the creeping abuses that had been totally commonplace under Somoza. Critical to this role has been Amnesty's documentation of abuse to the left and right of the political spectrum.

It is this kind of work that over the years has given Amnesty its credibility. Working both sides of the street, hitting left-wing regimes as hard as right, it has convinced an increasing number of government officials (even if they refuse to admit it publicly) that it is not an ideological tool of social democracy, nor of American foreign policy nor of communism. It is, in fact, its own master, attempting, albeit imperfectly, to be true to its statutes and its rank-and-file membership.

Ultimately, what is impressive is that Amnesty has developed a method of work that pressures it to be detached and independent-minded even when, as in Nicaragua, the cause of the revolution undoubtedly appeals to many members of the Amnesty staff.

5. West Germany: the Baader-Meinhof Gang

Passions are not supposed to be engaged inside Amnesty International. There is a method and a purpose that transcends the passage of ideologies and movements that is meant to raise Amnesty personnel to the status of angels, unsoiled by the struggle, torment and conflicts beneath. Of course the reality is a poor shadow of the image. Amnesty is full of men and women with convictions, passions and ideologies.

It is in fact remarkable that Amnesty most of the time is so credibly impartial, does cast its net so wide, is independent of the superpowers and maintains an internal discipline that gives it credence in the four corners of the world. But there are events, usually close to home, that make Amnesty's life difficult, that tax its strengths and tempt its virtue. The Baader-Meinhof gang was one of these. The West German branch of Amnesty International took up the cause. And it proceeded to cajole and push London HQ to get involved in a case about which some members felt very dubious.

The guerrilla group, the Baader-Meinhof gang, which functioned in West Germany during most of the 1970s, was an outgrowth of the student turbulence of the 1960s. It called itself the Red Army Faction but the world knew it by its two leading lights, Ulrike Meinhof and Andreas Baader. Ulrike Meinhof, the daughter of two art historians, had been a gifted journalist and an ebullient star of Germany's radical-chic circles before she joined the guerrilla group. Andreas Baader, the son of an historian, was the original driving spirit of the organization and he was said by one critic to have 'infatuated all those who ventured close to him with a Promethean mission of fire and immolation'.

Their purpose was to overthrow the bourgeois state. They

developed their maximum strength at a time when much of German society seemed inward-looking, concerned only with its own comforts and protection, and instinctively hostile to social and political reforms that would diminish its security and cosseted well-being.

For most of their active lives, the leaders of the Red Army Faction were in prison, organizing from their cells, via a network of lawyers, friendly guards, friends and family, a means of escape. The great headline-hitting dramas – the escape to South Yemen, the shoot-out in the library of the university, the murder of Schleyer (head of the West German industrialists' federation), and the final audacious act of hijacking a Lufthansa airliner to Somalia – were all efforts at escape or obtaining ransom for release. Nevertheless, such was their ruthlessness, their organizational powers, their determination, that they seemed on occasion to rock the very stability of the state. Even when isolated from the outside world in white-washed cells, lit twenty-four hours a day, they managed to communicate and organize. They seemed possessed of a laser-like purpose that could cut through prison walls and reach their targets unimpeded.

The Baader-Meinhof liaison began while Andreas Baader was serving a prison sentence for politically motivated arson. He had been allowed to continue his sociological research and received permission to visit the Sociological Institute in West Berlin. On one of his visits in May 1970, Ulrike Meinhof led a raid to release him. The library was stormed with pistols and tear gas, and an attendant was critically wounded.

Baader and Meinhof fled to Jordan and started their training in guerrilla warfare in a camp of the Popular Front for the Liberation of Palestine. On 9 August, they slipped back into West Germany.

The next two years were punctuated by bank raids, shootings and bombings. Within Germany, there was a great groundswell of support for them, which reached beyond traditional hard left circles into the liberal intelligentsia. 'Safe-houses' were easily available. The police found it difficult to trace them, but in the end they cornered them.

On 1 June 1972, after a fierce gun battle in Frankfurt, Andreas Baader and two companions were arrested. A week later, Gudrun Esslin, Baader's mistress, was arrested while shopping in an elegant Hamburg store, her revolver visible. A week after that, a disillusioned leftist, whose house was considered 'safe' enough to give Ulrike Meinhof a refuge, phoned the police.

Three years were to pass before the five hard-core members of the gang were brought to trial for murder, attempted murder, robbery and forming a criminal association. A special, fortified courthouse was built in which to try them.

Initially they were kept in solitary confinement, which was usual for prisoners accused of violent, politically motivated crimes. Although they were allowed visits by lawyers, priests, family and, on occasion, representatives of Amnesty, their lawyers launched a protest campaign against what they called 'isolation as torture'.

They said that they were being subjected to 'sensory deprivation' in silent cells, painted all in white, with the lights burning through day and night. In fact, only Ulrike Meinhof, who in November 1974 was sentenced to eight years in prison for freeing Baader, suffered a lengthy period of solitary confinement.

Either because of the campaign or because of re-thinking by the prison authorities, their conditions did improve. The gang members were allowed to share a cell. They could have more exercise, watch colour television and play table tennis. Their cells were lined with over 2000 books. Unlike common law prisoners, men and women could mix freely. As Paul Oestreicher, then chairman of British Amnesty, observed after a visit, it looked more like a student hostel than a prison.

The months of detention were punctuated by hunger strikes and protests. They were still not satisfied with their conditions. The campaign to ameliorate them became more intense after one of the gang, Holger Meins, died during a hunger strike. Outside members of the gang shot dead the president of the West Berlin Supreme Court. They said it was revenge for the death of Meins.

German public opinion was polarized between those who thought it was time for the government to crack down with all means at their disposal and those, including people of the stature of Heinrich Böll, for whom the state was becoming an ugly monster that allowed for no flexibility or tolerance.

Members of the German Amnesty group could not help being infected by the atmosphere. Although national sections are not supposed to take up issues in their own country, the German Amnesty members became deeply involved, pressing London to investigate the charges of torture and other human rights abuses.

After a long period of investigation, Martin Ennals wrote letters in November 1974 to individual ministers of justice in each of the *Länder* where Baader-Meinhof prisoners had been detained – they were by now scattered around Germany in a number of prisons.

During one of the hunger strikes, a private mission of mediation was undertaken by the Reverend Paul Oestreicher. In a public statement issued in December and confirmed by the International Executive Committee, Oestreicher said:

> In the opinion of Amnesty International at the present time, the allegation of so-called torture by isolation is not justified. As such, the organization cannot intervene. That Amnesty International is ready and willing to help find a solution in the present crisis is demonstrated by my presence in Germany.

In February 1975, there was a new crisis. The prison authorities had smelt it coming, but no one seemed to work out what form it would take. The gang had called off their hunger strike, and were assiduously using gymnastic equipment to build up their strength.

Baader issued one of his secret cell circulars – it was sent to Ulrike Meinhof and Gudrun Esslin and communicated via one of the gang's many secret channels. It read:

> to g/u. [Gudrun/Ulrike, probably.]
> i no longer bothered about it: i had n radio + have the

sequence + analyzed the reporting that will still have to be done in the newspapers in the next few days: sequence of decisions, Fundamental decisions (important!) n diagram of the times they need be able decide: to become grand Crisis staff (state ministers, presidents, minister of interior, minister of justice, buback [Buback, chief federal public prosecutor]) air flight times etc. hanna [Hanna-Elise Krabbe] is to do it. that is very important + must go quickly. i will pass on the stuff from wednesday.

On 24 April the import of this murky message became all too clear; six outside members of the gang captured West Germany's embassy in Stockholm, demanding the release of those imprisoned. They must be flown out of the country, they insisted. If there was any delay, the twelve hostages they had taken would be shot dead one by one.

When the police entered the building, the terrorists shot and killed the military attaché. When the deadline passed, they shot the ecomomics attaché. Then the Swedish government decided enough was enough. It had reached the same conclusion as the West German government – there could be no more blackmail. Countess Marion Donhoff, the publisher of *Die Zeit*, summed it up when she recalled the old Frederickian maxim: 'Better that a man die than Justice disappear.' The police stormed the embassy. One terrorist died and the other five were captured.

Nearly three years after the original June arrest, the trial began in May 1975 in the most secure penitentiary courtroom ever devised.

The government, meanwhile, in an attempt to outwit the Red Army Faction's lawyers who seemed in many ways to be part and parcel of the gang, passed laws restricting their rights. Within days of the opening of the trial, all the lawyers defending Baader were excluded from the case on suspicion of participating in or abetting the crimes of which their clients were accused.

Although Amnesty did not challenge the German government directly on this, they drew attention to it in their regular published reports. They also kept up their pressure to ameliorate the near-solitary confinement that many of the Red Army Faction prisoners experienced.

In the spring of 1977, there was a modest shift in government policy. The prisoners were given permission to use larger rooms and to associate with groups of up to ten fellow prisoners. This was in addition to the other concessions granted three years before.

Members of the gang, meanwhile, despite high-pressure courtroom tactics, were becoming increasingly demoralized. The chances of rescue after the Stockholm fiasco were low. Gang members in prison began to quarrel among themselves.

Ulrike Meinhof's will was the first to crack. On 15 May 1976 she was found hanged in her cell. The others, however, maintained their morale, discipline and daring for another year.

In April 1977, after 103 weeks of trial, Baader, Esslin and Jan-Carl Raspe were found guilty of four murders and thirty-nine attempted murders. They were each sentenced to life imprisonment plus fifteen years for offences including bombings, using firearms and founding a criminal organization.

Despite the vigilance of the prison authorities, the imprisoned gang members continued to pass orders to the outside world. On 31 July 1977 Jürgen Ponto, the head of the Dresden Bank, was shot down in his home. The prison authorities reacted by attempting to end the agreement allowing the prisoners to meet in larger groups. The prisoners began a combined hunger and thirst strike.

On 12 August, Martin Ennals sent letters to the German authorities requesting information on the transfer of Red Army Faction prisoners to single cells. The next day, Amnesty expressed concern about the lives of thirty hunger strikers. A week later, two leading members of the West German section of Amnesty, with the consent of the International Executive Committee (though breaking the Amnesty mandate on the non-involvement of national sections in the affairs of their own country), visited the prisoners and officials involved. On the same day, Amnesty International requested its membership to send appeals to the West German authorities. On 26

August, an Amnesty delegation was sent to West Germany.

While attention was focused on the hunger strike, the gang struck again. On 5 September 1977, industrialist Hans-Martin Schleyer was kidnapped. His chauffeur and three-man security guard were machine-gunned to death. The price for Schleyer's freedom was the release of the prisoners and travel to the country of their choice. The government this time was in no doubt it could not give in. Schleyer was later found in the boot of an abandoned car, murdered.

Amnesty was now being increasingly criticized. In the eyes of some, Amnesty had come dangerously close to being seen as a friend of a ruthless band of terrorists who were still totally engaged in their effort. These were not prisoners cut off from their political friends, isolated and badly treated. They seemed able still to call the shots and direct the campaign for their release. Did not Amnesty, by pressing for a looser prison regime, give them more opportunities to organize their deadly work? It was one thing for Amnesty to work for the amelioration of the lives of passive prisoners, but to work on behalf of such activists was almost to be a part – or at least a tool – of their cause.

Amnesty's reply was to insist that their job was to stop human rights violations. Prison was meant to rehabilitate prisoners, not to 'break' them. It should be possible to build a high-security prison that was liberal within the walls, even while entry and exit was carefully controlled. Besides, Amnesty said, there seemed to be no correlation between the degree of isolation of the prisoners and the number of violent events organized by the gang outside. Even during the most severe isolation, the gang seemed to have ways of communicating between its members and with the world outside.

On 13 October a Lufthansa airliner with sixty-eight passengers and crew was hijacked by members of the gang. It was flown to Somalia and the bargaining began. It was a long-drawn-out process, carefully orchestrated by the Bonn government which, with the connivance of the Somali government, was secretly flying an élite group of commandos into Somalia. On 18 October they stormed the plane in a lightning surprise attack. The passengers were freed. Hours later, Andreas Baader and his friend Jan-Carl Raspe were found shot in their cells. Gudrun Esslin was found hanged, and a fourth, Irmgard Müller, attempted to cut her throat, but survived.

Amnesty was invited to the autopsy but decided not to go, because of the lack of warning time given. Nevertheless, the local German authorities claimed they had been in attendance.

The prisoners, since the Schleyer kidnapping, had all been in solitary confinement. But, as a search of their cells revealed after their death, it had not stopped them setting up a communications network. The police discovered batteries, cables and electrical plug combinations. The terrorists made contact with each other through the prison radio system, even though the lines connecting their cells were cut. In a cell which had once been occupied by Baader, and in the cell in which Raspe died, police found a hollow space in the wall that could have been used for hiding the gun used in the suicides. It is possible they even masterminded the hijacking, although a number of observers, who have tried to study how they kept their chain of command so effective so long, have concluded that a number of their lawyers were senior figures in the gang.

In May 1980, Amnesty issued the results of their long-awaited enquiry into the use of isolation for prisoners held in connection with politically motivated crimes in Western Germany.

Amnesty said that more than a hundred Red Army Faction prisoners had been subjected to the isolation treatment at some time. The memorandum quoted findings of the European Commission for Human Rights, the Council of Europe and medical research to emphasize that isolation can gravely damage health. Symptoms, it said, included psychosomatic disturbances, low blood pressure and circulation problems, including dizziness and headache, disorders of the stomach and intestines, sleep disturbance, difficulty in concentrating and speaking, hallucinatory symptoms in extreme cases, and emotional disturbances, including depression and ultimately suicidal tendencies.

Amnesty argued that security and humane treatment were not contradictory goals, and asked the German government to seek alternatives to solitary confinement and 'small-group isolation'. It ended with a quotation from a Council of Europe report: 'In institutions where a higher standard of security is needed, this reasonably high standard against the outside world generally allows a more liberal regime inside the institution.'

The German authorities rejected the Amnesty conclusions. They invited Amnesty to inspect their prisons and said that Amnesty had overlooked the fact that members of the Red Army Faction had refused to accept more contact with non-political prisoners. They had demanded to be put into groups of at least fifteen politically motivated prisoners. They even attacked other prisoners. To the extent that the gang were isolated, it was by their own choice or when they abused the opportunities for contact.

Amnesty disagreed with this assessment, countering that not all the Baader-Meinhof gang had rejected contact with non-political prisoners and criticizing the distribution of the remaining Baader-Meinhof prisoners around numerous jails, making it difficult for them to associate even in small groups.

Amnesty stresses that it is part of its mandate to raise its banner against 'torture, or other cruel, inhuman and degrading treatment or punishment'. No one following the case of the Baader-Meinhof gang could be unaware of Amnesty's commitment to stick by its own standards. But they came dangerously near to being used by a group that had no sympathy for the values Amnesty stood for and which sought to overthrow the kind of West European democracy that allowed Amnesty to flourish. Nevertheless, it seems in retrospect they were right to intervene and insist on a decent prison regime. Only if the German authorities could prove that isolation broke the political and military chain of command of the Baader-Meinhof gang would they have a duty to rethink their role.

Looking back, the Baader-Meinhof effort was not the organization's finest hour. Against the better judgment of some of its members, Amnesty allowed the German national group to push it in deeper than the case properly deserved. The Baader-Meinhof gang's imprisonment, measured against Amnesty's terms of reference and other interests, was a marginal affair. But in terms of energy, emotion and time it became much more than that.

6. China: Amnesty Raises the Curtain

When Amnesty International published its blockbuster report, 'Political Imprisonment in the People's Republic of China', in November 1978, Thomas Hammarberg, then the chairman, made a simple but revealing observation: 'Official government statements and Chinese laws confirm the patterns of political imprisonment described by former prisoners. We are not dealing with a situation where the government says one thing and the prisoners say another.'

The report was one of the most detailed and thorough ever produced by Amnesty, creating enormous press interest. It revealed what only a few China specialists had been aware of — that China's great revolution, and later economic and political success, where nearly everyone* is fed and absolute poverty has been abolished, was bought for a great price — the near abolition of personal freedoms and the creation of a repressive machine that was often arbitrary and on occasion quite savage. Whereas the Soviet Union has long been charged by a wide spectrum of critics with being brutal and uncaring in its treatment of dissidents, China had for decades lived with the indulgence, even the favour, of outside Western observers who saw the economic and social progress but ignored the abolition of civil liberties.

The tide of opinion was changed by the Chinese themselves. The death of Mao-tse-Tung in September 1976 allowed the shutters to be raised on the interiors of Chinese life. Amnesty was one of the first outside organizations to look inside. As Hammarberg said, they found the government confirming all they discovered themselves.

* Reports of famine in 1981 and calls for food aid suggest that even the 'economic success' image is seriously flawed.

For the moment, however, it looks as if that period of daylight was all too brief. The shutters have been lowered again, not by any means as closed as they were under Mao, but enough to make Amnesty's job of prisoner adoption increasingly demanding and exercising.

The Amnesty 1978 survey examines the evolution of Chinese law, the judicial process and penal policy. It is detached and exhaustive, and the picture painted is as detailed as a traditional Chinese landscape. The faces on the figures crossing the bridges to torture, imprisonment and, often enough, execution are vivid and real. The inscrutable mask had been dropped for a moment. More of the real China is there to see.

The writing of the Amnesty report was a painstaking affair. Information in China is not easy to come by. The size and diversity of the country, the complexity of the issues, the restriction of movement and the lack of access to information all made the investigation excruciatingly difficult.

Nevertheless, there were government documents that were useful although they gave information only on official principles, practices and institutions, and little on individual prisoners and their treatment. The human picture was filled in by the information supplied by ex-prisoners, friends, acquaintances and refugees. Amnesty did not, was not allowed to visit China.

On the Peking Road in Canton an enormous poster was stuck up one night in mid-November 1974. The poster stretched for one hundred yards of wall. It was a plea, written at incredible length, with 20,000 Chinese characters, for the 'rights of the people'. It attacked the 'suppression' and 'miscarriages of justice' since the Cultural Revolution began in 1966. And it demanded a proper socialist legal system which would be applied to everyone.

The authorities described it as reactionary. They traced the authors, who had signed the poster with a pseudonym, and they were brought before a 'criticism meeting'. Two of three men arraigned, having admitted their 'guilt', were sent to work under surveillance in the countryside in the province of Guangdong.

The third author was a young man named Li Zhengtian, from a 'good' family background, who, as a young graduate, had participated actively in the Cultural Revolution, although he had been caught out in one of its many twists and turns and in 1968 was sentenced to three years' imprisonment. Bravely he had put his address at the local arts college on the bottom of the poster. He refused to admit 'guilt' and strenuously argued that the message contained in the poster was right. His case dragged on, but in the spring of 1975 he was sent to work 'under the supervision of the masses' in a mine in Guangdong.

The matter did not end there. In June 1977, a traveller to Canton claimed to have seen a court notice announcing that Li Zhengtian had been sentenced to life imprisonment.

Later, there were reports that Li Zhengtian had died in detention. Amnesty, however, continued to treat him as a prisoner of conscience and regularly the authorities in Peking and in Yunna and Guangdong were bombarded with letters and cards. In early 1979 he and the two others, alive and reasonably well, were released.

Li's case is only one of many outlined in the Amnesty report, which also drew attention to the new atmosphere since the death of Mao. It reprinted part of an article published in the Chinese *People's Daily* in July 1978 arguing for a 'criminal code', a 'civil code' and a set of 'rules of legal procedure on the base of which the "masses of the people" could "institute legal proceedings under the law so as to protect their legitimate interests".'

The truth is that in China politics and law are intimately entwined. The Chinese constitution defines certain groups of people as 'class enemies'. They are deprived of their civil and political rights merely because of their 'class origin' or political background. As the report said, 'political considerations have always been taken into account in the treatment of offenders, and this trend has been marked since the Cultural Revolution.' Visitors who have had the chance to talk to Chinese judges confirm this. 'Law', says the Amnesty report, 'is mainly used to enforce official policy,' and is phrased so as to make regulations 'applicable to any opponents of those in power, depending on the current policy line'.

The 'class enemies' concept is a far-reaching one. Mao in his writings, which have profoundly influenced state legal policy, argued that classes still exist after the revolution and that class struggle must continue through the period of socialist construction.

Class enemies are broken up into sub-groups, some not well defined. Besides 'landlords', 'rich peasants', there are 'counter-revolutionaries', 'rightists' and just 'bad elements'. The 'rightists' label was later dropped and in the 1978 constitution a new category introduced – 'the new-born bourgeois elements'.

Mao went so far as to declare that the concept of 'the people' varies in different periods of history. 'This argument', says the Amnesty International report, 'puts into broader perspective the policy of repression of political dissent', as it implies that anyone can in fact become the 'object of the dictatorship' – in other words be deprived of freedom – 'depending on the political necessities of the period.'

One case mentioned in the Amnesty report sharply illustrates the impact of this hopelessly politicized philosophy. Deng Quingshan was a member of a rural production brigade, the basic work unit in a commune. In 1970 he was arrested and accused of 'slandering Chairman Mao'. He was said to have 'bad background' – because of a difference of opinion between his brother and the officials running the brigade several years before. He was convicted on a charge of slander, sentenced to fifteen years in prison, plus a further three years' deprivation of civil rights after release. Amnesty's investigation could establish no basis for such a punishment.

Another case was that of a twenty-year-old girl, Lin Xiling, who besides being a party member was one of the leaders of the student movement at the People's University in Peking. She was a fourth-year student who came from a poor family but had worked herself into university via a spell in the People's Liberation Army art group. At the time of Mao's 'Let a Hundred Flowers Bloom' movement, she was an active critic of Chinese society. She, along with other student intellectuals, lambasted the leadership for the lack of democracy and the system of privileges based on political alignment. When the right to air this kind of criticism was abruptly stopped in 1957 and the official press started its anti-rightist campaign, Lin was arrested. She is reported to have been detained in Peking prison and later sent to a labour camp. According to a Chinese student, she was serving a twenty-year sentence. Other sources have reported that she was still imprisoned in the mid-1970s. Her present fate is unknown.

Although the Chinese themselves have begun to question this sweeping use of the 'class label' type of accusations, and although they've reduced its use, the practice has not been abandoned. And the penalties can still be severe. Moreover, the social stigma may hang over the victims for the rest of their lives. Even family members of the accused are not immune, since family background is seen as an influence in the crimes committed by the accused.

Until new laws were adopted in January 1980, there was no habeas corpus in China. A suspected political offender could spend years in a dark cell before being brought to trial. Usually, the aim of the authorities is to 'persuade' a detainee to confess in writing his misdeeds. It is common practice to ask detainees to write lengthy reports on their past thinking, relations'and activities. The accused cannot refuse to write such reports because this is officially considered a lack of co-operation with the government and is practically treated as an offence in itself.

Torture and coercion to extract confessions are, according to the law, prohibited. In practice the pressures are formidable. 'In some cases,' observed the Amnesty report, 'it is reported that *non-stop* interrogation is used to "crack" a case.' In addition,

tellingly named 'struggle meetings' can be organized to bring pressure on the accused to confess. These meetings can go on for hours, even days, and may become so tense that insults, threats, various forms of humiliating procedures and even blows are used by the people in the audience to undermine and weaken the prisoner's will.

It is a peculiarly Chinese invention, combining intimidation, humiliation and sheer exhaustion. Briefly described, it is an intellectual gang-beating of one man by many, sometimes even thousands, in which the victim has no defence, even the truth . . .

. . . After three or four days the victim begins inventing sins he has never committed, hoping that an admission monstrous enough might win him a reprieve. After a week of struggling he is prepared to go to any lengths.

The Chinese legal system hinges on these confessions. When the confession is made and the dossier prepared, the police authorities then forward the material to a judge for trial. The trial is a formality. Trial is a misnomer. In many cases, it is merely a meeting to announce the sentence.

Amnesty quotes a judge from Shanghai who, describing a case of embezzlement in 1976, said: 'The day after the judgement was decided upon, the trial took place.'

When the Gang of Four went on trial at the end of 1980, it was clear that little had changed since Amnesty had written its report two years before. Madame Mao's attempt to present a defence was dealt with abruptly and her claim to be innocent of the charges was brushed aside without debate.

In fact, if political offenders attempt to defend themselves in court, this can be regarded as an aggravating circumstance. In February 1978, a court notice publicly announced that a political offender named He Chunshu had been sentenced to death for writing and distributing a 'counter-revolutionary' leaflet. The notice said that He Chunshu had 'obstinately refused to admit his crime' and that 'the wrath of the people was very great'. The court, it concluded, had no choice but to sentence him to immediate execution. The notice further claimed:

After he became a teacher in 1956, he maintained a reactionary attitude, deeply hated our party and socialist system. In 1963, he started secretly writing a large number of counter-revolutionary articles. After the Great Proletarian Cultural Revolution started, the criminal Chunshu frantically engaged in counter-revolutionary sabotage activities; he wrote and stencilled a counter-revolutionary leaflet of more than 200,000 words containing counter-revolutionary articles; using the names of seven counter-revolutionary organizations, he mailed it to Soviet revisionists, American imperialists, reactionary Hong Kong newspapers, to some foreign consulates and embassies in China, to institutions and press organizations in our country, to about 10 units and people. [In it] he viciously attacked our great leader and teacher . . . the political campaigns launched by our Party, he attacked the Proletarian Cultural Revolution, the dictatorship of the proletariat; he greatly praised social-imperialism, spread his counter-revolutionary ideas, foolishly tried to overthrow the dictatorship of the proletariat and to restore capitalism.

On occasion, in a case like this, the death penalty is imposed but suspended for two years. Then the offender's attitude is examined to see whether he should be executed or his sentence commuted.

The Amnesty report also examined prison conditions and the treatment of prisoners in China. Since the revolution, depending on the varied political and economic conditions, the prison regime has varied considerably. Nevertheless, the complaints were common – too harsh punishment, inadequate food, lack of proper medical care, forced labour where not only is the work arduous but the prisoner is watched to see what his attitude is.

Political education and thought reform are an important aspect of the prison reform programme. Regular study sessions are held for prisoners 'to express and correct' their thoughts about current political events. Study sessions will often begin with 'sincere talk' in which prisoners account for their behaviour and criticize that of fellow prisoners. There are periodical evaluations, lasting days or even weeks, and which involve several phases: self-examination, mutual denunciation, crime-confession and admission of guilt.

Deviations from expected behaviour in prison can result in 'warnings', 'de-merits' and ultimately solitary confinement which is 'not only a period of physical isolation, but a punishment involving confinement in a tiny cell and significant reduction in food rations. The offender may also be handcuffed and chained during the entire period of punishment to break his resistance.'

A former prisoner, who had been held in the prison at Sechen Ho in Tibet, reported that during the five months he was there, seven prisoners had spent the entire period in solitary confinement. Their offence? Complaining about the treatment or refusing to express 'proper thoughts' during political education sessions.

The Amnesty report, although sent to the Chinese government six months ahead of publication, received no comment or corrections. Officially, it has not been answered, nor have Amnesty's enquiries about individual prisoners over the years of investigation. Only very recently have the solicitations of Amnesty adoption groups elicited the occasional reply. Nevertheless, it is known that extracts from the report have been published in Chinese unofficial journals, which would have reached a restricted circle – young activists, intellectuals and some party officials.

The report came out while Deng Xiaoping, the vice-chairman of the party and the most influential personage in the ruling class, was pushing China into a period of political liberalization. Only a few months after the publication of the report, there were large-scale releases and rehabilitations. Several million people had their reputations and jobs restored. The 'Democracy and Human Rights Movement' began and wall-posters flourished. Unofficial publications appeared and were even tolerated. In the spring of 1978 a new constitution was enacted. And in the autumn, the minister of public security said there was the urgent need to revise existing laws and to draft a criminal law, a civil law and a code of criminal procedure. In the *People's Daily*, he was quoted as saying that letters from people in various parts of the country had revealed that cadres 'have violated

laws, wantonly abused their powers, and bullied and oppressed the masses and encroached upon people's rights.'

The press, in fact, has carried many similar acknowledg-
ments about past miscarriages of justice and the problems
involved in redressing them.

Seven new laws, revising the criminal statutes, were
submitted for approval at the Fifth National People's Congress
in the summer of 1979. According to the director of the
Commission for Legislative Affairs, the new laws stipulate the
protection of a citizen's rights, against infringement by 'any
person or organization'. To extort confessions by torture, to
gather a crowd 'to beat, smash and loot' and to detain illegally
and prosecute on false charges are to be strictly forbidden.
Nevertheless, the liberalization legislation seems ambiguous.
'Counter-revolutionaries', defined sweepingly as anyone who
'attempts to overthrow the political power of the dictatorship
of the proletariat and the socialist system', are still to be
prosecuted. Besides this, a number of the more restrictive old
laws have been left standing. Moreover, the political atmosphere which would allow liberalization to develop and
strengthen is wanting. In late March 1979 the government took
steps to ban posters and books 'opposed to socialism and to the
leadership of the party'. Several human rights activists were
arrested including Wei Jingsheng, the twenty-nine-year-old
author of perhaps the best-written and most outspoken of the
wall-posters, 'Democracy – the Fifth Modernization'.

At his trial Wei Jingsheng was convicted of passing on
'military secrets' to a foreigner and of conducting 'counter-
revolutionary propaganda and agitation' through his writings.
He was sentenced to fifteen years' imprisonment.

Soon after his arrest, Amnesty adopted him as a 'prisoner of
conscience'. His detention and trial were carefully watched and
recorded by Amnesty's research department. The hearing,
which lasted only a few hours, was not open to foreigners nor to
the general public, but reports on it by the official press and an
unofficial transcript of the trial which was illegally circulated
reveal that procedures have changed little if at all since
Amnesty published its report. No defence witness was called,

and the alleged 'secret' nature of the information was not considered. In fact, it seems that the information given by Wei Jingsheng to a Western journalist concerning the China-Vietnam border conflict, was not particularly secret and was circulating widely among Chinese citizens.

A month later, three young men were arrested at 'democracy wall' while distributing the unofficial transcript of the trial. At the end of the year the authorities closed 'democracy wall' as part of the official campaign to 'restore law and order' and to put an end to unofficial publishing and discourage potential dissenters.

In a major speech in Peking in January 1980, Vice-Premier Deng Xiaoping stated that the central committee of the Communist Party was preparing to submit a motion to the National People's Congress that would delete from the constitution provisions legalizing wall-posters. He went on to say:

'Factionalist elements still exist . . . There are also so-called democrats and dissidents who openly oppose the socialist system and the CCP leadership, such as Wei Jingsheng and his ilk . . . Although they sometimes say that they support Chairman Mao and the CCP, they actually want to oppose the CCP leadership and socialism . . . They are quite capable of banding together under certain conditions and forming a sabotage force capable of causing a great deal of turmoil and damage . . .

'It is the unswerving principle of our Party to persevere in developing democracy and the legal system. However . . . they must be carried out step by step and in a controlled way. Otherwise, they may only encourage turmoil and impede the four modernizations, democracy and the legal system . . .

'It is absolutely impermissible to publicize any freedom of speech, publication, assembly or to form associations which involve counter-revolutionaries. It is absolutely impermissible for any persons to contact these people behind the Party's back . . . Where does the paper come from? These people do not have printing presses. Are there any Party members in the printing works who print these things? Some of the people who support these activities are Party members and quite a few of them are even cadres. We must tell these Party members clearly that their standpoint is very erroneous and dangerous and if they do not correct it immediately and completely they will be liable for Party disciplinary punishment.

A few months after the speech, the constitution was amended and the 'four great freedoms' deleted – 'the right to speak out freely, air views fully, hold great debates and write big-character posters'.

Wei Jingsheng, although the best known of Amnesty's prisoners of conscience, is only one of many on Amnesty's books. They include Ren Wanding, the leader of the Chinese Human Rights Alliance and Chen Lu, a member of the same group. Very little has been heard of them since their arrests, and the charges against them are not known. There is also Kung Pingmei, the eighty-year-old former Roman Catholic Bishop of Shanghai, who is still imprisoned after twenty-five years of detention. And since the autumn of 1979 Amnesty has continuously appealed for death sentences – more numerous – to be commuted.

But the most demanding case for Amnesty has been the trial of the Gang of Four. A political trial, the ramifications of which went to the very roots of the Chinese revolution, Amnesty decided that it needed special attention. Amnesty feared that the trial might set the standard for trials to come.

When the prosecution demanded on 29 December 1980 that Jiang Quing, Mao-tse-Tung's widow, receive a death sentence, Amnesty sent out to local Amnesty adoption groups one of its Urgent Action messages. It asked the groups to send telegrams to the Chinese Prime Minister 'expressing concern at the pending possible execution of Jiang Quing.'

As with other Amnesty cases in China, there was no way of knowing if Amnesty's campaign had any impact on the authorities. Nevertheless, Madam Mao's death sentence has been suspended: for the moment, she and the other members of the Gang of Four are still alive. But like many other political prisoners, they remain incarcerated, unlikely to benefit from the short-lived, highly-circumscribed period of liberalization which for a moment seemed to be the new China, but which now lies in pieces, the victim of insecurity, rivalry and dissension among the ruling group.

7. The Central African Republic: Bokassa and the Dead Children

The Emperor Bokassa was a wilder creation than could ever have been dreamt up by Evelyn Waugh even in his most satirical moments. A man who cut off the ears of his prisoners, murdered his former finance minister in the privacy of his palace cabinet room, engaged the full facilities of the French diplomatic service in tracking down an illegitimate daughter in Indo-China, conceived while he was a wartime sergeant in the French forces, who would receive the French ambassador in his underwear and would conduct a serious conversation with him in an empty room in the palace, furnished only with a mattress. No novelist could have created such a character. Yet this was only a part of him.

According to a Commission of Inquiry consisting of five senior African jurists, sent into the Central African Empire in the wake of Amnesty's revelations, 'riots in Bangui [the capital city] were suppressed with great cruelty by the security forces and in April 1979 about a hundred children were massacred at the order of Emperor Bokassa who almost certainly participated in the killings.'

'Almost certainly,' the report said, 'no one will ever know the precise truth of the degree of Bokassa's bestiality,' a man who considered himself the 'father and protector of children', who had himself crowned emperor with a golden crown and a golden throne specially made in France with French 'aid'. Nevertheless, there is no good reason to doubt eye-witness reports that he kept pieces of his victims in his refrigerator and feasted on them in private orgies.

The discovery and exposure of the child-murders was one of Amnesty's major breakthroughs. No great detective work was necessary, just diligence and persistence, putting together the pieces of an incomplete picture. But no one else had either the facilities or the interest to do it. In the end, not only did Amnesty reveal one of the most horrible events of the last decade; the disclosure also provoked the French government into sending in paratroopers to depose a tyrant who had become an embarrassment.

Amnesty had been watching the Central African Empire for some time. A number of happenings over the years had caused alarm and persuaded Amnesty researchers to give more than passing attention to unusual pieces of gossip or small items of news carried by the wire-services, such as the beating of thieves and cutting off of ears, and a report by an Associated Press journalist, Michael Goldsmith, on appalling conditions in Bangui prison. Amnesty also over the years had received a trickle of letters. But not until 1979 was there enough information to prove a systematic pattern of abuse.

Bokassa, whose father was assassinated when he was six and whose mother committed suicide a week later, seized power from his cousin in 1966, systematically eliminating all rivals, including his once-favoured aide, Alexandre Banza, whom he had murdered in 1969. Since 1966, judicial standards in the country had declined fast. There had been many 'disappearances' with relatives uninformed of the fate of their loved ones. Imprisonment was harsh, with a high mortality rate among political prisoners – mostly high civilian and military officials suspected of trying to overthrow Bokassa, or ordinary people suspected of trying to organize opposition movements. The Porte Rouge section of Ngaragba prison in Bangui had earned itself a notorious reputation. It contained three cells where political prisoners were herded in almost on top of each other. Food was inadequate, medical aid insufficient and prisoners were denied any contact with their families.

Cruel and inhuman punishments seemed to have become Bokassa's speciality. In July 1972, President-for-life Bokassa (this was in the days before he had been crowned emperor) decreed that thieves should have their left ear cut off. Three thieves were immediately dealt with. When thefts continued, Bokassa reacted by ordering that forty-five suspected thieves, who were being held awaiting trial, should be severely beaten by soldiers. Bokassa joined in himself, hitting prisoners with a big stick. Three of the thieves died. The corpses, along with the other beaten prisoners, were put on public display in the town. When he was told that Dr Kurt Waldheim, the UN Secretary-General, had protested, Bokassa, bursting into one of his frequent rages, called him 'a pimp, a colonialist and an imperialist'.

Bokassa hit the headlines every so often. But by and large, the world passed him by. The French government, which kept itself well-informed, kept its information to itself. The press was not greatly interested in this African backwater. Amnesty maintained its watch, almost alone, as it does on dozens of other seemingly unimportant countries.

The Amnesty alert began in January 1979. Bokassa had issued an order compelling all students in the empire to wear special uniforms, costing about $30 each, way beyond the means of most parents. Besides, the government and its multitude of agencies rarely paid its employees with anything approaching regularity.

The students began to protest and then to rampage. In the Bangui suburb of Miskine, sympathetic crowds joined in. Shops were vandalized, including one called 'Le Pacifique', owned by Bokassa's beautiful wife, Catherine.

Bokassa sent the soldiers in. Armed with machine pistols, they began shooting indiscriminately. They were met by a bow-and-arrow attack in which maybe as many as a hundred soldiers died. Bokassa asked President Mobuto of Zaire to send in troops to help quell the unrest.

An Amnesty International representative in Paris got the first wind of what had been going on from brief press reports. The information was enlarged upon when she went to a meeting of the Union National des Etudiants Central Africain held at the Bourse de Travail in Montreuil. Apart from the communist deputy-mayor of Montreuil, hers was the only white face in the auditorium. She approached the students after the meeting. They were sceptical of Amnesty with some reason.

Amnesty had not in recent years given their part of the world much detailed attention. Nevertheless, they told her that their estimate of the deaths was around four hundred.

As more information came out in the news, based on interviews with travellers and businessmen, press estimates also climbed to four hundred. Although the journalistic reports were thin, Amnesty became concerned; experience had shown that when demonstrations are put down, arrests are likely. The Research Department set to work to contact people who had recently been in the country or might know what was going on. They spoke to the relatives of prisoners, Central Africans living abroad, particularly in France, who had contacts on Bangui, and foreigners who had visited the Central African Empire. Their aim was to contact as many independent sources as possible and to cross-check the details in each account.

In mid-February, Amnesty was receiving reports suggesting that important heads of schools and lycées had been arrested, as well as an unknown number of students and some civil servants from the Ministry of Education.

During February and March, Amnesty worked hard to try and get names. It was difficult, as it often is in this kind of situation. Even people living outside the country were frightened that to give a name to Amnesty, which might then publicize it, would result in retribution. The prisoner could be killed and the family persecuted. Iran, Uganda, Ethiopia and Equatorial Guinea are all countries in which Amnesty has recently had a similar problem.

Eventually, however, Amnesty was given the names of three prominent headmasters who were in prison. It was felt their reputations were sufficient to give them a measure of protection.

By the middle of March Amnesty still only had the names of a handful of prisoners. It knew there were many more but it was hard to get hold of reliable information as there was no free press, no foreign news reporters based in the country, and no normal means of communication to transmit information. Amnesty's suspicions were aroused that Bokassa was engaged in a particularly nasty piece of repression, but they had insufficient facts to go public. There could clearly be much error, exaggeration and sheer misinformation in the material they had collected so far.

Nevertheless, Amnesty sent a cautiously worded telegram to Bokassa on 14 March. Amnesty expressed its concern at the reports of detainees held since 1973 and new prisoners detained since January. They asked Bokassa to grant a general amnesty to all those detained for their beliefs. The cable read:

> Amnesty International, a movement independent of all governments and political parties, which intervenes on behalf of prisoners of conscience throughout the world . . . has the honour to communicate its serious concern about the fate of military and civilian detainees, some of whom have been held for several years and a considerable number of whom have been detained since the events of January 1979. We ask for special amnesty for people detained for reasons of conscience.

Ten days later Bokassa replied. He said that everyone imprisoned had been released on his fifty-eighth birthday, a month before. Amnesty International, he said, could come to Central Africa to confirm this.

Amnesty attempted to see if there was any truth in his reply. Contacts did confirm that there had been prisoners released in early March. Yet there were many cases where families had had no contact with imprisoned relatives. Moreover, this wasn't the first time that Bokassa had announced an amnesty, only for news to filter out later that political prisoners were still locked up. Amnesty decided to step up its investigation.

They learnt that further arrests had taken place. This time it was the parents of the students who had participated in the January demonstrations. Then, on 21 April, Agence France Presse reported that these parents had been put on trial. According to the despatch, the ruling Central Committee had 'examined the retrograde character of the events that had occurred in the capital and condemned the disorder, hate and subversion organized by students and supported by an occult force.' The report, however, did not say what the events were. About this time, Amnesty learnt of the arrest of the Minister of Information, Barthelemy Yangongo, and others, accused of distributing tracts on behalf of an illegal opposition group, the Fronte Patriotique Oubangien.

In early May, Amnesty's Paris office was approached by a number of people who had stories of events they said occurred between 17 and 20 April, relating to the arrest and disappearance of a group of children. The Amnesty representative in Paris admits with some embarrassment that if she hadn't been away on holiday, Amnesty would have started to receive the critical information some days earlier. One important informant was waiting on her doorstep for her to return. This often happens to Amnesty. After it becomes known that Amnesty is working on a case, people who think they have information get in touch.

Sometimes they are private individuals who accidentally have run across an event or piece of information. On occasion, they are high officials, ashamed at what their colleagues are up to and seeking to unburden themselves. On 8 and 9 May, Amnesty received information from four sources in Paris, each independent of the other. Some were old and established contacts.

Again, as is often the case, there were discrepancies in the information:

Some alleged that the children, once arrested, had been taken to the Imperial court at Barengo.
Some said that all the children had been taken to the central prison, Ngaragba.
Some said the arrests had taken place in four districts; another said five districts.
All said the children were of school age, not university students.
Some said a few were as young as eight, with most between the ages of twelve and sixteen.
Others said they were between ten and fifteen years of age.

There were also differences in pin-pointing the cause of the arrests.

In London, Amnesty set to work to try and sort out the conflicting stories.

While in the middle of this they were visited by a new contact, a priest, Joseph Perrin, who had lived in Bangui between 1971 and 1976 and who returned there for a week's stay just after the killings had taken place. Father Perrin talked to more than fifty people about what had happened and passed on the information in the form of a detailed letter to Amnesty International when he returned to Europe.

Father Perrin had a wealth of detail – from people who had heard the screams of young voices in the prison; from a family who had had five sons taken away; about a boy killed with the pocket-knife he was carrying. He'd also talked to some children who had been arrested, imprisoned and then released. One of them told him that they had seen sixty-two dead children.

This report seemed to fill out the flesh on the earlier testimony. The situation was serious enough to go public. On 11 May Amnesty sent a telegram to Bokassa expressing its deep concern. It also alerted the International Year of the Child Secretariat in New York.

Three days later Amnesty issued a news release which was both direct and circumspect. Amnesty was careful not to describe the context of the incident since they were unsure of it. Nor did they publicize the allegations that Bokassa himself had been personally involved. These were not, in Amnesty's view, satisfactorily corroborated. Nor did Amnesty say that the children had been taken to the Emperor's court and killed. The details of the transfer from prison to court seemed too murky. For Amnesty, it had been a piece of investigation in the normal line of business. The slow, sometimes arduous sifting of facts.

The press release, in fact, was a model of restraint. Only in paragraph four did the bombshell explode:

On 18th April more than 100 children are known to have been taken to Bangui's central Ngaragba prison where they were held in such crowded conditions that between 12 and 28 of them are now reported to have died from suffocation. Other children are reported to have been stoned by members of the Imperial Guard to punish them for throwing stones at the Emperor's car. Some have been bayonetted or beaten to death with sharpened sticks and whips.

Amnesty said it had received reliable reports that between 50 and 100 children had been killed in prison. A witness said the bodies of 62 dead children had been buried by government officers during the night of 18 April alone.

To Amnesty's surprise, the press leapt on the story. Bokassa, the child-murderer, was page one news. The French foreign minister, Jean Francois-Poncet, was more cautious. He talked of 'conflicting reports' and his colleague, the minister of co-operation, referred to what he called 'pseudo-events'.

Information now began to pour into Amnesty in Paris and London: reports from foreigners who had been there, first-hand testimonies by people who had been at the prison. By June, Amnesty had built up an authoritative picture that nobody has credibly disputed.

The trouble had begun in January with the beating-up by some schoolchildren of two security guards sent to spy on them, following their protests about wearing school uniforms. The repression had been more severe than realized in January 1979. Between 400 and 500 people had been killed.

The arrests of the schoolchildren had begun three months later on the morning of 18 April. Most of those arrested were boys between the ages of twelve and sixteen, but some of the children were as young as eight, nine, ten and eleven. Any who attempted to resist arrest or shouted anti-government slogans were beaten up and in some cases killed on the spot.

The children were flung into the backs of trucks, and beaten with rifle-butts, whips and sticks with nails in them. By the time the trucks arrived at the prisons, many of the children had died, some from their wounds, some from being crushed alive by the weight of the others on top of them.

When the children reached the prison of Ngaragba the

guards began hurling stones at them. Several more died. As many as thirty children were crammed into each cell, which was only two metres square and had tiny windows letting in only whiffs of air. The heat was overpowering. There was no food and no water. By next morning twenty-two of the children in one cell were dead. According to a survivor of this cell, more children were pushed into the cell and a further eleven died.

Other children were tortured and killed. Some of the survivors claimed that they saw Emperor Bokassa inside the prison personally directing and participating in the killings. Another survivor described how a group of twenty boys was taken outside Bangui and killed when stones were dumped on top of them.

Amazingly, forty or so survivors were let out of the prison on 20 and 21 April. It is they who gave much of the information that Amnesty's investigation has been built on.

At first the French government was loath to recognize the Amnesty charge. Then, as the accusations gathered strength, it sought to defuse them. The chosen vehicle for this was the meeting in late May in Rwanda of the Francophone African heads of state including President Giscard d'Estaing.

They decided to send a team of five respected African jurists, from the Ivory Coast, Liberia, Rwanda, Senegal and Togo to investigate the atrocities. It would have been difficult, given the unanimity of the Francophone States, for Bokassa to have refused their request to investigate. It was, however, the first time the African nations had done anything of this kind. And it set a precedent which African nations, led by Nigeria and Senegal, have built on, seeking to establish an African Human Rights Commission, with the power to investigate and criticize. The Commission of Inquiry was a very successful first effort. It managed to interview Bokassa himself as well as senior ministers and the prime minister. It took testimony from the local Red Cross, priests, teachers, students and schoolchildren. Its report also contains interviews with ten children who were incarcerated in the Ngaragba prison, but who survived. Two of these survivors had been presumed dead by their captors and had been taken with a truck-load of dead bodies to the cemetery. In the confusion they managed to escape before being buried alive.

The Commission, besides confirming Amnesty's principal findings, also describes a number of events which Amnesty had not publicized: how local Red Cross officials were fired on by soldiers in January; reports on the personal participation in the killings by Bokassa and also by General Maimokola and Colonel Inga, senior members of the Central African Empire's armed forces. It also explains how the dead bodies were disposed of – some were taken to the cemetery, others to military camps and others thrown into the Ubangi river which flows past Ngaragba prison.

The report was made public in August. By that time several of those who had given evidence to the Commission had been executed or arrested.

In September the French sent in their paratroopers to over-throw Bokassa. For a long time France's close friend and ally, Bokassa had finally become an impossible embarrassment. No one criticized the invasion, not even the most anti-French of the African countries. There was, it seems, a crude element of self-interest in the French decision to go into the Central African Republic. President Giscard d'Estaing, when he had been minister of finance, had formed a close personal link with Bokassa. The French journal, *Le Canard Enchaîné*, revealed in its issue of 10 October 1979 that it had documents proving that Giscard had accepted a present of diamonds from Bokassa, to the value of $250,000.

Giscard did not deny it at first. His press statement was an ambiguous declaration that amounted in the eyes of some observers to a confession. It said that it was usual for presents to be exchanged when members of a government visited foreign countries but that they 'never had the character nor the value of those mentioned in the press'. What the communiqué did not mention was that when such gifts are exchanged in the course of foreign visits, they are donated publicly. Bokassa's gift, however, was not made during a public visit. It was a private present sent by special messenger. Later, just before the 1981 May election, Giscard announced he had sold the diamonds and that they were worth much less than had been said, and he had sent the proceeds to a Central African Republic charity.

The scandal gave rise to a theory as French scandals always do – that Giscard sent in the paratroopers not only to depose Bokassa, but to hijack his papers and correspondence before Bokassa could blackmail (any more?) Giscard. While the French paratroopers were sorting out Bokassa's soldiers, other troops were removing Bokassa's archives to the French embassy. This was witnessed by a number of French correspondents.

Whatever the truth in these allegations, which were to haunt Giscard right through his re-election campaign in the spring of 1981 and contributed to his defeat, there is no gainsaying the fact that Giscard's relationship with Bokassa had been un- usually close and Bokassa was adept, politically at least, at exploiting it. Giscard loved to hunt in Bokassa's private hunting area, a large tract of jungle in the east of the country, accessible only by private plane. It was Giscard's *chasse gardée*. Accompanied by Bokassa, he could shoot elephants, giraffes, and the rare white rhino. (Bokassa claimed, in an interview in the *Washington Post* just before the French election, that he gave Giscard a 3000-square-mile hunting preserve.)

Giscard's family also had close connections with the country. His cousin, Jacques Giscard d'Estaing, represented French interests in Bokassa's attempt to get uranium mining started. Another cousin, Francois, had banking interests in the country. Both have been accused by *Le Canard* of having received diamonds.

Giscard made things worse by choosing Central Africa for his first presidential visit to Africa, by being the first President to congratulate Bokassa after his crowning, and calling his host during a visit 'a cherished relative', an endearment which Bokassa used to love repeating. Take this 'imperial press release' for example: 'On October 2nd the head of the French State, M. Valéry Giscard d'Estaing, left Paris to visit his relative in the Château de Villemoran (one of the emperor's four estates in France). The Central African monarch and President Giscard d'Estaing met at a family lunch. Gifts of Central African objets d'art were given to the French head of state by His Majesty Bokassa I, thereby combining business with pleasure.'

Peculiar though Giscard's personal relationship was, it was in fact rooted in a longstanding foreign policy which had been laid down by General Charles de Gaulle. The thinking was simple, and simplistic.

Bokassa's strength in French eyes was that he was staunchly anti-communist. In the context of mid-African geopolitics, this was an important consideration, particularly when the support for the West nearby appeared rather precarious. Zaire, although also pro-West, has long been subject to unpredictable upheavals. Congo-Brazzaville has been hostile to the West. Chad is continuously in a turbulent state (and in early 1981 was effectively taken over by Libya).

Outside powers have long shown an interest in the Central African state. The Soviet Union has a large embassy and Bokassa enjoyed teasing France and upping the French economic commitment by doing deals with the Soviets. With Libya, too, he has played fast and loose. In 1976, when Colonel Gaddafi visited Bangui, Bokassa announced he'd become a Muslim. Again, a reminder to France of his real worth.

De Gaulle began the serious courting of Bokassa. Bokassa was given a grandiose official visit to Paris, complete with a wreath-laying ceremony at the Tomb of the Unknown Warrior, a triumphal drive down the Champs-Elysées, a gala night at the theatre and a ceremonial dinner at de Gaulle's residence. De Gaulle's dinner speech was sycophantic. He lauded the Central African government's achievements and added, 'Mr President, I insist on saying that this is the case more than ever and that your personality has contributed much of it.'

Eight weeks after his visit to France, Bokassa liquidated his former finance minister, Alexandre Banza, in circumstances, according to *Le Monde*, 'so revolting that it still makes one's flesh creep.' The *Le Monde* report continued, 'Two versions concerning the end circumstances of his death differ on one minor detail. Did Bokassa tie him to a pillar before personally carving him with a knife that he had previously used for stirring his coffee in the gold-and-midnight blue Sèvres coffee set or was the murder committed on the Cabinet table with the help of other persons? Late that afternoon, soldiers dragged a still identifiable corpse with the spinal column smashed from barrack to barrack to serve as an example.'

The French press did its best to highlight these allegations and Bokassa was furious, convinced that French diplomats had leaked the story. He slapped France across the face by nationalizing the diamond mining company. A little later, France's foreign minister, Maurice Shumann, attempting to placate Bokassa, sent him a carefully worded message: 'You have understood quite well that there is nothing in common between what some more or less well-informed journalist thinks he can print and the brotherly respect in which the French government has always held the Central African Republic and its head.'

Bokassa is now gone – in exile on the Ivory Coast, sentenced to death in absentia the day before Christmas 1980.

Will there be any great changes? Hopefully the wanton cruelty will not reappear.

President David Dacko, installed by the French paratroopers in September 1979, has moved reasonably effectively on the human rights front. Political prisoners were released from Ngaragba and a start made to reorganize the security forces.

Politicians who had worked for Bokassa and members of the security forces were arrested. However, there seemed to be some caution about bringing the politicians to trial – it was said they might reveal information embarrassing to Giscard. The major trial had only thirty-four people in the dock, including members of the security forces, a doctor, a nurse and various government officials. Six of the accused were sentenced to death. Three of them were alleged to have been closely involved in the murders of the children. One, Joseph Mokoa, had been the head of Bokassa's hit squad and was responsible for the deaths of at least forty military officers and one hundred civilians as well as the children.

Amnesty International repeatedly appealed for the sentences

to be commuted. They were allowed to appeal, but were finally executed by firing squad in January 1981. Other, minor trials have taken place in which the former minister of the interior, Jean-Robert Zana was acquitted (December 1980); the former minister of defence, Louis Lakouma, was also acquitted; and Bokassa's eldest sister, Catherine Gbagalama, was convicted in December 1980, but given a suspended sentence and released.

Dacko called elections in March 1981 and won by some 50,000 votes. There were, however, charges of ballot-rigging and, in the violent demonstration that followed, people were killed by security guards.

For its part, France's immediate concern has been to get the country's economy moving again and to make sure the country is not subverted by Libya. In January 1981, France reinforced its military presence in the Central African Republic in an attempt to reassure the regime that it would not go the way of neighbouring Chad and be gobbled up by invading Libyan tanks. This has been France's priority. Encouraging Dacko to prosecute Bokassa's political retinue and henchmen is not. It remains to be seen whether President Mitterrand will change his predecessor's policy on this.

Amnesty's power, it seems, does not extend to changing the fundamental *Realpolitik* of France's African policy. Amnesty can have an impact on events when they have exceeded what even the hardest diplomats and political practitioners can tolerate. But it can only have marginal influence on the political relationship that creates the environment that spawns and nurtures such behaviour.

8. Brazil: Sixteen Years of Torture

Antonio das Mortes, the work of a young Brazilian film-maker, Glauber Rocha, tells the story of a small village in the north-east of Brazil. A group of land-hungry peasants have in their despair taken to banditry. The local landowner and police chief decide that they need the special skills of Antonio das Mortes, a professional murderer. Antonio arrives and meets the peasants' leader in the village square.

Soon the peasant is dead, a knife through his heart. The peasants weep and dance and begin the struggle to carry their leader up the mountain. Antonio is overcome. He asks the landlord to open the granary and help the near-starving people. The landlord refuses. In a vision Antonio sees the peasant leader crucified on a gnarled tree. A virgin appears. She asks Antonio to seek revenge. Antonio is persuaded. He climbs down into the village and with the help of the police chief's drunken assistant, who has befriended him, he takes on the landlord's private army and wipes it out.

Fact or fiction? Mostly fact. Antonio das Mortes did exist and so did the Cangaceiros, the bandits, and their leader, Lampiao. In the mid-1930s, these land-hungry peasants with their wide-brimmed hats studded with bright metals were ruthlessly wiped out. In the late 1950s they were replaced by the more sophisticated *ligas camponesas* (peasant leagues) organized by a Marxist lawyer from Recife, Francisco Juliao. They systematically occupied land and threatened to obstruct landlords who did not agree to a programme of land reform. They, too, however, were suppressed.

It is difficult, visiting Piloezinhos, a tiny out-of-the-way village in the north-east of Brazil, to think that this story is the local living history. Around the quiet, ordered village square, the houses of the richer peasants built in a simple Portuguese colonial style with yellow or blue façades and red clay tiles for the roof. Behind are the coconut and banana groves. Behind them are the homes of the landless, rudely built from sticks and clay. Rising into the mists are the orange groves, the sisal estates and the sugar plantations of the *latifundiario*, the large landowners who, from far away – Recife or even Rio – still give the orders and take most of the money. At first sight, it is the kind of place Gauguin would make famous. At second sight, it is a Picasso mask.

This village is one of thousands in the Nordeste – the poorest part of Brazil. The land is distributed here more unequally than anywhere else on the globe, by a tenure system imposed in the sixteenth century. The *latifundiario*, only 4 per cent of the population, own 70 per cent of the land.

Every day a child dies in Piloezinhos. The undertaker lives in Guarabira, the small market town five kilometres down a pot-holed road. In his shop front are the stacked layers of children's coffins: blue with white crosses on top. More often than not the children go alone to the cemetery to bury their companions. Fathers often hear of their children's deaths only when they come back home on occasional holidays. Most of the young men of Piloezinhos are away in the big cities. Emigration has hit the village like a small plague. To escape the harshness of feudal servitude, to provide some hope of improvement for their children, the men trek to Rio de Janeiro and Sao Paulo.

After a few years of commuting in six-month trips, the men usually send for their wives and children. They lose the beauty of Piloezinhos but gain the companionship of their family. One man I talked to felt differently. He had just come back from Rio. He said he would never take his five daughters to the *favela* (shantytown). He could not bear to watch them be corrupted by the filth and the crime.

The will to live in Piloezinhos is slowly ebbing. An old man on the bus coming back from the weekly market in Guarabira told me that his landlord had said this was the last year he could rent his small piece of land. His landlord was going to put down the land to sugar cane. The man no doubt could work for eighteen *cruzeiros* a day (65 pence) cleaning sugar cane. That, however, is difficult work for an old man. But what else? He would never find work in the town.

In Guarabira lives the local Catholic bishop, Dom Marcelo Carvalheira. A youthful fifty-two-year-old, dressed in slacks and open shirt, Dom Marcelo is a passionate opponent of an economic system which he believes is driving the people to destitution. 'Things have always been bad,' he argues, 'now they are getting worse. Since the commercial farmers came in, buying out the feudal owners and putting down the land to sugar cane or cattle ranching, tens of thousands of families have been evicted. One has only to go to the market-place to see that their standard of living is falling dramatically.' Dom Marcelo's bed is an old door supported on bricks. There is no mattress. In 1969 he was jailed for two months, falsely accused of being part of Carlos Marighella's urban guerrilla group. The military regime fought the Vatican tooth and nail when his name was suggested for bishop.

On one of the Fridays of Lent in 1979, Dom Marcelo organized a 'way of the cross' procession that would go through the lands of the evicted peasants. On the eve of the procession, the local police commander came to visit him with an imposing group of subordinates, all heavily and ostentatiously armed. 'They urged me to give up the procession, alleging it was a political act and would lead to retaliation from the landowners. There was even talk that they would resort to shooting and the bishop's life would be in danger,' the prelate recalled. The procession went ahead – uneventfully, although nervously. A number of Brazilian clergymen have died for taking this kind of stand.

Recently, he told me, the Brazilian bishops' conference issued a document entitled 'The Church and the Problem of Land'. It quotes the 1975 farm census to the effect that 1 per cent of the farmers own nearly half Brazil's land. 'Everywhere we hear the cry of these suffering people,' the bishops wrote, 'who are either threatened with the loss of land they have, or are powerless to get any.'

Within the diocese, Dom Marcelo has set up a human rights

office. Manned by a local lawyer, himself the son of a peasant, and a team of volunteers, it has started to challenge landlords in the courts. In theory, the law protects the rights of tenants and sharecroppers. In practice they are ignored or abused.

Another group, led by a nun, Valeria Rezende, and a handful of lay volunteers, has successfully helped evicted tenants to build their own well, construct houses on the edge of the town and organize their children to build their own schools.

Simultaneously there is the long-term work of welding the tenants into a body that can make its weight felt at the time of a mass eviction. For the church workers in Guarabira, events in Algamar, in the same archdiocese, provided inspiration. Seven hundred families were evicted from one estate. The tenants refused to go. Earlier last year, the archbishop of Joao Pessoa, Jose Maria Pires, and the neighbouring archbishop of Recife, Helder Camara, were photographed by the press and television helping the tenants drive the landlord's new cattle herds off their bean patches. President Joao Baptista Figueiredo was forced to intervene. Under an old law that allows expropriation in cases of social tension, he handed over one-sixth of the estate to the peasants. The case continues in the courts, pursued by the archdiocese's human rights lawyer.

At the moment, the church's work is still a drop in the ocean. Piloezinhos, it is likely, will be even poorer this time next year. More children will be dying. More landless will be erecting their forlorn houses. But there is a distant hope. Give it another three years and maybe it will be a different story.

On 4 August 1980 Amnesty International issued an 'urgent action' appeal, very different from those it had been putting out regularly during the previous eight years of reporting on Brazil. It read:

On 28 July 1980 Wilson Souza Pinheiro, president of the Agricultural Workers' Union in northwest Brazil, was murdered when unidentified gunmen invaded the union's headquarters. In a separate incident, another rural workers' union leader, Raimundo Lima, was shot dead by gunmen;

according to reports, the gunmen had been hired by landowners in the Araguaia river area.

Amnesty International is becoming increasingly concerned about the violent repression of smallholders and squatters in rural areas as landowners attempt to systematically expel them from their land in order to further their business interests. Many peasants have come into conflict with local landowners while trying to defend their property and there have been reports that many peasants have been tortured, detained and even killed by hired gunmen or local police acting on the orders of the landowners . . .

. . . A local official in the Amazon is reported to have said 'The only way to solve land conflicts is by killing the head of the rural workers' union, the representatives of rural workers' federations and those priests who spend their time instigating the peasants.'

The press release in effect announced that the battle for human rights in Brazil was shifting away from the courts and prisons of the big cities, where torture, prison sentences, police and army practice were relatively easy to document, to the more nebulous feudal violence of the rural backwaters.

For Amnesty this presents new problems of definition. The human rights issues in Brazil of the 1980s are more localized, more in the hands of landlords and land-buyers. Moreover, Amnesty's statute does not allow it to address directly the problem of land purchase and consolidation of migration and dispersion. Only when someone is shot and murdered and there seems to be evidence that the act is tolerated by the police does Amnesty have grounds for getting involved.

Amnesty's strength is also its weakness. It is an international body with a wide membership reflected in a heterogeneous board. Approval of a new direction is not easy. Different constituencies have to be consulted. The various political leanings and biases of the membership weighed up. Amnesty is at its best when the issues are stark and clear. Then Amnesty's mandate is unequivocal – and the organization very effective.

The situation in Brazil in the early 1970s was very stark and very clear. It all began with the army coup in 1964 that deposed the left-leaning President Joao Goulart.

Brazil, which had begun to industrialize quite rapidly, had not adapted its institutions to the twentieth century. There was much social unrest and Goulart was being pushed leftwards at a pace even faster than he wanted to go. The army stepped in and the first four years of uneasy army rule began. It was welcomed not only by the upper class but also by the middle class, the church hierarchy, and the United States.

A series of institutional acts, constitutional amendments and executive decrees were introduced to strengthen the power of the executive. The power of congress, of state legislators and of the judiciary was progressively undermined. Elections of the president and state governor became indirect: in theory by congress and state legislatures; in practice by the military high command. The old political parties were suspended. Civil liberties were eroded. Hundreds of Brazilians were stripped of their political rights, jailed or removed from their jobs.

Urban guerrilla activity had begun, student protests were big and numerous. The country seemed to be polarizing fast. Then in 1968 there was what the Brazilians have called 'the coup within a coup'. Hardliners within the military establishment took power and cracked down hard on political dissidence. The programmes of censorship, repression and torture were intensified.

The military's most serious step was the promulgation of Institutional Act No. 5. In effect this gave the executive unlimited power of repression. Congress was closed, supreme court judges were suspended, criticism made practically impossible. Several hundred politicians and officials were deprived of what the Brazilians call *cassado* (political rights) and thousands of intellectuals, journalists, teachers, students and labour leaders were arrested. The opposition from the revolutionary left was crushed and its leader, Carlos Marighella, killed in a gun battle with the police.

For at least six years, the police and army appeared to have more or less a free hand to root out dissent as cruelly as they wished. Moreover, what the police couldn't get away with during duty hours, they did off-duty. The death squads, often off-duty or retired policemen, became notorious, intimidating the population with their threats and 'executions'.

Amnesty's involvement in Brazil began in 1965. In 1970 it sent a delegation to the Brazilian embassy in London to express concern about the continuous reports of torture they were receiving. In the course of two visits, they gave the embassy the information they had on the names of people who had died under torture, the suspected torturers, along with a proposed press release. The embassy forwarded the material to Brasilia. But there was no response. Amnesty put out its press statement, the first of many.

Amnesty kept up its pressure on the embassy, asking permission to send in a mission. A wide variety of countries have over the years accepted Amnesty missions, even particularly repressive ones like Guatemala and Zaire. Brazil refused, however. The Brazilian ambassador, Roberto de Oliveira Campos, wrote to Amnesty:

> In the event of the government feeling that at any time it would be in the national interest for members of the International Community to be given access to matters concerned with Brazil's internal jurisdiction, it would turn to the United Nations or the Organization of American States.

Amnesty was left with no alternative but to begin the laborious process of attempting to collate the material that was available in Europe. There were numerous exiles in Europe, all with their sources of information. The church, which was becoming more liberal, later radical, was also an important conduit.

By 1972 Amnesty was in a position to publish its *Report on Allegations of Torture in Brazil*. It was the first Amnesty report focusing exclusively on torture, and it was longer than usual. It had been meticulously researched, containing a wealth of detail, and it attracted a large amount of press publicity.

Governments asked for copies. Brazil's practices were on the map.

In one section there was an analysis of the procedure for political trials. Thousands of prisoners were being held for up to three years without trial. And the legal procedures were so structured as to make torture relatively easy to organize and implement. The report described three stages in the legal procedures – police investigations, police enquiry and the judicial hearing.

During the first stage the detainee could be in the custody of the military police or in the hands of a number of special security forces. These latter were paramilitary forces, constantly being renamed and reorganized. Their lines of authority were unclear and it was often difficult for concerned relatives and lawyers to find out where prisoners were being held or by whom. It became difficult for lawyers to present writs of habeas corpus, since they rarely knew where their client was. The detention of prisoners was often not even communicated to the official legal authorities. In a moving letter, one mother told of her attempts to keep track of her son. The letter was written to the Pernambuco legislative assembly:

Recife, 25 April 1971

Dear Sirs,

I, Ana Daura de Andrade Morais, mother of Carlos Alberto Soares, who is at present in prison charged with political activities contrary to the regulations of the present government, call on your Assembly.

Having learnt of the torture undergone by my son at the air force barracks, and having unsuccessfully tried, in every way possible, to see him, I call upon you to allow me, by virtue of my rights as a mother, to give him all the physical and mental assistance that his present state of health requires.

I therefore bring to the attention of your Assembly the events which I have witnessed and which I have undergone from the time of my son's arrest until now.

My son, Carlos Alberto Soares, was arrested on 7

February of this year (according to information which I later received). It was only on 27 February that I was able to see him in the headquarters of the Department for Social and Political Order. In March he was transferred to the Dias Cardoso barracks where I was given permission to see him once a week until 4 April, a Sunday: on my arrival on that day for my customary visit, I learnt that my son had been transferred to the air force barracks. The same day, I went to the air force base of Piedade where I was told simply that I could only speak with Colonel Camara during weekdays. So, I returned another day and Colonel Camara told me that my son was incommunicado but that he would soon be returned to the Dias Cardoso barracks.

On Monday 12 April there was a hearing in the Chamber of Military Justice, at which time I was able to see my son. He arrived handcuffed and showed evident signs of torture. His face was swollen and he had heavy bruising in the left eye and was bruised about the throat, behind the ears, on the neck and on the stomach. His legs and hands were enormously swollen and his fingernails were badly marked. My son was in an extremely weak condition. He asked me for swimming trunks because his testicles were swollen: I got the trunks for him the very same day and I handed them in at the air force police station, but I do not know if they were ever given to him since I have not been allowed to see him since. The Army Council ordered on the same day that an examination be carried out to establish the facts of the torture – this was performed during an examination undertaken by the doctors at the military hospital.

The following day, I went once more to the air force barracks in Piedade to ask Colonel Camara to allow me to see my son: permission was again refused. Colonel Camara then stated that my son would return to the barracks within 48 hours. This did not occur.

There was a new hearing in the court of Military Justice at which my son, Carlos Alberto, was to appear, but did not. I was very worried and returned once more to see Colonel

Camara. I begged him to allow me to see my son, even at a distance, but was again refused.

In addition to the fact of having seen visible proof of torture, as did all those present in the courtroom, I also received telephone calls ostensibly from the air force barracks, informing me that my son's torture continued even after his lawyer submitted a request that a medical examination be carried out on Carlos and that the traces of torture be officially verified. Today, Sunday 25 April, I went once again to the Dias Cardoso barracks and was informed that my son had not yet been transferred there.

Gentlemen, please be assured that I am aware of the charges against my son and of the penalties to which he will probably be condemned. I ask only that his rights as a defendant and my rights as a mother are not denied. I appeal to you to allow me to give physical and psychological assistance to my son, and to permit me, insofar as I am able, to bring him the moral support he needs.

Signed: Ana Daura de Andrade Morais

The Code of Military Penal Procedure allowed secret detention for a period of up to fifty days. This gave ample time for torture to be conducted and 'confessions' to be wrung out of the prisoners.

The second stage in the legal proceedings, the enquiry, was meant to be a 'provisional hearing'. This was when the 'confessions' were presented. There were many cases, however, of prisoners attempting at this point to rescind their testimony in the 'confessions'. They were then taken off for more torture.

The third stage, the judicial hearing, was heard before a military tribunal, made up of five judges, four military and one civilian, a qualified judge. The military judges were changed every three months, so for the longer trials the military judges had little idea what was going on. The judges often exerted strong pressure on the witnesses. Defence witnesses were intimidated not to appear.

The places of torture were widespread. One centre mentioned in Amnesty's report was the fifth floor of the

Ministry of the Navy in Rio de Janeiro, next door to the US naval mission. The screams and groans of the captives could be heard by the Americans. Another was at the prison of the 12th infantry regiment in Belo Horizonte. One of the best known was at the headquarters of the paramilitary organization, Operacao Bandeirantes, in Sao Paulo. OBAN, as it was locally known, worked in an elegant district of the city, Ibirapuera. The methods used by OBAN were described in a declaration signed by eleven well-known Brazilian journalists who had been imprisoned by OBAN.

Torture ranged from simple but brutal blows from a truncheon to more refined methods: the end of a reed was placed in the anus of a naked man hanging suspended downwards on the *pau de arara* (a horizontal bar from which the prisoner was suspended) and a piece of cotton soaked in petrol was lit at the other end of the reed. Pregnant women were forced to watch their husbands being tortured, and other wives were hung naked beside their husbands and given electric shocks on their sex organs. Children were tortured before their parents, parents before their children. At least one child, the three-month-old baby of Virgilio Gornes da Silva, was reported to have died under police torture.

Marcos Arruda was a young geologist who was picked up by the police and tortured by the OBAN. His case had attracted the attention of the Vatican and after his release, he sent on 4 February 1971, a moving letter to the Pope. It was reproduced in the Amnesty report. He wrote:

> I was arrested on 11 May 1970 in Sao Paulo on my way to dinner with a young lady that I had recently met. I learnt afterwards that she belonged to a political organization. She had been arrested several days previously, violently tortured and taken to Operacao Bandeirantes.
>
> I was picked up even before I reached the meeting place and taken off in a car (the licence plate was not an official one) by four armed policemen. We went to OBAN head-quarters. During the journey the leader of the group

ordered the young lady to show me her hands so that 'I could have an idea of what awaited me'. She lifted her hands, which were handcuffed, and I saw that they were greatly swollen and were covered with dark purple hematomes. I learned that she had been badly beaten with a type of palmatoria. Once the car stopped in the OBAN courtyard, they began immediately to punch and kick me in the presence of some people seated on benches in front of the main building. I was beaten as I went up the steps to a room on the top floor where they continued to slap me, hit me about the head and bang my ears with cupped hands (telephone torture); they took the handcuffs off and continued to hit me with their truncheons whilst questioning me.

They ordered me to strip completely; I obeyed. They made me sit down on the ground and tied my hands with a thick rope. One of the six or seven policemen present put his foot on the rope in order to tighten it as much as possible. I lost all feeling in my hands. They put my knees up to my elbows so that my bound hands were on a level with my ankles. They then placed an iron bar about eight centimetres wide between my knees and elbows and suspended me by resting the two ends of the iron bar on a wooden stand so that the top part of my body and my head were on one side and my buttocks and legs on the other, about three feet from the floor. After punching me and clubbing me, they placed a wire on the little toe of my left foot and placed the other end between my testicles and my leg. The wires were attached to a camp telephone so that the current increased or decreased according to the speed at which the handle was turned. They began to give me electric shocks using this equipment and continued to beat me brutally both with their hands and with a palmatoria – a plaque full of holes – which left a completely black hematome, larger in size than an outstretched palm, on one of my buttocks. The electric shocks and the beatings continued for several hours. I had arrived at about 14.30 and it was beginning to get dark when I practically lost consciousness. Each time that I fainted, they threw water over me to increase my sensitivity to the electric shocks. They then took the wire from my testicles and began to apply it to my face and head, giving me terrible shocks on my face, in my ears, eyes, mouth and nostrils. One of the policemen remarked, 'Look, he is letting off sparks. Put it in his ear now.' The group of torturers were under the command of Captain Albernaz and consisted of about six men, amongst them Sergeants Tomas, Mauricio, Chico and Paulinho.

The torture was so serious and long-lasting that I thought I would die. I began to feel completely drained; my body was covered in a cold sweat; I could not move my eyelids; I was swallowing my tongue and could only breathe with difficulty; I could no longer speak. I tried throughout this time to think of great men who had suffered horrible things for a noble ideal. This encouraged me to fight on and not give way to despair. I felt that my hands would become gangrenous because circulation was blocked for some hours. I moaned 'my hands, my hands!' and they continued to beat my hands with their clubs. I think I eventually lost consciousness. When I came to, they had lowered the bar and laid me out on the ground. They tried to revive me with ammonia but I didn't respond. They struck me on the testicles with the end of the stick; they burnt my shoulders with cigarette stubs; they put the barrel of a revolver into my mouth saying they would kill me. They threatened me with sexual abuse. Suddenly, my whole body began to tremble and I began to writhe as if shaken by an earthquake. The policemen were alarmed and called for a doctor from the first-aid post. They said I was a soldier who was feeling ill. They gave me an injection and refused to give me water although my body was completely dehydrated. They left me to sleep in the same room in which I had been tortured.

The following morning I was shaken violently by the shoulders. I realized that I was still shaking, my eyelids were shut, my tongue was paralysed and I felt strange muscular contractions on the right side of my face. My left leg was like a piece of wood, the foot turned downwards and the toes had contracted and would not move. The small toe was totally black. After enduring many insults, I was carried to the general military hospital of Sao Paulo. The sole of my left foot was again forcibly struck in order to try and return it to its normal position and to make it fit into my shoe. Despite shooting pains, the foot would not move. The torturers took me by the arms and legs and brought me like a sack to the courtyard where I was thrown into the back of the van.

I later learned that at the hospital they gave me only two hours to live. The military chaplain came to hear my confession. I asked the soldiers who were on guard in my room to leave us alone but they refused. In these circumstances, the priest could only give absolution *in extremis* in case I should die. For several days I was subjected to interrogation at the hospital despite the fact that my condition had not improved. The fifth day after I was admitted to hospital two policemen opened up the door to my room saying, 'Now that you are alone we are going to get rid of you. You are going to die . . .' and one of them began to hit me about the face and body. I tried to protect myself and to cry out but I was still shaking and could hardly move. In addition, my twisted tongue prevented me from crying out loudly. I could not see them well because my eyelids still would not move. The policemen continued to say, 'No one can hold out against Sergio Adao, you are going to die . . .' He went out for a moment with the other to see if anyone was coming and then returned to continue. Eventually, I managed to cry out loudly. They were frightened and left me . . .

I remained in the general hospital for about a month and a half. During this time I was visited several times for questioning. My family had been trying to help me and for over a month had been trying unsuccessfully to find me. I finally received a note which told me that they had discovered where I was. But I remained incommunicado without permission to see my family for five more months, and I received no visit from a lawyer throughout the duration of my detention.

When I was released from the hospital, my right eyelid was still paralysed (it remained so until the month of December) and I had a slight but constant shake in the shoulders, the left arm and leg; the latter, half paralysed, could not support any weight and I was obliged to use a broom stick for a walking stick.

I was sent back to OBAN, put in a cell, and told to write out a statement . . . I finished this in three days, at the end of which time I was brought face to face with the young woman whom I had been on my way to meet at the time of my arrest. It was six o'clock when I was carried into the room where she was kept. They wanted me to admit the name of the organization to which they believed I belonged and to give names of supposed comrades. They began to carry the young woman off into another room and gave her a strong electric shock in order to make me talk (they were afraid to torture me again in view of my poor physical condition). I heard the cries of the girl being tortured and when they brought her back into my room she was shaking and totally distraught. I was paralysed with fear at witnessing such cruelty and even more terrified when they threatened to do the same to members of my family if I didn't tell them what they wanted to know. They repeated the electric shock treatment to the girl and, seeing that they were not achieving anything, decided to call the doctor to examine me physically to see if I was fit to undergo more torture. The doctor ordered certain tablets and said that I should not be given food. They brought me back to my cell and were to return for me later. Having seen that they were ready to torture the young woman again, and possibly members of my family as well, I decided to try and protect these people and I agreed to write out another deposition.

I was carried into the room of a certain Captain Dauro,* who, along with another officer, offered me coffee and cigarettes and advised me in a friendly way to cooperate with them. I began by saying that I did not want to

---

* Other witnesses have referred to this captain as Dalmo.

cooperate with them since they represented the institutions of force and violence to which we are subjected and because they used such inhuman treatment when dealing with people against whom they had no proof. They were irritated and began to torture the young woman once again in order to make me talk. Finally, they used violence on me again, along with insults and moral attacks, threats concerning members of my family and even attempts to strangle me. They blindfolded me and pushed a revolver against my forehead – all to the same end. After several hours, they carried the young girl and me back to our cells. Major Gil, head of OBAN, and Captain Dauro, Captain Faria, jailer Robert, a huge lieutenant with ginger hair and moustache, a young feeble-looking black and three others, about whom I can remember nothing, took part in this torture session.

The following evening, when they came for me I was again suffering from contractions, my right side was paralysed, I dribbled, my body twitched constantly . . .

The next morning I was carried into court. My condition had considerably worsened and my seizures were continual and more visible. I was photographed, my fingerprints were taken and I was then brought into a room on the same floor as the torture room. A sergeant in a military police uniform with his name band covered with a sash, interrogated me calmly for forty-five minutes. He threatened me alternately with torture and death if I refused to confess. Later, he told me that he was a doctor and knew that I would die if he permitted me to be tortured again. In the end, he gave me an injection for my spasms and told me that I ought to be taken back to the hospital. Throughout the night, I was locked up in a bathroom and was then taken to a doctor, Primo Alfredo, who had recently been arrested. Throughout the night, we heard as usual the terrible screams of people being tortured. The following morning I was once again brought to the military hospital.

Two days later my condition began to worsen and I lost consciousness and became delirious – this condition lasted more than ten days. I learnt afterwards what had happened during that period . . .

. . . It is clear that my case is not exceptional as such events have become commonplace during the last few years in Brazil.

. . . I thank your Holiness for your interest and the action taken in an attempt to secure my release. I beg you to do the same for the other thousands of men and women who suffer the same treatment in Brazil and in other countries . . . unfortunate human beings who continue to be tortured . . .

Signed: Marcos Pena Settamini de Arruda

Amnesty has in its archives dozens of similar letters and testimonies. The constant outpourings of Amnesty, quoting these cases, publishing the worst in full, drew more attention to Brazil.

One telling example is the case of Luiz Rossi, professor of economics and head of the faculty of philosophy, science and letters at Penapolis University in the state of Sao Paulo, Brazil.

On the night of 15 February 1973 a small army surrounded his house in Aracatuba – a combined operation by local police and agents of Sao Paulo's political police, DOPS, backed up by military policemen armed with submachine-guns. They stormed into his house and ransacked it, confiscating books and documents. Nearly six hours later, at 1 a.m., they took away the professor and a visitor. Both men were taken to the army's regional headquarters at Lins. Maria Rossi and the children were kept at the house under surveillance for two days. Two days later Mrs Rossi, together with the Bishop of Lins, Pedro Koop, attempted to make enquiries at the army HQ. The army confirmed merely that it was holding the professor. Two days after that, Maria Rossi was told that he had been transferred, but not where to. From then on she could get no news as to his whereabouts. She was met by a wall of silence.

Amnesty International was alerted to the case in March by a newspaper cutting and an appeal from one of Luiz Rossi's university colleagues. The information arrived on 16 March.

Three days later, after checking it, Amnesty International headquarters issued urgent appeals to international educational and humanitarian organizations. A double adoption of the case was organized – by the West German Amnesty group No. 363, in Emden, and the French group No. 18, in Montpellier.

As reports that Luiz Rossi was being tortured came in, letters from Amnesty International members began to stream into Brazil; funds were raised to sustain the appeal and press coverage organized. (The whole system of urgent actions, now part and parcel of Amnesty's daily work, was developed as a result of this Brazilian experience. Amnesty was receiving such a continuous stream of well-documented reports of torture from Brazil that it was necessary to devise some system of fast response.)

The campaign, involving principally the two adoption groups in France and West Germany, continued non-stop until the first week in May. Then Maria Rossi wrote that she had been allowed to see her husband; she said he was 'well' and had been 'released'. 'Thank you for your interest,' she wrote.

It was a puzzling letter – in her own handwriting – which seemed to contradict most of Amnesty International's information about her husband's plight. Most peculiar of all, it had been mailed in an envelope bearing the name of the prison director.

Three days later Maria Rossi wrote again, explaining all. The prison director, Dr Lucio Vieira, had called her in and instructed her to reply to Amnesty International's correspondence on Luiz Rossi. He had told her she must say he was 'well' and had not been 'torn to pieces'. Obviously his secretary mailing the letter had not quite understood what she was supposed to do.

The truth was, Mrs Rossi said, that her husband had been subjected to prolonged physical torture and had been told she and the children would be tortured if he did not cooperate. But now he was no longer being tortured and was in fact well.

Amnesty International's letter campaign seemed to have had an impact on the authorities; enough to make Dr Vieira respond in the way he did; perhaps enough to end the torture. Whether the appeals and letters resulted in Luiz Rossi's release on 24 October 1973, Amnesty does not know for sure. But it is certain they helped Luiz Rossi in other ways. He wrote after his release: 'In my own name, in the name of my wife, of my children and of other Brazilians in similar situations, we should like to thank all the proofs of humanity and kindness that have comforted and helped us.'

Professor Rossi was to have been tried in March 1975 on charges of trying do restart the banned Communist Party. By then he and his family had fled Brazil.

Yet whatever progress was made on individual cases, the state of Brazil seemed as tight as a drum. The government felt secure. The economic miracle was in full swing with growth rates of around 10 per cent a year. Capital was pouring in and, whatever individuals or organizations might do, Western governments continued to be friendly.

In 1974 Ernesto Geisel became president. Although he was one of the chief architects and pillars of the 1964 military coup, he was more liberal than his predecessor General Medici. Words like *descompressao, normalizacao, abertura,* and *distensao* came into vogue. Press censorship was considerably relaxed and elections were held for congress and the state legislature. To the surprise of the military, the opposition party, the Movimento Democratica Brazileiro (MDB), won victories in most of the urban areas of Brazil, particularly in Sao Paulo. Many observers thought the regime might retreat at this point from its liberalization line. To its credit, it didn't, although much less was heard of the *abertura* – the opening. And renewed attacks were launched on 'communist infiltrators' in the media, unions, the bureaucracy and the university. Some of the more outspoken deputies were arrested.

Nevertheless, it was clear that the combination of outside pressure, spearheaded by Amnesty, but including internal pressure from the church, and economic growth were combining to persuade the regime that it could afford gradually to relax its hold. After all, its most ferocious critics were dead, imprisoned or in exile. The one exception was the church. Although a few priests had been killed, by and large this Catholic country respected its church, even when it moved to the left. And the church had become very radical.

Many outsiders have heard of Archbishop Helder Camara of Recife, who for years has been persecuted by the government, his house sprayed with machine-gun bullets, his assistant murdered, his words, written and spoken, banned. Yet what is not so often realized is that whereas fifteen years or so ago Archbishop Camara was a lone voice, he now represents mainstream opinion among the Brazilian bishops.

The church in Brazil, during the days of empire in the eighteenth and nineteenth centuries, provided one of the principal supports for elitist monarchical rule. Although with the birth of the Republic in 1889 church and state were separated, the church by and large remained a friend of the state, participating in state ceremonies and concentrating its energies on matters that were apolitical.

Around the late 1940s the writings of the French Catholic left – by people like Jacques Maritain, Emmanuel Maunier and the French Dominican, L. B. Lebret – began to be a major influence. Then in 1952 the Brazilian bishops established their own National Conference and appointed as secretary-general a young bishop, Helder Camara, who at that time was no radical. Indeed, as a young priest he had toyed with fascism; if anything, he was an evangelist who believed in big events, big rallies, in which good old-time religion was preached. At some point, however, he began to see that Brazil's rapid economic development was at the expense of the mass of the poor. A large comfortable middle class was being built up at the same time as the *favelas* grew and the peasantry sank deeper into apathy and wretched poverty.

Many bishops, however, were in profound disagreement with Camara's line of social and political reform. Many agreed with the government that the dangers of communist influence overrode other concerns. Yet gradually through the 1960s and early 1970s, as the old bishops retired or died and were replaced by younger men, more turned to Helder Camara and to the ideals of the Second Vatican Council, and the church became increasingly daring.

Now it is true that on social issues the church leadership is fairly united: it is socially committed and politically to the left. Two of its four Cardinals are particularly militant.

Slowly but surely under the pressure of the church, the press, which had been slowly liberalized, the legal profession and even parts of the business community, the regime loosened the reins. In June 1978 censorship was formally abolished. And in the national elections that year, the MDB was allowed to run a presidential candidate, albeit a general. The MDB was able to build on its 1974 success and many of its more outspoken candidates were elected. The Brazil magazine *Veja* referred to 'galloping democratic inflation', and the *New York Review of Books* printed an article entitled 'Is Brazil on the brink of Democracy?'.

In January 1979 the Law of National Security was reformed and penalties for crimes of subversion were reduced. An amnesty was formally approved in 1979. All but fifty-six of the political prisoners were released, and all the exiles, including the official communists, were allowed to return. Amnesty's fourteen prisoners of conscience were among the freed.

In August of that year, Amnesty International sent a cable to the recently elected president, Joao Baptista de Oliveira Figueiredo, welcoming the amnesty. It urged, however, a pardon to the remaining prisoners, and asked about the sixty known cases of people who were known to have been in police custody and tortured, but could no longer be traced. Receiving no response, later that year Amnesty started up a campaign on behalf of thirty political prisoners who had been excluded from the amnesty because they had been convicted of crimes of violence.

This issue of violence has always been a controversial point among Amnesty supporters. Amnesty only seeks the unconditional release of prisoners who have conducted non-violent opposition to the government. To define its terms of reference more loosely would have posed the risk of Amnesty ending up supporting guerrilla movements. At the same time it is often the case, as in Brazil, that the judicial proceedings are so unfair that one cannot depend on the court's findings of violence. Moreover, Amnesty has always been against torture and violence whatever the crime.

There is, it must be admitted, a narrow dividing line, and Amnesty workers are often tempted to broaden their concerns rather than narrow them. For their more conservative members, this is a worrying development. There are nagging doubts from some members that Amnesty play closer to the rule book when dealing with the oppressive regimes of the left.

In the Brazilian case, having come so far, it was difficult to let go at this point. The issue came to a head when political prisoners throughout the country began a hunger strike to protest at what they said were the arbitrary terms of the amnesty. Amnesty sent telegrams urging cases to be reviewed.

Two cases in particular drew Amnesty's attention – those of Rholine Sondo Cavalcanti and Luciani Almeida who were being held in the notorious Itamaraca penitentiary in north-east Brazil. They were serving terms of sixty-five and eighty-five years respectively. They began their hunger strike in December 1979 and by January were close to death. Amnesty increased its pressure and was ultimately successful. They were released.

By mid-1980 there were no political prisoners in Brazil. It was the end of a terrible sixteen years – thousands tortured and 325 political activists killed or 'disappeared' after being arrested by the security forces. Other problems were looming in their place. Brazil is going through a period of great economic transformation, which is producing tension and resentment among the factory workers, particularly in the Sao Paulo industrial belt. There are signs that the economic miracle is in trouble, and that the government, in order to contain the situation, might be forced into a new bout of repression.

Brazil is a nation of gross extremes. Most advanced among the developing countries, it has quadrupled its gross national product in fifteen years; but in the north-east, where one-third of its 130 million people live, the life expectancy of its poorer classes is less than Bangladesh's. Brazil's highest-paid can earn 500 times more than the lowest.

The sixth-most-populous country in the world, Brazil has an economic growth rate that most of the time reaches towards the 10 per cent mark. Yet the real income of its swelling proletariat has been decreasing since 1964.

This roster of contradictions forms the background against which the wizardry of its economic potentate, Antonio Delfim Netto, is meant to work. Netto's reputation, earned from the days when he began the 'miracle' in the late 1960s, is supposed to guide him through the quicksands of an inflation rate of nearly 90 per cent, and the spending on oil and debt repayments of nearly everything Brazil earns from its exports.

All this makes the political and economic community distinctly uneasy. Their nervousness is compounded by the way Delfim Netto is playing his hand – close to his chest. A senior international banker just back from a visit to Brasilia told me that it was impossible to obtain even the basic facts, such as the level of reserves and the planned rate of borrowing.

There are two principal schools of thought as to what is going to happen. The optimistic scenario has Delfim Netto bringing down the growth rate to around 5.5 per cent. He'll bully the foreign bankers to keep on rolling over the debts by playing one off against the other and by reminding them they cannot afford to pull the plug on a country that owes them so much. The combination of these policies will prepare Brazil to resume in a year or two the high road to growth, fuelled by new large loans.

The pessimistic school of thought looks at the balance-of-payments problem and the high inflation. Moreover, with the industrialized world in a recession, who wants to buy large amounts of Brazilian products? The international banks, too, are being leaned on by their host governments to be careful about over-extending their lines of credit. This leads the pessimists to conclude that Brazil's growth rate must come down to 4 per cent; better still, 3 per cent. Only in this way can the economy be brought into balance. The political price, it is realized, will be high. The real incomes of the workers will fall even faster than heretofore. The social services that were promised in more euphoric days will be cut. Workers who step out of line will be dealt with perhaps as in the days of General Emilio Medici and Delfim Netto's first 'miracle' – by bloody repression.

The truth of the matter is that even if the first scenario were possible in the short run, it is likely to bring on the second over the long run. Given Brazil's overwhelming backlog of social and political problems, 5.5 per cent growth is not enough to steer it into clear water. At that rate, the economy can do nothing for half of the million workers who join the labour force each year and add to the already teeming and mushrooming *favelas*. The wage squeeze, even under this milder formula, is savage enough to spur more strikes. Foreign investors and bankers will decide to step back a pace to see what is going to happen. Brazil's leaders, desperate to keep their reputation as good financial housekeepers, will pull the 4 per cent lever.

Is there any reason to think that the government will be able to pacify the resulting unrest? Although the increasingly powerful Lula,* the leader of the unofficial unions, is explicitly against violence, he also says, in his careful non-hyperbolic manner, that it may be difficult to hold the line. The workers, moreover, have important friends, not least the church, which is prepared to support them through a long period of confrontation. The bankers and investors may get scared long before President Joao Baptista Figueiredo gets back on top of things.

The tragedy of Brazil is that to be caught in this way is unnecessary. Brazil's ambitious road and dam programmes, its nuclear developments, its mammoth-scale industrial projects and freeloading credit for the big commercial farms consume large slices of the government's revenues. If, instead, the government diverted these expenditures in the direction of land reform, credit for the small farmers, water and sewerage for the *favelas*, and health care for the work force, and if it

* His real name is Ignacio da Silva, but everyone in Brazil knows him as Lula.

moved, as Lula suggests, to running Brazil with 130 million minds instead of with one, it might buy itself a measure of tolerance, even support. But Brazil is trapped in the contradictions of its gross inequalities. The signs of repression, if unclear as to their long-term implications, are still much in evidence.

During a march by striking metal-workers in October 1979 in Sao Paulo, police shot dead one of the marchers. The Cardinal of Sao Paulo, Evanisto Arns, as he has many times before when death has befallen a government opponent, said the funeral mass. More than 200 priests and half a dozen bishops walked through the centre of Sao Paulo. This led President Figueiredo to accuse the Cardinal of 'inciting' the workers.

In April the following year, Lula was arrested in an attempt to end a strike. He was held incommunicado in the Sao Paulo police station, along with sixteen other union officials. They were charged under a law that punishes 'incitement to strike' with a sentence of between two and twelve years.

Amnesty again sent telegrams. And at the same time, within Brazil there was an enormous upwelling of support for a man many regard as a future president. In the end, all the trade unionists were released on bail.

A year went by and an uneasy lull set in, only to be shattered when on Monday 23 February 1981, Judge Nelson da Silva Machado Guimares announced that the trial of Lula and twelve other trade unionists would take place in Sao Paulo two days later.

Lawyers for the accused made a desperate attempt to have the trial postponed after they had been told by the judge that the second army corps was imposing strict conditions on the trial. There would be only one lawyer and one relative for each defendant. Only fourteen journalists were to be allowed in the courtroom. There would be no foreign journalists and no foreign observers in the court. No one would be allowed near the court without army credentials. The lawyers were also told that the neighbourhood would be surrounded by eleven concentric security barriers, and 2000 men from the military police would occupy the area.

The lawyers objected to these conditions saying that there was not enough time to prepare the case and that the trial would contravene Brazilian law in that only when defendants and their lawyers have failed to appear on two occasions can a trial go ahead in their absence. The trial went ahead nonetheless. According to an informed newspaper report, it had become a point of honour for the most hardened section of the army, in particular the local army commander, General Mittoren Tavares, who led the repression of the strike the year before, to have Lula condemned to at least six years in jail. A jail sentence would automatically make it impossible for Lula to run for political office in the 1982 elections – and Lula with his new Workers' Party had fast become a political force to be reckoned with.

Lula, his friends and his lawyers, refused to attend the trial. In absentia, after a one-day trial, Lula and three others were given sentences of three and a half years. Five received terms of two and a half years and two were sentenced to two years.

At 11 p.m. that same night, Lula and the other unionists presented themselves to the authorities in Sao Paulo. They spent the night in jail. Meanwhile, the lawyers were attempting to launch an appeal. And numerous voices added to the pressure – the church, the international labour movement, many influential international newspapers and maybe some of Lula's important friends who include Lech Walesa, Pope John Paul II, and Helmut Schmidt.

Amnesty International sent telegrams to the minister of justice protesting at the way the trial had been conducted, at the virtual barring of international observers (including Amnesty International's delegate) from the proceedings, and calling for a review.

Twenty hours later, Lula and the other unionists were released from custody, their appeal having been allowed.

The military regime of General Joao Baptista de Oliveira Figueiredo may still be intent on making sure Lula serves his jail sentence, but it has been served notice that it is going to be a tough fight and one that is likely to trigger off a tide of international criticism and possibly a great degree of domestic unrest.

The rush to try Lula, the quick lock-up and the equally quick release, all reflect the government's indecision as it faces two options. If they allow the unofficial unions a free hand, there could be a rash of strikes and a great push by the workers, backed by their powerful friend, the Catholic Church, for heads to roll in the government economic team. On the other hand, to imprison Lula and his associates and to keep in place the tough labour laws could be even more provocative. The great groundswell of discontent that now exists right across Brazil could overflow its banks.

Amnesty, for its part, has tried to keep the pressure on the government to make sure that there is no retreat on human rights – convinced that the more the excesses of the past are exposed, the more difficult it will be to go back to the dark nights of the 1970s. For this reason, it has focused attention on the apparatus of torture which still exists for ordinary prisoners.

In its 1980 annual report, it described a recent example of routine brutality as printed in the Brazilian left-wing newspaper, the *Reporter*.

> Two workers, Adao Rosa, aged 56, and Alfredo Henrique Batista, aged 34, were arrested by military police on 5 March 1980 after having failed to pay for a drink in a bar. They were taken to a barracks in Vila Americana, Volta Redonda, and there tied up; their mouths were forced open and a truncheon was rammed down their throats. They were beaten about the ribs, head and chest. The military police officers eventually took them to hospital but on the way beat them again. Adao Rosa lost his spleen and his liver was perforated. Alfredo Henrique Batista's spinal column was injured and he suffered serious bruising to his throat and oesophagus.

Amnesty has also, as part of its 'purge torture from Brazil' effort, highlighted the disciplinary hearing being carried out by Sao Paulo State Medical Council. Five years ago a well-known Brazilian journalist, Vladimir Herzog, was summoned to appear at the military intelligence headquarters in Sao Paulo. Within hours of presenting himself, he was dead. The official verdict was that he had taken his own life by hanging. A death certificate gave the cause of death as suicide. Much later, the doctor who signed it admitted he had never seen the body. In October 1978 a Sao Paulo federal judge ruled that the Brazilian government was responsible for the death of Mr Herzog. The doctor who signed the death certificate, Harmy Shibata, later became head of the Sao Paulo Medical Legal Institute. Nevertheless, when the facts of the case emerged, he was summoned to disciplinary proceedings. That a man of his station could be disciplined by his peers was a sign of the progress towards liberalization being made in Brazil. Amnesty reinforced the domestic Brazilian pressure by sending their own medical representative to try to attend the disciplinary hearings. His presence attracted wide publicity in Brazil and has raised hopes that this may help propel forward investigations into ten other cases where doctors are accused of being involved in torture and signing medical certificates.

Brazil, as far as Amnesty is concerned, is now in a strange hiatus. There are no political prisoners, the house-cleaning goes on. But will the economy collapse and with it the political liberalization? And meanwhile, what should Amnesty do about the economic and political pressures, often violent, in Brazil's underdeveloped north-east and Amazonia? Inside Brazil there is a feeling among some observers that outside organizations like Amnesty are powerless or losing their interest just as the real hard drama is about to begin.

9. Tanzania: the Liberal Dilemma

In its 1981 annual report, Amnesty noted blandly that its chief concern in Tanzania 'was the continued refusal of the Zanzibar authorities to allow a "forced bride" to leave the country to achieve her freedom.' Tanzania today is one of the small number of countries in the world where there is little torture, only a few prisoners detained without trial, and none shackled to the prison wall.

But this has not always been the case. From the early 1970s to late 1979 Tanzania had around 1500 detainees held in indefinite detention, reports of torture were frequent, and prison conditions deteriorating.

Yet few of Tanzania's influential friends in the West wanted publicly to embarrass President Julius Nyerere. Some of them did use their private conversations with him and other senior officials to try and put pressure on the government. But Jimmy Carter and Andrew Young, US ambassador to the United Nations, needing Tanzania's help in resolving the Rhodesian war, decided not to call attention to Tanzania's human rights problems. Nor did the press pay much attention to the question, partly because most of the African correspondents and analysts are very pro Julius Nyerere.

Why does this man have such a hold on liberal affection? Nyerere is undoubtedly one of the most fascinating and engaging rulers alive in the world today. He began life as a teacher, mild-mannered, disciplined and effective. When nationalist politics emerged in the late 1950s, he soon became the chief spokesman for the Tanganyikan Nationalist Union and, when Tanganyika became independent in December 1961, its first Prime Minister. (At that time the off-shore island Zanzibar was a separate British colony. Only much later, after what looked like an attempted East German take-over, did Zanzibar merge with the mainland to form the united country of Tanzania.)

Nyerere always was an idealist. He wanted the nationalist struggle to abjure violence and to aspire not just to replace white rule with black rule, but to build a society where inequalities would disappear and the country would be run on the lines of the traditional African village in which everyone lent a helping hand to communal endeavours. He certainly was not a Marxist. He described himself as a Christian socialist. His Catholicism has always been important to him. A regular church-goer, he has written in theological magazines, and one of his most admired and admiring friends is the Anglican Archbishop, Trevor Huddleston.

Nyerere's most original socialist creations were the '*ujamaa* villages'. *Ujamaa* is a Swahili word meaning togetherness. From his early days, Nyerere had visions of an earthy village socialism where modern techniques such as the use of tractors and fertilizers could be managed by village teams and used in communal fields with the village selling and buying in from the outside world on a cooperative basis. He began his experiments in the early 1960s using Israeli experts who tried to set up sophisticated model kibbutzim. They failed to catch on. Then, over the next four years, Nyerere evolved his own concept, *ujamaa*. For years he talked about it, at first his ideas falling on deaf ears, for Tanzanian peasants were used to living on scattered family holdings and leading a fairly independent life. Although they did help each other in the fields at the time of maximum pressure at harvest time and although family and kinship ties were strong and ubiquitous, the notion of a village where everyone collected together and organized the land and other family aspects of life in a tight commune was alien.

Come the early 1970s, Nyerere decided that talking and thinking about *ujamaa* had gone on long enough. He wanted to push Tanzania forward, convinced that *ujamaa* would shake up the old structures and provide new dynamic economic units that would raise productivity two- or threefold.

The order was given that the peasants were to move. It was a momentous exercise, uprooting people whose families had farmed the same scattered and often uneconomic plots for hundreds of years. Many moved voluntarily, persuaded by Nyerere's rhetoric. But others had to be cajoled and pushed. In a number of cases, zealous local officials set fire to the old homes to force the peasants to move to the new.

The detailed planning work was shoddy. Villagers were herded together and told 'this is your village site', yet there was often no running water, no good agricultural land, and no road. The communal system did not work well, except in a few cases here and there. Later, Nyerere was to admit that even in his own home village, which he often liked to visit, *ujamaa* had not really taken hold. In the end, Nyerere put *ujamaa* on the back burner. Many villagers drifted back to their old homes, others stayed, but abandoned the communal field, although the villages kept calling themselves *ujamaa* villages as a kind of insurance policy.

All the while, Nyerere kept most of his critics at bay. His manner is disarming. He is often the first to articulate what has gone wrong. On many occasions he is self-critical. He rarely tries to cover up mistakes, and ministers who don't perform well are quickly shunted aside. He is accessible to the foreign press and is never hostile to his critics. His humour is effervescent and his charm engaging – not sugary or supine, but simple and straightforward. A visitor is made to feel comfortable and important. Moreover, his own life is relatively modest. He lives in an ordinary house by the sea, having decided that the state house bequeathed to him by the British was too much like a hotel. He is visibly without pomp. He has few pretensions and for all his mistakes is still extraordinarily popular in Tanzania. One serious blindspot, however, is that he does not like to deal with Amnesty. He never even replies to its letters.

He rules very much as the benevolent but strict headmaster. He changes his ministers with regularity, often because they don't live up to his own hardworking ideals. And he prefers to rule by direct appeal to the people, making effective use of the radio to reach into the most remote parts. Even so, there are occasions when he moves slowly to exert authority. For example, a number of regional police commanders and security officials were not charged until three years after they had been involved in a torture scandal.

The electoral system is peculiarly Nyerere's own. Early on he decided that Westminster democracy was too alien a concept to survive in Tanzania. Africans, he used to say, have long sorted out their problems by talking under the shade of a tree. Parties, with the professional duty of fighting each other for opposition's sake, were not suited to this tradition.

Nevertheless, although firm on the one-party government, he has always called regular elections. Local branches of the party are encouraged to put up a range of candidates to give the electorate a choice, and the electorate in turn has responded by voting out large numbers of MPs and ministers. Nyerere himself is never opposed.

The only serious opposition he has ever faced was an attempted coup in 1962 by junior army officers who were disgruntled about their pay. Although for two or three days the situation looked precarious, with Nyerere's whereabouts uncertain, in the end order was quickly restored when Nyerere called in British troops.

A less serious occasion was when his former radical foreign minister, Oscar Kambona, publicly broke with him. After some desultory manoeuvrings, which led to his imprisonment, he was allowed to go into exile where he made a futile attempt to build an opposition movement. (His brothers and cousin remained in prison without trial for another few years.) The movement quickly dissipated, although it managed at the height of its success to drop leaflets from aeroplanes over a few of Tanzania's larger towns. At one time Kambona tried to forge an alliance with Idi Amin of Uganda.

None of this quite explains Tanzania's build-up of political prisoners. In 1979, in the one conversation I had on the subject with Nyerere, he was quite matter-of-fact, although dismissive.

Detaining without trial doesn't worry me as much [as torture]. Torture is unlawful and criminally immoral.

Detention without trial is not. We do it under the law. The British recently did this and the Irish didn't like it. I think they took them to the European Court of Human Rights. If I were to go over those detention orders again, I could possibly say I was wrong here or wrong there. But this is not a moral matter, unless I was being personally vindictive.

The image of the benign but authoritarian headmaster is still the best available reflection of his character. A headmaster surrounded by too many inept, though probably not often corrupt ministers and senior civil servants, who do not keep a close enough watch on their subordinates' activities. But that only explains part of the reason for the prisoners. Some of the political prisoners like the Zanzibaris, the Namibians, and Kambona's relations were Nyerere's direct responsibility. Without a fully functioning, independent judiciary, political short-cuts are all too easy. And when one's friends in the outside world go along with it, then it is even easier.

One exception to this conspiracy of friendship was Amnesty International. Year by year it plugged away with its Tanzanian case-load, as documented in its annual reports. Martin Ennals visited Tanzania to try and see Nyerere but was refused an appointment. Again, when Vice-President Jumbe came to London, Amnesty tried to see him without success.

But although Amnesty did its day-by-day work, regularly reporting developments and seeking occasions on which it could influence ministers, this work was within the context of an unwritten rule among the London liberal intelligentsia not to expose Nyerere to public rebuke. His virtues, it was considered, far exceeded his vices. Those responsible for Tanzania in the organization were, and still are, very sympathetic to the regime, and somewhat hesitant about handing over information to journalists who might use it to savage Nyerere, particulary when Amnesty was engaged in sensitive negotiations with the Tanzanian authorities. Nor was the Tanzanian section of Amnesty given the resources to mount a proper investigative mission.

I remember I decided to write a column in the *International Herald Tribune* about political prisoners in Tanzania. It was 1978, the peak year for political prisoners in Tanzania. There was nothing in the press files, and none of my friends with contacts in Tanzania had more than skeletal knowledge of the situation inside Tanzania's jails. I approached Amnesty with some reticence, which probably raised their confidence in me. Besides, I was a known Tanzania-lover, having lived and filmed documentaries in the country for some years. All the same, there was obviously a certain anguish in handing over the information, although much of it Amnesty had already published in annual reports and elsewhere.

I published my article in February 1978, concluding with a reminder which I hoped the Shakespeare-reading (and translating) Julius Nyerere would enjoy — 'Lilies that fester smell far worse than weeds.'

A few weeks later I bumped into a Tanzanian from the BBC Swahili service who told me my column had been translated by them into Swahili and beamed into Tanzania.

In April and May 1978, two groups of political prisoners were released, including the Namibian and Zanzibari prisoners I'd written about.

I was pleased, assuming the Namibian negotiations and Amnesty's steady behind-the-scenes pressure had all contributed to changing Nyerere's mind. That was probably the truth of it. There is, however, a footnote to the story. One of the released detainees, Andreas Shipanga,* a former senior official in the Namibian nationalist movement, SWAPO, who had been under lock and key for two years, phoned up and announced he was in London and hoped to see me. He and Anthony

---

* Shipanga's release came at a time when it had become politically embarrassing for Nyerere to keep him in prison. The South Africans, negotiating with the Western five, United States, Britain, West Germany, France and Canada, on a Namibian settlement plan, were making great hay of SWAPO's political prisoners. Also Sam Njoma, SWAPO's leader, was judged to be too stubborn in the negotiations, a conviction held not just by the Western five but by the Front Line States. Nyerere probably thought to release Shipanga at that time might help pace Njoma towards an agreement.

Sampson, with whom he was staying, took me out to a fine lunch, a thank-you, they said, for getting him released. Nothing I said could convince Shipanga that it was otherwise. My column, he maintained, had broken through the 'conspiracy of silence' on Tanzania's political prisoners. He recounted, too, the sheer joy he experienced, hearing the Swahili version of my column coming into the tiny radio receiver he had hidden in his cell. It was the first indication he had that anyone outside, apart from his wife, was interested in what happened to him.

A happy story, perhaps overdrawn. It was Amnesty who had done the hard work of logging the long list of prisoners who disappeared into Tanzania's jails, monitoring their lives, examining the reports smuggled out on torture, sifting the fact from rumour, deciding who was being fed adequately and who was not, and attempting, without any cooperation from the Tanzanian legal authorities, to measure the degree of innocence of those detained.

It was painstaking work, carried out thoroughly and with expertise. The only problem was that it had lain unexposed by the media.

The full story of Tanzania's political prisoners is worth recounting. It shows how quite separate developments, if not properly handled through open court procedures, can accumulate into a major human rights issue. For Nyerere's Tanzania there were three main problems — domestic criminality and police behaviour, Zanzibar and the assassination of its first post-revolutionary president, and the guerrilla war in Namibia.

In 1972 a small group of Zanzibaris and mainland Tanganyikans murdered Zanzibar's leader, Sheik Abeid Karume. It was an assassination widely welcomed, not least in Tanzania, for Karume had been a potentate of quite ruthless cunning and merciless repression. Since his revolution, when he deposed the traditional sultan, he had run Zanzibar with Stalinistic finesse. Every opponent or potential opponent was eliminated. Zanzibar was a constant embarrassment for Julius

Nyerere; every attempt to edge it towards moderation or full union was ineffective. He felt that if he pushed any harder the regime might turn towards East Germany, which had close contacts with the regime, thus becoming a potentially de-stabilizing force for the mainland. He felt obliged to return political opponents of Karume to Zanzibar, even though he knew they would be tortured and murdered.

The assassination was followed by a big round-up, and after a trial in Zanzibar in 1973, thirty-seven were found guilty of treason although they were allowed no defence counsel. Some were sentenced to death; others were given long terms of imprisonment. The prisoners' appeal was heard in late 1976 by the Supreme Council of Zanzibar's only political organ – the Afro-Shirazi Party. The Attorney-General of Zanzibar acted as both prosecutor and defence counsel. In the end, death sentences were confirmed on six people and seventeen others were committed to between thirty and thirty-five years' imprisonment.

Amnesty's adoption groups had been writing letters pro-testing against the court procedures; Amnesty had also asked the Tanzanian authorities to investigate allegations of torture. Amnesty was convinced by evidence obtained from numerous sources that torture was widely used in Zanzibari prisons. It also became apparent during the court proceedings that a number of the prisoners were quite ill but receiving no medical attention. None of the prisoners had been allowed visitors, even from their families.

Thirteen of the thirty-seven prosecuted had been arrested on the mainland. Nyerere refused to hand them over to the Zanzibari authorities. Instead they were incarcerated on the mainland without ever appearing in a courtroom – this seemed to be the behind-the-scenes deal he and the Afro-Shirazis had worked out. The Zanzibari authorities were allowed to interrogate them. They were also tortured, though when Nyerere heard about it, he ordered it to be stopped.

Amnesty International began to receive disturbing infor-mation on their conditions. Letters were smuggled out of Ukonga prison in Dar-es-Salaam. One detainee, Amirali Ramji, who was released, corroborated the information. The diet was poor, there was no medical treatment by qualified personnel, no exercise, and restrictions on visits and correspondence. To receive a letter from outside was to run the risk of brutal punishment. One of the Zanzibari detainees was Abdulrahman Mohamed Babu, a former Tanzanian minister of economic affairs, who had been quite close to Nyerere at one time. He had been one of the original Zanzibari revolutionaries and soon after the 1964 revolution became Zanzibari minister of defence and external affairs. (In the 1950s, he lived in London, worked as a postman, attended classes at the London School of Economics and was active in the Movement for Colonial Freedom.) He was, however, too pro-Chinese for the Zanzibari regime and he was transferred to the mainland where Nyerere appointed him a minister. Babu was particularly ill, suffering from hypertension, stomach disorders and eye trouble. He was rapidly becoming blind. Amnesty made him a prisoner of the month.

The second main group of political prisoners in Tanzania were members of Southern African liberation movements. Nyerere, who was and still is involved up to his neck in Southern African politics, offering base training facilities to a number of movements, had also allowed Tanzania to become the jail-house for dissidents in these movements. The largest group was from SWAPO, which was engaged in trying to dislodge the South Africans from Namibia, which legally was a United Nations trusteeship territory. SWAPO had gone through a period of turbulence and one group, led by Andreas Shipanga, had broken with Sam Njoma, the movement's rather hard-line president. Amnesty adopted him as a prisoner of conscience.

The Zambian authorities, concerned about the sometimes violent feuding, arrested eleven of Shipanga's faction. The Zambian Appeal Court, however, issued a writ of habeas corpus in Shipanga's favour. Not to be outmanoeuvred, the Zambian government transferred the eleven to Tanzania, to avoid being compelled by the court to release them. There was no provision in Tanzania for habeas corpus for people held under the Preventive Detention Act. Ironically, the government of Zambia, acting under instruction from the Zambian Appeal Court, later requested their return. Tanzania refused to comply.

Nyerere has always been very single-minded about the liberation movements. As he views it, Tanzania and Zambia gave them enormous facilities including financial and military help. If they were going to squabble with each other, rather than fighting the enemy, he was not going to tolerate it. The dissidents would be locked up. This was war. (Similar actions were taken by Britain and the United States during the Second World War.)

There were also in Nyerere's jails a group of non-political prisoners, who were languishing without trial. The man who became a particular focus of Amnesty concern, just because his case was so outrageous, was James Magoti. He was arrested in 1976 and charged with the theft of a large sum of money from a bank in Dar-es-Salaam where he was the manager. He was, however, never brought to trial. Amnesty was convinced that he had been severely tortured by the secret security police. He was blindfolded, hung by the wrists from a high bar, beaten on the legs and ears, burned on the sexual organ with cigarettes, tortured with electrical shocks and a bottle was inserted into his anus. Afterwards, he was given some medical treatment, but was not admitted to hospital.

Magoti, although supposed to be a common criminal, was held under the Preventive Detention Act, which had been enacted to deal with political cases where the government wanted to hold someone against whom it had insufficient evidence to bring to court.

Amnesty kept lobbying the Tanzanians, writing letters to the government, pressing it to investigate the allegations of torture. After a long while, four railway police detectives were arrested. Two of them, security officers, were later convicted of the use of torture and sentenced to three years' imprisonment.

Amazingly, although the Tanzanians also arrested a group of soldiers and charged them with the theft, they kept Magoti in prison.

The Amnesty pressure continued, but Magoti remained untried in prison. His wife and brother were also detained in the same prison. In the end, Amnesty adopted him as a prisoner of conscience.

This, then, was the situation at the end of 1976: four groups of prisoners, all important Amnesty cases. In 1977, the situation improved: some of the Zanzibaris who had been given shorter sentences were released and all the death sentences were commuted. In April 1978, Babu and the Zanzibaris held on the mainland were set free. Amnesty regarded this as a great victory. Some of its local adoption groups had been working on the case persistently without a single response from the Tanzanian government. Only in February 1978 did they receive a circular letter from the Tanzanian minister of health, Dr Stirling, stating that all detainees had an adequate diet and regular visits from doctors. The circular criticized Amnesty which, the minister said, had been 'supplied with false and malicious information by persons whose aim is to damage our country in every way possible'.

Three months later, on African Liberation Day – the fifteenth anniversary of the founding of the Organization of African Unity – President Nyerere ordered the release of twenty members of various South African liberation movements, including Andreas Shipanga.

Amnesty immediately cabled Nyerere to congratulate him. It also cabled the South African Prime Minister John Vorster to remind him of the undertaking given during his talks in Vienna with the US Vice-President, Walter Mondale. The agreement had been that if SWAPO detainees were freed, Vorster would seriously consider releasing the political prisoners he held from Namibia. Amnesty received no reply.

In December, the remaining fourteen prisoners convicted in the 1973 treason trial were released from their jail in Zanzibar.

The year came to an end, however, with James Magoti still in prison.

Not until the summer of 1979 did Amnesty see their efforts rewarded. Magoti, along with more than half the hundred or more people held in Tanzania under preventive detention legislation, was allowed free. Magoti was still, by Amnesty accounts, suffering from the after-effects of the severe torture he had experienced. His brother Adam, moreover, had died in jail a few days earlier. Amnesty attempted to get information on the case from the Attorney-General but was rebuffed. Magoti was never compensated and he is still denied state employment, which severely restricts his opportunities.

In the same year, a determined effort was made by the government to eradicate torture from the Tanzanian prison system. Nyerere told me, when we discussed it, he regarded torture as wicked and unnecessary. However, the evidence suggests that he was not as quick to stamp on it as he claims.

The worst torture case of all had taken place in Mwanza and Shinyanga. It began when Nyerere in 1975 was informed about a wave of unsolved murders in the region. At his prompting, a special security meeting was called, chaired by the Prime Minister. The Mwanza regional police commander, Isaias Mkwawa, and a regional security officer, Godfrey Ihuya, were told to initiate a special operation.

In the next two days 374 people were picked up and detained in Kigoto Interrogation Centre where torture was used systematically. A number of prisoners died. Men and women prisoners had been stripped naked, tied and beaten. Hot chili peppers were inserted into the anus, sexual organs, eyes, nostrils, ears and mouth. Food was denied them and the victims were made to crawl over sharp stones.

The deaths became known, the situation was investigated and two years later Mkwawa and Ihuya were sentenced to seven years' imprisonment for causing death by torture. Nyerere asked for the resignations of the home affairs minister and the minister of state in the President's office, and of the local regional commissioner. They were detained under the Preventive Detention Act and tried in 1980 and 1981. Although the ministers resigned, one is still on the central committee of Nyerere's party and the other is serving as Tanzania's ambassador to Egypt.

Amnesty has received only isolated reports of torture since, and the siuation in Tanzania looks better than it has for years.

Amnesty, however, points out that in Tanzania the Preventive Detention Act remains on the statute book and a hundred or so prisoners are still detained under it. The Act, Amnesty has told the Tanzanians, does not incorporate in the detention orders the legal safeguards which are included in the International Covenant on Civil and Political Rights which Tanzania has signed and ratified.

Tanzania is almost back where it should be and, maybe, where Julius Nyerere wanted it to be all along. The 1970s have been a difficult and stormy decade. The overthrow of, first, Portuguese colonialism in neighbouring Mozambique and, second, the Smith regime in Rhodesia were gruelling and demanding exercises, straining the resources, both material and political, of Tanzania. The union with Zanzibar was consummated, the political parties finally merged and Zanzibar's political boss, Jumbe, effectively integrated into Tanzania's governmental structure by being named vice-president.

Were the detentions unavoidable in such a situation? A difficult question to answer with a flat no. Nevertheless, if there had been no Preventive Detention Act, other ways of dealing with complex issues, like what to do with dissident Zanzibaris, would have had to be found. The normal courts would have had to be taken more seriously and the Zanzibaris made to understand that short-cuts to justice were not part of a parcel of the Tanganyika connection. Yet with the Act on the statute book, it was all too easy to have recourse to it.

In all this, the Amnesty factor is hard to plumb. It was a constant pressure, an irritating embarrassment for a president with deep Christian principles. But reasons of state were also a powerful countervailing force. Perhaps if Amnesty had raised its profile and encouraged other liberal voices who had the confidence of Julius Nyerere to do the same, the principles would have triumphed over the reasons of state sooner rather than later.

10. The USSR: Stalin's Legacy

It was the theme of Alexander Solzhenitsyn's masterpiece, *The Gulag Archipelago*, that the penal system of the Soviet Union was not an excrescence nor an aberration but rather an integral element in the functioning of its institutions.

In 1979, Goronwy Rees, in his now-famous review in *Encounter* of Solzhenitsyn's book, compared its revelations to those made centuries before in Dante's *Divina Commedia*, only to make the counter-point that

> the comparison fails, for the *Divina Commedia* is a creation of sublime art and imagination, while *The Gulag Archipelago* is a work of the harshest and most relentless realism; while again, in the *Divina Commedia* the human soul emerges from the depths of sin and suffering until it can once more see the stars, but from the darkness of *The Gulag Archipelago* there is no such release.
>
> It is only in their vast scope and immensity that the two books resemble each other; in everything else there is no likeness between the messages they offer to suffering humanity. Only in reading *The Gulag Archipelago* one cannot help thinking again and again that the tortures inflicted by Dante on the souls of the damned in the *Inferno* are as nothing compared with those perpetrated in the Archipelago on the living flesh of for the most part innocent men and women.

The Gulag Archipelago exposed nakedly the unique contribution of terror, cynicism, hypocrisy, ruthlessness, stupidity and inefficiency, which provides the ideological infrastructure of the Soviet state. Solzhenitsyn wrote his account, based on his own direct sources, his own experience of being an inmate inside one of the prison camps, and in his own style, full of rage and violent revulsion.

Amnesty International has been documenting the activities of the Soviet penal system for the best part of its twenty years' history. Amnesty picked up from where *The Gulag Archipelago* left off. The problem Amnesty has addressed is less a question of liquidation than rigorous punishment. It may not be Stalin's Russia, but Brezhnev's Russia is run by many of the same men who served him.

The political repression these days in the Soviet Union is on a small scale compared with its past. The Stalinist era of the Gulag consumed perhaps as many as 17 to 20 million mortal victims altogether. Today, according to Amnesty, we are counting in the thousands (around 10,000 people imprisoned for their political or religious beliefs).

It is true that repression has always been an integral part of the Russian political system. In the early nineteenth century, there were dissident groups like the 'Decembrists', a group of high-bred officers who wanted to overthrow the tsar and install a liberal monarchy. The plot was uncovered, the ringleaders hanged, and the rest sent to banishment in Siberia. One of their sympathizers was the poet, Pushkin. He got away with being banished from Moscow to St Petersburg.

In the mid-nineteenth century, the great novelist Dostoyevsky was arrested. He was accused of being a member of a secret Socialist society. He was sentenced to be shot, only to be reprieved at the last moment. He spent four years in penal servitude.

Nothing done by the tsars, however, compared with Stalin's rule of terror, repression, murder, execution and exile. An interesting footnote to this frightening period was the growing use of psychiatric hospitals for incarcerating political prisoners, an abuse which during the present Brezhnev era was to become one of the dominant forms of punishment. But during Stalin's repression it was used by sympathetic psychiatrists as a way of giving refuge to prisoners who otherwise would have been criminally prosecuted.

*

This all came before Amnesty was set in motion. In the year of Amnesty's birth, the eminent Soviet physicist, and inventor of the Soviet H-bomb, Andrei Sakharov, could write: 'Our country has started along the path of cleansing itself from the filth of Stalinism.' And he quoted Chekhov: 'Drop by drop we are squeezing the slave out of ourselves.'

This was Krushchev's time: the years of thaw when the weight of state control was markedly loosened. Even *One Day in the Life of Ivan Denisovitch* could be openly published. Religious persecution, however, worsened.

The thaw did not last long. By the mid-1960s Amnesty was involved in the case of two writers, Yuli Daniel and Andrei Sinjavsky, who spent over five years in hard-labour camps. They became Amnesty prisoners of conscience. There was a string of other lesser-known writers and intellectuals who entered Amnesty's books. Soon Amnesty was deeply involved in the problem of Russian dissidents.

A number of observers, not just the Soviet government, believe Amnesty devotes a disproportionate amount of its energies to Eastern Europe and the Soviet Union. Compared with Latin America, they say, the number of political prisoners is small. In Poland there have been in the last twenty years only a handful. And in modern-day Hungary, Amnesty has no prisoners of conscience. Even in Czechoslovakia there are probably less than a hundred. As for torture, it does not exist as a formal instrument of state policy in any Warsaw Pact country. Brutality, hard labour and bad treatment, including systematic starvation, but the rack and the *pau de arara* cannot be found.

All this is true, but it misses an essential point. These countries for a long time have had frozen political systems, where to walk on the ice of political free expression is a dangerous act that can bring about a loss of job, the removal of privileges and access to higher education for one's children. Such is the degree of control, such is its longevity, that everyone knows the rules. The few who do dissent find that imprisonment, the psychiatric hospital or the labour camp is their punishment. Most do not tempt fate and the system survives intact without the need for a repeat of Stalinist terror. The repressive system, once in full command with opposition eliminated, keeps its grip with the merest reminders of what has been. The events in Poland, of course, belie the truth of this observation. It remains to be seen how far Moscow will tolerate its liberalization, or whether it will attempt to turn back the clock as it did earlier in Hungary and Czechoslovakia.

The Helsinki Final Act was signed in 1975 by most of the European nations, together with the United States and Canada. It was meant to be a confirmation of the post-war boundaries of Europe and an agreement on what the East and West meant by human rights. On paper it looked like a magnificent achievement. Détente was reaping its own reward. The worlds of two opposing economic systems were drawing closer.

The reality was light years away. Since 1975 Amnesty has counted well over six hundred Soviet citizens who have been imprisoned for 'anti-Soviet' activities of various kinds. (That does not include those already in prison in 1975 nor the many times this number restricted or harassed by extra-judicial persecution. Also it is likely that the total of those imprisoned is more than six hundred. Official secrecy, censorship, and the threat of retaliation against reformers keep much of the news away even from the sharp eyes and ears of Amnesty.) One thing is clear, however: Amnesty *has not heard of a single case in which a Soviet court has acquitted anyone charged with a political or religious offence*.

The problem begins with the constitution of the USSR itself. This and the laws that are derived from it impose restrictions on the freedom of speech, association, religion and movement. Soviet legislation bans 'agitation and propaganda' and 'slanderous fabrications' meant to weaken the Soviet regime. The official commentary on the code makes clear that a conviction can only be won if it is proved that the accused *intended* to weaken the state or *knew* they were spreading false slander. In practice, Soviet courts ignore this requirement and sentences are usually severe. The guiding language written during the reaction to Stalin's arbitrary terror has been shunted aside.

The groups persecuted range over a wide political and

religious spectrum. They include the 'Helsinki monitor' human rights activists who have sought to embarrass the Soviet authorities by quoting back to them the document signed by the government. There are the national rights campaigners, striving for cultural autonomy and in some cases for political independence, in particular Ukrainians, Lithuanians, Latvians and Estonians. There are the Tartars who have attempted to resettle in the Crimea, their ancestral homeland from which they were forcibly deported in 1944. There are the unofficial workers' groups: although pale shadows of Poland's Solidarity, they have branches dotted around the country. There are conscientious objectors, including Baptists, Jehovah's Witnesses, Seventh Day Adventists, Pentecostals and Jews.

Mainline religious groups themselves, although supposedly now tolerated, are often persecuted. Three Seventh Day Adventists were imprisoned in 1979 for operating an unofficial printing press and several Russian Orthodox believers have been imprisoned or exiled. There are maybe hundreds of others who have been similarly dealt with, but on whom Amnesty does not have hard information.

The charges vary. They can be for 'anti-state activities' or 'intentional actions violating public order in a coarse manner and expressing a clear disrespect towards society', but the authorities prefer to dress the charges up: 'violating the work ethic', 'hooliganism', 'parasitism', or avoiding 'socially useful' work are favourites.

Usually, the arrest of Soviet dissenters comes only after a sustained period of harassment. Intensive police surveillance, house searches, questioning, even dismissal from employment are the tools most commonly used. Dissenters can be pulled into a police station and left in the cells for a day or two on 'suspicion', or, more seriously, can be jailed by local judges for up to fifteen days on trumped-up charges of 'disobeying a policeman' and 'petty hooliganism'.

If this harassment does not silence the critics, then they will be charged under the criminal law. Although the law sets a nine-month limit on pre-trial detention, often political or religious prisoners are held for a year or more. They are incarcerated in 'investigation-isolation' prisons where the naked light burns in the cell day and night, windows are painted over and toilets are often nothing more than a slop bucket. Torture is not used during interrogation, although the treatment during questioning can be rough. A few slaps and pushes may not be in the same class as being hooded with a tyre lined with quick-lime, but they can be quite effective, particularly when no visits from family or friends are allowed and lawyers are kept at bay until the preliminary investigation is declared complete. Even then, the lawyer is no great bulwark of liberty, and is allowed only an hour or two to talk to the prisoner. Only those lawyers listed by the KGB can defend in cases where the charge is treason or 'anti-Soviet agitation'. The too-energetic lawyer does not stay on the list. The trial, although said to be open, is normally packed with invited groups. Friends and relatives often find it impossible to gain access.

The maximum term of imprisonment for these kinds of offences is fifteen years, followed by another five years of exile. In practice, further convictions can be administered during detention. Some prisoners of conscience, such as the Ukrainian Danylo Shumuk, have been repeatedly imprisoned: his successive jail terms now total more than thirty years.

Prisoners, on conviction, are sent to one of four types of institutions. The most severe is a prison, although rarely do political or religious prisoners get sent to these unless they keep repeating their offence. The next most severe is a 'corrective labour colony with a special regime', then there are 'strict', 'reinforced' and 'ordinary regime' labour colonies. Most prisoners on Amnesty books go to either strict or ordinary regime colonies, followed by a period of internal exile to a remote region with a severe climate. Very occasionally, dissidents are exiled abroad.

Only rarely are prisoners paroled. Amnesty has not succeeded in getting any prison terms reduced. One of the rare cases of early release was a group of dissenting Baptists.

The distances to the labour camps are often enormous. The journey can take days, weeks, even a month. The prisoners are transported in overcrowded, poorly ventilated railway wagons, often with common criminals who beat them up and occasionally sexually assault them. Food and water are inadequate. Thirty prisoners can be crammed into a compartment meant for eight to ten.

During the heatwave of 1972, several hundred prisoners had to scream when the train passed through populated areas in order to attract attention. Only by embarrassing their guards did they get permission to drink or gulp fresh air. Prisoners reported on another occasion that seventeen people died of suffocation in Kazan in April 1979. They were locked up in an airless van, left standing in the sun.

The labour camps are surrounded by barbed wire, with watch-towers in the corners, guns trained on the prisoners.

Prisoners complain of overcrowding, noise, lack of ventilation and inadequate heating. Prisoners are only allowed one blanket, even in the severest weather. Amnesty have received reports of prisoners being punished for wearing extra clothing in winter or for stripping off part of their uniform in the heat of the summers.

Food for the prisoners is scarce and the diet rigid. An unpublished decree issued in 1972 sets out thirteen different diets, depending on sentence, type of work, punishment and medical authorization. A typical diet is rye bread, groats, cabbage and strictly rationed quantities of rotten meat or fish.

According to recognized standards, a man working on active physical labour needs between 3100 and 3500 calories a day. In the camps he gets only 2500 and if he is in the punishment cell, it goes down to 1300 with a diet every other day of rye bread, hot water and salt.

Food parcels are allowed, and prisoners can use their prison wages (usually 10 per cent of the normal pay for this kind of work) to supplement their diet. But these privileges are often suspended as a punishment. Medical care is inadequate and the medical posts are often undermanned and occupied by unqualified personnel. Cases have come to Amnesty's notice of seriously ill prisoners being left to finish a term in the punishment cell before receiving treatment.

Work ranges from timber-cutting to woodwork, sewing and making parts for factories. Or it can be construction, building factories in the cold and the ice, so tellingly portrayed in *One Day in the Life of Ivan Denisovitch*. There is a lack of safety devices or regulations and accidents are common.

Political education classes, usually of low intellectual content, are held at least once a week.

Letter-writing is a hazardous business. Details about camp life are censored and letters are arbitrarily seized. Although prisoners legally are entitled to a number of parcels each year, often they are not allowed to be delivered, a form of punishment. The prisoners, virtually starved for most of the time, overworked and without medical treatment are worn down and down.

In its favour, the regime of the camp is said to be a notch up on the regular prisons where the common criminals go.

The Western press have given much publicity to the misuse of Soviet psychiatric hospitals to imprison political prisoners. In fact, according to Amnesty, only around two hundred people were forcibly confined to psychiatric hospitals for exercising human rights between 1 June 1975 and 31 May 1979, although there are many others whose confinement began before 1975.

Enforced hospitalization need not be by order of a court. There are so-called civil procedures where the individual is confined on the authority of a psychiatrist: later approval is confirmed by a panel of three other psychiatrists.

Alternatively, the courts are used, after a person has been charged for an offence but an expert commission has decided the prisoner is 'not accountable' for the offence. In this situation most prisoners have not been allowed to attend their hearings. They are often held in camera.

In both cases the diagnosis is superficial. Official psychiatrists often follow a loose and vague definition of schizophrenia which requires no manifestation of external symptoms.

A group of prominent psychiatrists suggested in 1973 that people who commit 'anti-social' acts may require psychiatric confinement, even though they are 'seemingly normal'.

An officially appointed psychiatrist in the case of a woman accused of 'anti-Soviet agitation and propaganda' told a court: 'The absence of symptoms of an illness cannot prove the absence of the illness itself.'

Another psychiatrist described a dissenter as 'delirious' because 'his behaviour bore the mark of anti-Soviet views'. Asked by the defence counsel, 'What form did his delirium take?', the psychiatrist replied, 'He did not respond to correction.'

Some of the official diagnoses of dissenters have to be read to be believed: 'nervous exhaustion brought on by her search for justice', 'reformist delusions', and 'mania for reconstructing society'.

If a prisoner is lucky, he is confined to an ordinary psychiatric hospital. In many cases, however, he is sent to a special hospital, a more secretive institution, under the direct authority of the Ministry of Internal Affairs. They are meant to be maximum security institutions holding the specially dangerous, such as psychopaths. Confinements can be up to fifteen or twenty years, even indefinite, release, it is said, being conditional on the attitudes and behaviour of the prisoner.

The special hospitals are run on prison lines; several of them are housed in former prison buildings. The most notorious is the Dnepropetrovsk Special Psychiatric Hospital, located next to a corrective labour colony. The very mention of it can bring human rights activists out in a cold sweat.

Security and discipline in these special hospitals come before medical care. They are staffed by the Ministry of Internal Affairs. Criminal prisoners are recruited to serve as orderlies. Amnesty International has received many reports of arbitrary, sadistic and sometimes fatal beatings.

Drug abuse to the inmates by the medical staff is well documented. Most commonly used are powerful tranquillizers, including chlorpronazin, haldol, insulin and sulphur. In accepted medical practice their use is carefully regulated. In Soviet psychiatric hospitals they are used indiscriminately and routinely − as a form of punishment and pressure. Drugs are given without the corrective for side effects. They are often administered incorrectly and painfully. Prisoners can be reduced to vegetables.

One dissident, Vladimir Gershuni, smuggled a letter out to Amnesty about his hospital experience. He was a bricklayer before his arrest, when he was found to be carrying *samizdat** documents in his pocket. He wrote:

> I complained of feeling poorly after a dose of haloperidol, and asked that the dose be reduced. This led to my being prescribed even more aminazine than I was already receiving . . .
>
> During a hunger strike in January 1971 (I had been given aminazine ever since my arrival) I felt steadily worse and worse, and after making a complaint, I began to get aminazine injections in the maximum dose . . . I couldn't sleep at all, yet the same dose was administered to me for twelve days in a row, until they became convinced that I was still not sleeping, and that the injections had not made me give up my hunger strike . . . I have been given two tablets of haloperidol twice daily . . . This medicine makes me feel more awful than anything I have experienced before; you no sooner lie down than you want to get up, you no sooner take a step than you're longing to sit down, and if you sit down, you want to walk again – and there's nowhere to walk.

Some prisoners have spent decades in these hospitals with no way of knowing when they will be released. Vasily Shipilov was first arrested in 1939 while studying in a religious seminar. He was sentenced for 'counter-revolutionary activities', and ten years later was ruled mentally ill. His case was unknown until it was uncovered in 1978 by a Moscow Human Rights group – the Working Commission for the Investigation of the Use of Psychiatry for Political Purposes. The Commission found that he had been given insulin as a form of shock treatment. He

---

* Unauthorized publications, usually typed, carbon copied and privately distributed.

was suffering from fits because of the insulin and regular beatings. The Commission noted: 'Since 1960 Shipilov has been held in the Sychyouka Special Psychiatric Hospital where the head of the ninth section, Elena Leonievna Maximova, has told him repeatedly, 'You'll be here until you renounce your religion, unless they kill you.' He was released in 1979, thirty years after committal.

Amnesty has made a point of bringing all their information on psychiatric abuse to the various international medical organizations where Soviet doctors and psychiatrists meet their colleagues from the outside world. Although it is obviously embarrassing for the Soviet participants, there is no way of knowing if it has any measurable impact on changing the system.

In 1974, a group of dissidents took the bold step of trying to set up a branch of Amnesty in the Soviet Union. Martin Ennals, Amnesty International's secretary-general, went to Moscow at their request to talk with members of the Committee of Human Rights. They had already told him they were anxious to make the attempt and were prepared to take the risk. Ennals advised them not to. He was worried on two counts. First, the atmosphere in the USSR was not conducive to its success. Secondly, the KGB could use their organization as a channel to infiltrate Amnesty. However, they were determined to go ahead and Ennals gave way. Ennals emphasized that if they wished to join Amnesty and form an adoption group, they must stick to the principles of the movement, particularly that of no involvement in the politics of their home country.

The group was established and Valentin Turchin, a physicist and computer specialist, elected as chairman. Other members of that first Amnesty group in Eastern Europe were the Ukrainian writer Mykola Rudenko, the biologist Sergei Kovalyov, the physicist Yuri Orlov, the mathematician A. Albrekht and Andrei Tverdokhlebov, another physicist.

Back home in London, Ennals put the wheels of Amnesty into motion. The secretariat sent to Moscow the names of three prisoners for adoption: one prisoner from Spain, one from Sri

Lanka, and one from Yugoslavia. The group had trouble surviving. The first two or three letters arrived but after that they were intercepted. Kovalyov was arrested and sentenced to seven years' imprisonment. Tverdokhlebov's flat was searched twice and he, too, was arrested by the KGB. He was sentenced to five years 'internal exile' for disseminating 'fabrications known to be false which defame the Soviet state and social system'. On the same day, Rudenko was detained in Kiev, and later imprisoned. He was banished from the Ukrainian Writers' Association on the grounds of having 'joined a bourgeois organization'. Orlov, too, was later arrested. Amnesty says that some of the group were picked up for dissident activities that pre-dated their Amnesty organizing efforts. This may be true, but undoubtedly the authorities were irritated by their growing international links, which Amnesty represented.

From time to time, the Soviet press launches into full-scale attack on Amnesty. The most serious was contained in the columns of *Izvestia* in August 1980: another, in March 1981, made similar points. Amnesty's 217-page report on conditions in the USSR had been published five months before. Clearly Amnesty was now becoming well known in the Soviet Union and the authorities wanted to tarnish its image.

Its main line of attack was that Amnesty was 'maintained by imperialist secret services' and went on to charge that Amnesty staff had links with British and US intelligence agencies. It stated that President Jimmy Carter's national security adviser, Zbigniew Brzezinski, had 'assumed the role of ringleader for the organization's activities'. *Izvestia* also accused Amnesty of saying 'not one word' about human rights violations in the USA, Israel, El Salvador, the United Kingdom and South Korea.

Amnesty did not rebut the *Izvestia* article until the charges had been carefully examined. Three months later Secretary-General Thomas Hammarberg issued a reply: 'We are an open, democratically run movement. We are not funded or controlled by any government or secret service. Amnesty International is entirely supported by its members and donations from the public. Its accounts are open to public inspection.'

Hammarberg went on to point out that the candidates for all posts in Amnesty are screened before they are appointed, to guard against infiltration and to protect confidential sources of information. The charges about not investigating certain countries could be easily shown to be false, merely by looking through Amnesty International reports.

The *Izvestia* article did cause some damage. Thomas Hammarberg decided it would be unwise to send one Amnesty member, named (falsely) in the *Izvestia* article as a CIA agent, on a planned mission to an African country. Hammarberg was worried that someone who read the report might consider it true and take some action against him.

There was, however, one point on which *Izvestia*'s criticism was fair – the USA. During the late 1960s, when black militancy was at its most active stage, and confrontation with the police and the National Guard was commonplace, many blacks were sentenced to inordinate terms in jail for what were often relatively minor offences. Blacks, anyway, had long been subject to discriminatory jail sentencing. For the same offence whites could usually expect a more lenient sentence. Amnesty does not appear to have tackled this contradiction; admittedly, the problems of definition and delineation in a field of law full of grey areas would not be easy. Only recently has it adopted a handful of US prison inmates as prisoners of conscience.

Nevertheless, by no stretch of the imagination can the situation in the USSR be compared with the USA or any other Western European country. Nowhere else in the industrialized world, even in Eastern Europe (apart from East Germany, Bulgaria and Romania), is the authoritarian net drawn so tightly. The government and the party are all-powerful. Omnipotence is their creed and freedom an alien concept to be resisted at every point and on every occasion.

11. Human Rights?

Harlan Cleveland, who used to be Adlai Stevenson's intellectual right hand and coined that wonderful phrase 'the revolution of rising expectations', pin-pointed in a recent speech with a sharpness that is breathtaking the great revolution in human rights that has taken place in the last forty years.

We may be living, even if we're not yet noticing and articulating, one of those profound, tidal shifts in human values that come along only once a millennium in the long history of the human condition.

The old business was rights *conferred or arrogated* – granted by God if possible, but if necessary seized by force and maintained by claims of superiority on account of rank, early arrival or self-anointed citizenship, and always ultimately by force.

Sure, the Hammurabi code saved aristocrats from being mutilated or tortured by their peers; and a citizen of ancient Rome, if condemned to die, could choose to be beheaded rather than tortured to death in the public arena. But even such rights as these were not inherent; they were handed down from higher authority. Not inalienable rights but the alienation of rights was the rule. Duties, not rights, were the substance of tradition for Hebrew, Chinese, Greek, Hindu, Buddhist and Christian alike. The right called divine was typically privilege – the right of the few to tell the many what to do, and for whom to do it.

In Islam, the third 'religion of the book', the Koran comes out for equity in property, fairness towards slaves, and generosity towards the destitute – but again, not as rights of the deprived but duties of the more fortunate.

In Marxism, too, that fourth 'religion of the book' (and the first to worship a book by an economist), the value of the individual resides clearly enough in the social order. It was only last month that a Soviet magazine indicted Andrei Sakharov for 'pathological individualism'.

The kernel of human rights was always there – in the idea that Adam was created in the image of God, and in the practice of a few of the many – the civil disobedience which brought Daniel to the lions' den, the claim of the early Christians that Rome governed by transgressing the dictates of the divine, the resentment of oppression that brought the Puritans to America – all precedents for Martin Luther King who violated American laws as contrary to the laws of God.

Only with the Enlightenment comes the idea that every human being has rights that are to be recognized, even protected, but are not conferred, by society. Today, three crowded centuries and a hundred revolutions later, the content of these rights is still debated and no one's minimum list is anywhere fully realized. Yet as we grapple with the implications of this late-starting, parochial, Western idea, we sense that it is on its way to universality.

Every religion, every revolution has begun as an assertion of universal truth and wound up at an essentially provincial community. This has come to be true of Christian orthodoxy; it is true as well of its Marxist heresy. But the idea of human rights – the notion that societies should be managed 'as if people mattered' – is so fundamental, so 'natural', so obvious once revealed, that it just may be the first revolution to achieve a global reach, the first 'world-class' superstar in the history of political philosophy.

To try to determine how it came to be like this is not easy. It is to probe the mind of Eleanor Roosevelt who presided in 1948 over the great act of codification of the Universal Declaration of Human Rights. It is to ask whether without Martin Luther

King, the American blacks would have so successfully upset most forms of institutional discrimination in the United States and thus freed a great superpower to feel less inhibited about using its massive influence on the side of human rights as well as realpolitik, even though the pulls between the two produced searing contradictions.

It is to ask Peter Benenson why the idea of a voluntary organization, independent of government and big money, devoted to the release of political prisoners, suddenly crystallized in his mind. We know from things he's said that Eleanor Roosevelt and Martin Luther King were influences, yet in his own chemistry there was his Jewish background, the bell of the Holocaust still tolling, and his Catholic belief, shaped in part by the peasant Pope, John XXIII, who stripped layers off an ossified, even corrupt church and revealed the freshness of the liberating teaching of Jesus of Nazareth beneath.

Origins of movements are always impossibly difficult to plumb and Amnesty International and its cause, the freedom of man's conscience in the political arena, is no exception. Nevertheless, it's clear that it has evolved to the point where its status is unquestioned – although many would like to demolish it rather than build it up – and that it has a continuing ability to reach out and strike chords that an increasing number of people want to hear.

Jimmy Carter's human rights policy can come and it can go, the United Nations Human Rights Commission can drag on painfully its debate on the pros and cons of a Torture Convention, the Soviet Union can, with its behaviour at home and in Poland, tear up the Helsinki accords, but Amnesty's image does not appear dulled.

It is quite peculiar – and it's no wonder that totalitarian governments can't really believe it's not funded by someone's secret service – that a relatively small voluntary organization, staffed overwhelmingly by women and by young people under forty (the World Bank and the IMF are its polar opposites), should play such a major role in the public life of governments right around the globe.

What are its strengths? First, its ability to get the facts right most of the time. Anyone who has worked in a newspaper or a government knows that getting the facts is extraordinarily difficult. Yet the number of times Amnesty has been shown up to be badly wrong are few and far between. Western diplomats growl under their breath about Amnesty exaggerations, but the criticism never seems properly to surface. Governments who are criticized denounce Amnesty, but even though they have been given an Amnesty report a month or two before it is due to be published, they rarely, if ever, take the opportunity to try and put the record straight.

Amnesty has a credibility with the media, with parliamentarians and with public opinion, that, it is fair to say, is as strong and as wide-reaching as any other international organization, with the possible exception of the Red Cross and UNICEF.

Richard Reoch, Amnesty's press officer, a friendly Canadian who never tires of recounting funny stories, told me this one. Amusing it is, but accurate too.

I remember a series of phone calls with a correspondent at the London bureau of the Associated Press news agency who kept trying to pin down exactly what we considered to be a political prisoner and how many of them there really were in Rhodesia. After he had got from us a breakdown of all the known categories of such prisoners, he rang off.

About two hours later he was back on the phone, politely telling me that he had been on to the Foreign Office and he had been told there were no political prisoners in Rhodesia. So he was back to ask Amnesty International what we had to say about *that*. What we had to say about that was to remind him of the statistics on political prisoners provided to us by the British administration in Rhodesia a month or so earlier, and the subsequent official figure which clearly indicated that several thousands of those prisoners were still held.

There was a brief silence on the other end of the phone and then the newsman cursed. Obviously recalling his long chat with the Foreign Office, he abandoned objectivity. 'No matter how long I stay here in London on this assignment,

I'll never fathom the deviousness of the British government,' he spluttered. Then he regained his composure. 'Okay,' he said, 'give me the facts again.'

Thomas Hammarberg, Amnesty's secretary-general, says he worries about Amnesty's temptation to come up with hard conclusions from what is too often a shallow research base. It's easy to understand his concern. In this book, two studies, of Guatemala and the Central African Republic, reveal the almost tenuous way conclusions are drawn.

The dilemma is obvious — is it better to keep quiet and wait until absolutely incontrovertible evidence arrives, by which time hundreds more may be tortured or dead, or is it not the more responsible course to come out with the reasonably watertight, but not perfect, case one has, and take the risk?

The dialectic between the two approaches is continuous among Amnesty's staff and members. The fact that so rarely has Amnesty had to issue corrections or apologies is proof of their good judgment. The Central African exposé was a vindication of their sense of responsibility — as much checking as could be done and a low-key press release at the end. In Guatemala, as I followed the Amnesty trail under my own steam, I often wondered if the facts would show up a little less hard, slightly softer round the edges, than the Amnesty researchers had painted them. On occasion they did, but then on occasion they were harder and sharper. Was Amnesty right to publish and say that the political murders were organized direct from the president's office? We don't know the answer to that one yet (although an editorial in the *Washington Post* in April 1981 noted that US intelligence sources had confirmed the Amnesty conclusions). My guess is that Amnesty will turn out to have been right, not because they had a team of a hundred investigators, evidence under oath, subpoenaed documents, and iron-clad proof — on the contrary, they had only a couple of people, who were simultaneously working on a dozen other countries — but because long practice in this arena, a disciplined caution, gives great depth to their judgments. They tend to know, unlike a court or a parliamentary investigation, who they can believe and who they can discount. This poses certain risks, but their record of success is their shield.

There is, nevertheless, one blemish on their copy book – its handling of the Baader-Meinhof gang. It is not that Amnesty doesn't have the facts, it does, but in this particular case it appears to interpret them in a manner that suggests it uses a harsher set of guidelines when dealing with the Western democracies than with the outside world.

One member of the Baader-Meinhof gang, Ulrike Meinhof, did undergo a long period of total isolation. Usually, however, apart from short periods after a major act of violence, the detainees have been allowed the company of other members of the gang albeit for too short a period of the day. They have, unlike common criminals, been allowed often to keep the company of the opposite sex. They have, with the regular and frequent visits of their lawyers, access to books and the media, been given great privileges.

The Baader-Meinhof, with their fasts to death – the latest was in the spring of 1981 – demanding political status and the right to associate in large groups, should not be the cause that wins any of Amnesty's sympathy. It is a nihilistic group, its ideals long buried, seeking only the violent destruction of a democratically elected state, one, it could be added, that has produced the most successful left of centre government in post-war Western Europe.

Some time ago, it was an issue of strong debate with Amnesty whether the organization should aid prisoners accused of violent crimes. In the end, Amnesty decided that they could not become prisoners of conscience but they would be helped if subjected to torture, serious ill-treatment, or threatened with execution.

There is no overwhelming evidence that the Baader-Meinhof prisoners are in these categories. And to give them the benefit of the doubt on the 'isolation is torture' issue is to take an unnecessary step towards a group of people, who, if back on the streets, would gladly shoot many of the people attracted to Amnesty International.

The other great strength of Amnesty has been to widen the appeal of human rights. It is often argued that Amnesty's concerns are a product of the Western world, that they do not apply to the Third World where the priorities are material needs and economic development. It has always been a rather phoney criticism. After all, the Third World group at the United Nations has probably spent more time on civil and political rights for blacks in Southern Africa than on any other single issue. The former Philippines senator, José Diokno, answered the point well in his 1978 Sean MacBride lecture delivered to Amnesty International's council:

> Two justifications for authoritarianism in Asian developing countries are currently fashionable . . . One is that Asian societies are authoritarian and paternalistic and so need governments that are also authoritarian and paternalistic; that Asia's hungry masses are too concerned with filling their stomachs to concern themselves with civil liberties and political freedoms; that the Asian conception of freedom differs from that of the West; that in short, Asians are not fit for human rights.
>
> Another is that developing countries must sacrifice freedom temporarily to achieve the rapid economic development that their exploding populations and rising expectations demand; in short, that governments must be authoritarian to promote development.
>
> Well, the first justification is racist nonsense. The second is a lie: authoritarianism is not needed for development; what it is needed for is to maintain the status quo . . .

Amnesty by its early decision to have its adoption groups take on one political prisoner from the West, one from a communist country, and one from the Third World, has encouraged a world-embracing viewpoint to develop. It has refused to accept that the *pau de arara* in Brazil is any more a part of the Latin American tradition than ducking and stretching on the rack during the Spanish Inquisition were part of the Christian tradition. Amnesty has also helped throw into relief the fact that there are many developing countries, some very poor, who have an active and militant awareness of the importance of human rights – and it is growing. In Africa three years ago, there was Bokassa in Central Africa, Amin in Uganda, Nguema in Equatorial Guinea, Smith in Rhodesia, and military regimes in Mali, Nigeria and Ghana. Now all these countries have shaken off their tyrants or strongmen and have moved, admittedly with varying degrees of success, to the restoration of democracy and human rights. Whatever the failings today, as in Obote's Uganda, the map of Africa has been transformed in a relatively short time. The hunger for the non-economic values is obvious.

This is not to say this is all Amnesty's achievement. Jimmy Carter, Cyrus Vance, and Andrew Young must take a large part of the credit. So must churches, unions and other organizations such as Freedom House. Amnesty, however, has been in the forefront of this evolution and has built up respect in Africa that, as far as one can tell, looks solid and full of potential. Amnesty International's representative in Paris, pointed out to me how much success they now have in Francophone Africa as a result of their Bokassa exposé. Before, that part of the world had been almost a closed book.

Amnesty's future, twenty years on, what is it? It has outlived three secretary-generals, its virginity was long lost when it was pressured and possibly penetrated by British Intelligence, and its independence, experience and vitality are safely vouchsafed when it could show it was able to live with and without the concern and favour of a superpower.

It's a very mature political animal as it comes up to twenty-one, still trim, a staff of only 150, still lean, a budget of only £2 million which would barely keep going the affairs of a couple of US Congressional committees, and it still has much to do.

The superpowers seem determined to take the world through another dark age. As the Soviet Union turns the screws in Afghanistan and Poland and keeps repression in Ethiopia and Libya well fuelled, and as the Reagan administration helps kill off protest and reform in Central America and rolls back political evolution in Southern Africa, the causes and people that cry out for Amnesty's succour multiply.

Economic problems in the industrialized countries tempt people to be more self-centred and chauvinistic and the need is reinforced for Amnesty's vigilance to remind the still relatively comfortably-off of a world beyond their immediate bread, butter and automobile concerns.

In the world at large, new techniques of torture are being refined by regimes who refuse to trust their people with the right to choose their political leaders. They are relying on psychological torture more than physical. They are holding the prisoners they have tortured until their scars and bruises heal before releasing them. They are learning that the *falanga*, electric shocks and drowning, leave less evidence than more traditional methods. Set against this, Amnesty's medical advisers are applying new techniques for examining torture victims and for developing their treatment.

Also as Amnesty develops, it becomes conscious of 'grey areas' that its 'mandate' seems to constrict it from acting upon. In Brazil, where official torture, after sixteen years, seems practically to have ceased, Amnesty finds it difficult to take up the cases of the peasants who are kicked off their land, often at the point of a gun or the end of a boot. This is not official violence or torture. But the police and the courts often look the other way. The authorities in the capital may wish to stop it, but their legal deterrents pale before the economic incentives they have given to the large landowners in the north-east and the Amazon. It's frontier violence, reminiscent of the American wild west.

The peasants, because they do not go to jail and are not hunted down by official death squads, cannot go on Amnesty's books. Amnesty appears helpless in the face of countless deaths and appalling suffering.

Thomas Hammarberg, for one, is conscious of this problem. Amnesty has evolved before and maybe will evolve again. It is a difficult decision to make. Undoubtedly, part of Amnesty's strength, not least its ability to command a wide spectrum of support, has been its narrow focus. If it takes on too broad a mandate it could well lose its cutting edge.

It is right for Amnesty to feel its way slowly and a step at a time and in Hammarberg it has a secretary-general who is both careful and sensitive, aware of the problems but, rightly, not always sure of the solutions.

The burden of being a member of Amnesty, a member of staff, its secretary-general or chairperson is immense. The responsibility it has arrogated to itself is mighty and the expectations of those who look to it for help to save their bodies and lives often overpowering.

But there are the great moments too. In June 1980 there occurred one of those.

Amnesty had sent one of its teams to Colombia, to investigate the repeated allegations of torture. Instead of the usual quiet, going-through-the-back-door kind of affair, the trip became a public extravaganza.

Local and regional newsmen followed the Amnesty delegates everywhere, even up to the gates of the prisons.

In the evenings, during their journey round the country, people flocked to see them. At one point they were seeing as many as four hundred people an evening, from dusk until midnight. In one town they had to hire the hotel ballroom just to accommodate the unannounced petitioners.

The government, too, took Amnesty very seriously. It opened the prison gates and let the investigators poke into the corners.

When the mission presented its conclusions – it had decided that there was overwhelming evidence of widespread official torture – the three main newspapers in Colombia carried Amnesty's full text, all 13,000 words. The country erupted into an unprecedented national debate. The president went on national television and spoke for nearly an hour in an effort to repudiate Amnesty's criticisms.

A year later one can see the impact. The Colombian government has done much to clean its house. The government announced an amnesty. The allegations of torture are less frequent, the number of political prisoners much reduced.

The Colombian mission, it was said, was amazing, even exhilarating. But for every carnival, there are a hundred nights in the desert; for every release, another batch of prisoners; for every family reunited, another torn asunder; for every shout of exultation, a cry of suffering, as the heavy door shuts out the daylight for one more prisoner, leaving him to nurse his own wounds and wait, when the morning arrives, for the tread of the official torturer or executioner.

These are the people whom Peter Benenson had in mind when, on 28 May 1981, Amnesty International's twentieth anniversary, he returned to the steps of St Martin-in-the-Fields to light again the original Amnesty candle. It was a moving moment. He offered a new slogan for the movement, 'Against Oblivion', and declared:

> We have lit this candle today as an act of rededication to our work. I would like you to remember, together with me, not our success, because I think that has been relatively lean, but all our failures. I think that the candle burns not for us but for all those whom we failed to rescue from prison, who have died in prison, who were shot on the way to prison, who were tortured, who were kidnapped, who 'disappeared'. That's what the candle is for . . .
>
> I have lit this candle today, in the words of Shakespeare, 'against oblivion' — so that the forgotten prisoners should always be remembered. We work in Amnesty *against oblivion*.

Statute of Amnesty International

*As amended by the 12th International Council, meeting
in Leuven, Belgium, 6–9 September 1979*

Object

1.   Considering that every person has the right freely to hold
and to express his or her convictions and the obligation to
extend a like freedom to others, the object of Amnesty
International shall be to secure throughout the world the
observance of the provisions of the Universal Declaration of
Human Rights, by:

 a) irrespective of political considerations working towards the
    release of and providing assistance to persons who in
    violation of the aforesaid provisions are imprisoned,
    detained or otherwise physically restricted by reason of their
    political, religious or other conscientiously held beliefs or by
    reason of their ethnic origin, sex, colour or language,
    provided that they have not used or advocated violence
    (hereinafter referred to as 'Prisoners of Conscience');

 b) opposing by all appropriate means the detention of any
    Prisoners of Conscience or any political prisoners without
    trial within a reasonable time or any trial procedures
    relating to such prisoners that do not conform to
    internationally recognized norms;

 c) opposing by all appropriate means the imposition and
    infliction of death penalties and torture or other cruel,
    inhuman or degrading treatment or punishment of prisoners
    or other detained or restricted persons whether or not they
    have used or advocated violence

Methods

2.   In order to achieve the aforesaid object, Amnesty International shall:

a) at all times maintain an overall balance between its activities in relation to countries adhering to the different world political ideologies and groupings;

b) promote as appears appropriate the adoption of constitutions, conventions, treaties and other measures which guarantee the rights contained in the provisions referred to in article 1 hereof;

c) support and publicize the activities of and cooperate with international organizations and agencies which work for the implementation of the aforesaid provisions;

d) take all necessary steps to establish an effective organization of national sections, affiliated groups and individual members;

e) secure the adoption by groups of members or supporters of individual Prisoners of Conscience or entrust to such groups other tasks in support of the object set out in article 1;

f) provide financial and other relief to Prisoners of Conscience and their dependants and to persons who have lately been Prisoners of Conscience or who might reasonably be expected to be Prisoners of Conscience or to become Prisoners of Conscience if convicted or if they were to return to their own countries, and to the dependants of such persons;

g) work for the improvement of conditions for Prisoners of Conscience and political prisoners;

h) provide legal aid, where necessary and possible, to Prisoners of Conscience and to persons who might reasonably be expected to be Prisoners of Conscience or to become Prisoners of Conscience if convicted or if they were to return to their own countries, and where desirable, send observers to attend the trials of such persons;

i) publicize the cases of Prisoners of Conscience or persons who have otherwise been subjected to disabilities in violation of the aforesaid provisions;

j) send investigators, where appropriate, to investigate allegations that the rights of individuals under the aforesaid provisions have been violated or threatened;

k) make representations to international organizations and to governments whenever it appears that an individual is a Prisoner of Conscience or has otherwise been subjected to disabilities in violation of the aforesaid provisions;

l) promote and support the granting of general amnesties of which the beneficiaries will include Prisoners of Conscience;

m) adopt any other appropriate methods for the securing of its object.

Organization

3. Amnesty International shall consist of national sections, affiliated groups and individual members.

4. The directive authority for the conduct of the affairs of Amnesty International is vested in the International Council.

5. Between meetings of the International Council, the International Executive Committee shall be responsible for the conduct of the affairs of Amnesty International and for the implementation of the decisions of the International Council.

6. The day to day affairs of Amnesty International shall be conducted by the International Secretariat headed by a Secretary General under the direction of the International Executive Committee.

7. The office of the International Secretariat shall be in London or such other place as the International Executive Committee shall decide and which is ratified by at least one-half of the national sections.

National Sections

8. A national section of Amnesty International may be established in any country, state or territory with the consent of the International Executive Committee. In order to be

recognized as such, a national section shall (a) consist of not less than two groups or 10 members (b) submit its statute to the International Executive Committee for approval (c) pay such annual fee as may be determined by the International Council (d) be registered as such with the International Secretariat on the decision of the International Executive Committee. National sections shall take no action on matters that do not fall within the stated object of Amnesty International. The International Secretariat shall maintain a register of national sections. National sections shall act in accordance with the working rules and guidelines that are adopted from time to time by the International Council.

9.   Groups of not less than three members or supporters may, on payment of an annual fee determined by the International Council, become affiliated to Amnesty International or a national section thereof. Any dispute as to whether a group should be or remain affiliated shall be decided by the International Executive Committee. An affiliated adoption group shall accept for adoption such prisoners as may from time to time be allotted to it by the International Secretariat, and shall adopt no others as long as it remains affiliated to Amnesty International. No group shall be allotted a Prisoner of Conscience detained in its own country. The International Secretariat shall maintain a register of affiliated adoption groups. Groups shall take no action on matters that do not fall within the stated object of Amnesty International. Groups shall act in accordance with the working rules and guidelines that are adopted from time to time by the International Council.

Individual Membership

10.   Individuals residing in countries where there is no national section may, on payment to the International Secretariat of an annual subscription fee determined by the International Executive Committee, become members of Amnesty International with the consent of the International Executive Committee. In countries where a national section

exists, individuals may become international members of Amnesty International with the consent of the national section and of the International Committee. The International Secretariat shall maintain a register of such members.

11.   Deleted.

International Council

12.   The International Council shall consist of the members of the International Executive Committee and of representatives of national sections and shall meet at intervals of approximately one year but in any event of not more than two years on a date fixed by the International Executive Committee. Only representatives of national sections and elected members of the International Executive Committee shall have the right to vote on the International Council.

13.   All national sections shall have the right to appoint one representative to the International Council and in addition may appoint representatives as follows:

10 – 49 groups	:	1 representative
50 – 99 groups	:	2 representatives
100 – 199 groups	:	3 representatives
200 – 399 groups	:	4 representatives
400 groups or over	:	5 representatives

National sections consisting primarily of individual members rather than groups may in alternative appoint additional representatives as follows:

500 – 2499	:	1 representative
2500 and over	:	2 representatives

Only sections having paid in full their annual fee as assessed by the International Council for the previous financial year shall vote at the International Council. This requirement may be waived in whole or in part by the International Executive Committee.

14.   Representatives of groups not forming part of a national section may with permission of the Secretary General attend a meeting of the International Council as observers and may speak thereat but shall not be entitled to vote.

15.   A national section unable to participate in an International Council may appoint a proxy or proxies to vote on its behalf and a national section represented by a lesser number of persons than its entitlement under article 13 hereof may authorize its representative or representatives to cast votes up to its maximum entitlement under article 13 hereof.

16.   Notice of the number of representatives proposing to attend an International Council, and of the appointment of proxies, shall be given to the International Secretariat not later than one month before the meeting of the International Council. This requirement may be waived by the International Executive Committee.

17.   A quorum shall consist of the representatives or proxies of not less than one quarter of the national sections entitled to be represented.

18.   The Chairperson of the International Executive Committee, or such other person as the International Executive Committee may appoint, shall open the proceedings of the International Council, which shall elect a Chairperson. Thereafter the elected Chairperson, or such other person as the Chairperson may appoint, shall preside at the International Council.

19.   Except as otherwise provided in the statute, the International Council shall make its decisions by a simple majority of the votes cast. In case of an equality of votes the Chairperson of the International Council shall have a casting vote.

20.   The International Council shall be convened by the International Secretariat by notice to all national sections and affiliated groups not later than 90 days before the date thereof.

21.   The Chairperson of the International Executive Committee shall at the request of the Committee or of not less than one-third of the national sections call an extraordinary meeting of the International Council by giving not

less than 21 days' notice in writing to all national sections.

22.   The International Council shall elect a Treasurer, who shall be a member of the International Executive Committee.

23.   The International Council may appoint one or more Honorary Presidents of Amnesty International to hold office for a period not exceeding three years.

24.   The agenda for the meetings of the International Council shall be prepared by the International Secretariat under the direction of the Chairperson of the International Executive Committee.

International Executive Committee

25.   a) The International Executive Committee shall consist of the Treasurer, one representative of the staff of the International Secretariat and seven regular members, who shall be members of Amnesty International, or of a national section, or of an affiliated group, elected by the International Council by proportional representation by the method of a single transferable vote in accordance with the regulations published by the Electoral Reform Society. Not more than one member of any national section or affiliated group may be elected as a regular member to the Committee, and once one member of any national section or affiliated group has received sufficient votes to be elected, any votes cast for other members of that national section or affiliated group shall be disregarded.

b) Members of the permanent staff, paid and unpaid, shall have the right to elect one representative among the staff who has completed not less than two years' service to be a voting member of the International Executive Committee. Such member shall hold office for one year and shall be eligible for re-election. The method of voting shall be subject to approval by the International Executive Committee on the proposal of the staff members.

26.   The International Executive Committee shall meet not less than twice a year at a place to be decided by itself.

27.   Members of the International Executive Committee, other than the representative of the staff, shall hold office for a period of two years and shall be eligible for re-election. Except in the case of elections to fill vacancies resulting from unexpired terms of office, the members of the Committee, other than the representative of the staff, shall be subjected to election in equal proportions on alternate years.

28.   The Committee may co-opt not more than four additional members who shall hold office until the close of the next meeting of the International Council; they shall be eligible to be reco-opted. Co-opted members shall not have the right to vote.

29.   In the event of a vacancy occurring on the Committee, other than in respect of the representative of the staff, it may co-opt a further member to fill the vacancy until the next meeting of the International Council, which shall elect such members as are necessary to replace retiring members and to fill the vacancy. In the event of a vacancy occurring on the Committee in respect of the representative of the staff, the staff shall have the right to elect a successor representative to fill the unexpired term of office.

30.   If a member of the Committee is unable to attend a meeting, such member may appoint an alternate.

31.   The Committee shall each year appoint one of its members to act as Chairperson.

32.   The Chairperson may, and at the request of the majority of the Committee shall, summon meetings of the Committee.

33.   A quorum shall consist of not less than five members of the Committee or their alternates.

34.   The agenda for meetings of the Committee shall be prepared by the International Secretariat under the direction of the Chairperson.

35.   The Committee may make regulations for the conduct of the affairs of Amnesty International, and for the procedure to be followed at the International Council.

International Secretariat

36.   The International Executive Committee may appoint a Secretary General who shall be responsible under its direction for the conduct of the affairs of Amnesty International and for the implementation of the decisions of the International Council.

37.   The Secretary General may, after consultation with the Chairperson of the International Executive Committee, and subject to confirmation by that Committee, appoint such executive and professional staff as are necessary.

38.   In the case of the absence or illness of the Secretary General, or of a vacancy in the post of Secretary General, the Chairperson of the International Executive Committee shall, after consultation with the members of that Committee, appoint an acting Secretary General to act until the next meeting of the Committee.

39.   The Secretary General or Acting Secretary General, and such members of the International Secretariat as may appear to the Chairperson of the International Executive Committee to be necessary shall attend meetings of the International Council and of the International Executive Committee and may speak thereat but shall not be entitled to vote.

Termination of Membership

40.   Membership of or affiliation to Amnesty International may be terminated at any time by resignation in writing.

41.   The International Council may, upon the proposal of the International Executive Committee or of a national section, by a three-fourths majority of the votes cast deprive a national section, an affiliated group or a member of membership of Amnesty International if in its opinion that national section, affiliated group or member does not act within the spirit of the object and methods set out in articles 1 and 2 or does not observe any of the provisions of this statute. Before taking such action, all national sections shall be informed and the Secretary General shall also inform the national section, affiliated group

or member of the grounds on which it is proposed to deprive it or such person of membership, and such national section, affiliated group or member shall be provided with an opportunity of presenting its or such member's case to the International Council.

42.   A national section, affiliated group or member who fails to pay the annual fee fixed in accordance with this statute within six months after the close of the financial year shall cease to be affiliated to Amnesty International unless the International Executive Committee decides otherwise.

Finance

43.   An auditor appointed by the International Council shall annually audit the accounts of Amnesty International, which shall be prepared by the International Secretariat and presented to the International Executive Committee and the International Council.

44.   No part of the income or property of Amnesty International shall directly or indirectly be paid or transferred otherwise than for valuable and sufficient consideration to any of its members by way of dividend, gift, division, bonus or otherwise howsoever by way of profit.

Amendments of Statute

45.   The statute may be amended by the International Council by a majority of not less than two-thirds of the votes cast. Amendments may be submitted by the International Executive Committee or by a national section. Proposed amendments shall be submitted to the International Secretariat not less than three months before the International Council meets, and presentation to the International Council shall be supported in writing by at least five national sections. Proposed amendments shall be communicated by the International Secretariat to all national sections and to members of the International Executive Committee.

Amnesty International News Releases, May 1980 – June 1981

1980

4 May AI expressed fears that former members of an East Timor independence movement have been executed after surrendering under an amnesty offered by *Indonesian* authorities. A number 'disappeared' after being rearrested by Indonesian troops, and others have been missing since they surrendered.

9 May AI urged the authorities in *Iran* to conform to internationally agreed standards for trials and treatment of prisoners, to which Iran is committed by international treaty. A report sent to the new government found that many people had been sentenced to death and executed without fair trials.

20 May AI launched a campaign against human rights violations in *Zaire*. Hundreds of people have been arbitrarily arrested and then confined indefinitely in remote camps in the jungle and bush where deaths by summary execution, torture or starvation are common.

20 May AI received a written response from the government of *Zaire* in reply to the report and memorandum on arrests and ill-treatment of prisoners.

22 May AI received an assurance from the chairperson of *Uganda*'s ruling Military Commission about former President Godfrey Binaisa.

26 May AI urged President Carter to establish a presidential commission to study the death penalty in the *United States of America*, and examine whether executions violate the country's international commitments to human rights.

28 May AI said that prisoners held in connection with politically motivated crimes in the *Federal Republic of Germany* were kept in conditions that could – and sometimes did – cause serious physical and psychological damage.

3 June AI appealed to President Carter of the *United States of America* to intervene personally with Governor George Busbee of Georgia to stay the execution of Jack Howard Potts, scheduled to take place on 5 June 1980.

9 June AI reported that torture in *Turkey* had become widespread and systematic; that most people being arrested by police and martial law authorities were tortured; and that in some cases it was alleged to have ended in death.

12 June AI launched an international campaign to persuade the *Iraqi* authorities to halt their increasing use of the death penalty, often imposed by special courts for non-violent political activity.

16 June AI called on the *Jamaican* Committee on capital punishment and penal reform to pave the way for the abolition of the death penalty.

30 June AI said that the authorities in *Romania* used a wide range of legal and extra-legal penalties against those breaching official limits on the expression of political, religious and social views.

30 June AI publicized reports that two Argentinians had been tortured to death after being seized in *Peru* and that three others had been secretly taken back to Argentina.

16 July AI warned that proposed United States security assistance to *El Salvador* would worsen the widespread murder and torture of peasants and suspected opponents of the government. In a letter to US Secretary of State Edmund Muskie, AI said that since early January 'at least 2000 Salvadoreans have been killed or "disappeared" while in the hands of conventional and auxiliary security forces'.

28 July AI reported that ten political prisoners being held without trial in *Angola* were seriously ill after more than three weeks on a hunger strike.

5 August AI announced that a fact-finding mission to the *Republic of Korea* had been refused entry. The mission was to investigate reports of large-scale arrests and torture of political prisoners.

8 August AI appealed to the new military leader of *Bolivia* to release all political prisoners and to publish a list of people imprisoned or killed since he took power on 17 July 1980. AI estimated that 1000 people had been arrested since the coup, and cited reports of summary executions, arbitrary arrests and torture.

21 August AI publicized an eyewitness account of *Bolivian* troops rampaging through a mining town, killing, abducting and raping. As many as 900 people had 'disappeared' from Caracoles after the attack. The town is in a mining region whose inhabitants are suspected of political opposition to the new military leaders.

29 August AI appealed to the newly appointed prime minister of *Iran* to halt executions and the imprisonment of people for their beliefs or origins. AI was saddened to see continued human rights violations since the Iranian Revolution 'and especially the large number of executions'.

2 September AI called on the government of *Israel* to set up a public and impartial enquiry into persistent complaints of brutality towards people arrested on suspicion of security offences in the Occupied Territories.

9 September AI reported that political arrests and systematic torture of suspects increased sharply as *Chile* approached the seventh anniversary of the military coup that brought its present government to power.

15 September AI called on the United Nations General Assembly to declare the death penalty a violation of fundamental human rights. The supreme governing body of

AI, meeting in Vienna, urged its national sections and members to seek support for such a declaration.

17 September AI was appalled by the death sentence passed by a *South Korean* military court on opposition leader Kim Dae-jung. The trial of Kim and twenty-three co-defendants, who received prison sentences, failed to meet international standards of fairness.

22 September AI sent the government of *Colombia* detailed and conclusive evidence of widespread arbitrary arrests and systematic torture of political prisoners by government forces.

29 September AI urged President Saddam Hussein of *Iraq* to enquire into reports that political suspects had been given slow-acting poison while in custody. The organization had received detailed evidence about three people, two of whom had been examined by doctors in the UK after leaving Iraq.

12 October AI launched a worldwide week of action on behalf of victims of political repression. Prisoner of Conscience Week 1980 was organized around the theme 'the different faces of imprisonment', spotlighting the different methods of repression – including abduction, house arrest, prosecution on false criminal charges and short-term arrest.

15 October AI announced it had submitted a series of detailed recommendations to the government of *Spain*, designed to protect political detainees from torture.

22 October Willy Brandt, Pierre Trudeau and Morarji Desai were among thousands of prominent people from around the world who joined in an AI appeal to the United Nations for international action to abolish the death penalty.

3 November AI called on President Zia ul-Haq to release all prisoners of conscience held in *Pakistan* and to take immediate steps to halt torture, floggings and executions.

6 November AI asked the government of the *United States of America* to clarify what treatment and status Haitians seeking asylum in the US would receive. AI had reports that they were to be sent to a military camp in Puerto Rico.

12 November AI rejected accusations by the *Soviet* newspaper *Izvestia* that it was 'maintained by imperialist secret services'.

28 November AI said that a new constitution proposed by the military rulers of *Uruguay* would institutionalize a system marked by repression and torture, and give a semblance of legality to violations of basic human rights which have been occurring since the military took full power in 1973.

3 December AI published medical evidence of ill-treatment amounting to torture inflicted on political detainees held incommunicado in *Spanish* police stations.

9 December AI appealed to the heads of government of each of the forty-three nations represented on the United Nations Commission of Human Rights in an effort to prevent the execution of *South Korean* opposition leader Kim Dae-jung.

10 December The *Amnesty International Report 1980* highlights the political death toll: people were murdered by government forces or executed for political reasons in more than thirty countries during the twelve months reviewed.

1981

21 January AI said that courts in the *Soviet Union* were passing severe sentences in a sustained crackdown on dissenters, more than two hundred of whom had been imprisoned during the previous fifteen months.

23 January AI appealed to President Chun Doo-hwan of *South Korea* for the immediate and unconditional release of opposition leader Kim Dae-jung.

25 January AI urged the authorities in *China* to commute the death sentences passed by a special court on Jiang Ching and Zhang Chunqiao in the 'gang of four' trial.

4 February AI appealed to the government of the *German Democratic Republic* to review the country's criminal laws to bring them in line with its international commitments on human rights.

13 February AI cabled the government of *Nicaragua* to express concern about reports that the Ministry of Justice had ordered the closure of the independent Nicaraguan Commission on Human Rights.

18 February AI said that a long-established government programme of murder and torture in *Guatemala* was run from an annex to the National Palace, under the control of President Romeo Lucas García.

25 February AI reported that *Bolivian* troops and government agents had killed, tortured and abducted people in total disregard of law and constitutional principles since a military junta took power in a coup in July 1980.

2 March AI launched a worldwide campaign to persuade the *South Korean* authorities to stop political imprisonment, torture and unfair trials.

20 March AI appealed to French President Valéry Giscard d'Estaing to use his power to prevent France's first execution since 1977.

9 April AI called on the government of *El Salvador* to guarantee the safety of people named on an apparent death list of 138 names published by the Salvadorean army.

10 April AI reported it had sent a legal observer to attend the trial by a military court of five men accused of plotting to overthrow the Bangladesh government. The five include a colonel, two retired army officers and two men who have never been in the armed forces.

14 April AI reported it had appealed twice in recent weeks to authorities in the *Federal Republic of Germany* to improve conditions for prisoners held in connection with politically motivated crimes. A number of these prisoners are on hunger strike, and their situation has made it urgent for the authorities to consider recommendations for improvements made by Amnesty International in 1979.

29 April AI published detailed medical findings supporting other convincing evidence that political prisoners are tortured in *Iraq*. Beatings, electric shock, burning and sexual abuse are among the tortures documented in case histories of fifteen Iraqis, all of whom were examined by doctors outside the country. The Iraqi government described the report as 'without any foundation', and emphasized that torture was banned by the nation's constitution and laws.

22 May AI appealed to the *Bangladesh* authorities to order a retrial before an independent court of five men convicted yesterday on charges of attempting to overthrow the government.

27 May AI said human rights face a crucial test in the 1980s, with the right to dissent under widespread attack. In an appeal issued to mark its twentieth anniversary tomorrow, the movement called for urgent international efforts to meet the challenge, through both public opinion and international law. It pledged to intensify its own efforts and said it hoped to double the number of people taking part in its campaigning over the next two years.

3 June AI made public a detailed written dialogue in which it urged the *Vietnamese* government to abolish 're-education' camps officially said to hold some 20,000 people who have not been charged or tried.

National Sections of Amnesty International

AUSTRALIA

Amnesty International
Australian Section
PO Box No. A159
Sydney South
New South Wales 2000

New South Wales

Amnesty International
New South Wales Branch
PO Box A611
Sydney South
New South Wales 2000

Queensland

Amnesty International
Queensland Branch
180-182 Roma Street
Brisbane
Queensland 4000

South Australia

Amnesty International
South Australia Branch
18 King William Road
North Adelaide
South Australia 5006

Tasmania

Amnesty International
Tasmania Branch
c/o Mrs Sue Forage
Box K968 GPO
Hobart
Tasmania 7001

Victoria

Amnesty International
Victoria Branch
277 Inkerman Street
St Kilda
Victoria 3182

Western Australia

Amnesty International
Western Australia Branch
Box X2258
GPO Perth
Western Australia 6001

AUSTRIA

Amnesty International
Austrian Section
Esslinggasse 15/4
A-1010 Wien

BANGLADESH

Amnesty Bangladesh
GPO Box 2095
Dacca

BARBADOS

AI Barbados Section
PO Box 65B
Brittons Hill
Bridgetown
Barbados

BELGIUM

Flemish Branch

Amnesty International
Blijde Inkomststraat 98
3000 Leuven

French-speaking Branch

Amnesty International
145 Boulevard Leopold II
1080 Brussels

CANADA

English-speaking

Amnesty International
Canadian Section
PO Box 6033
2101 Algonquin Avenue
Ottawa
Ontario K2A 1T1

Toronto Office
10 Trinity Square
Toronto M5G 1B1
Canada

French-speaking

Amnistie Internationale
Section Canadienne
  (Francophone)
1800 Quest, Boulevard
  Dorchester, local 400
Montreal
Quebec H3H 2H2

COSTA RICA

Please send all correspondence via the International Secretariat

DENMARK

Amnesty International
Frederiksborggade 1
1360 Copenhagen K

ECUADOR

Senores
Casilla de Correo 8994
Guayaquil

FAROE ISLANDS

Amnesty International
c/o Anette Wang
PO Box 1075
Trondargøta 47
3800 Torshavn

FINLAND

Amnesty International
Finnish Section
Munkkisaarenkatu 12 A 51
00150 Helsinki 15

FRANCE

Amnesty International
French Section
18 Rue Theodore Deck
75015 Paris

FEDERAL REPUBLIC OF
GERMANY

Amnesty International
Section of the FRG
Heerstrasse 178
5300 Bonn 1

GHANA

Amnesty International
Ghanaian Section
PO Box 9852
Kotoka Airport
Accra

GREECE

Amnesty International
Greek Section
22 Kleitomachou Street
Athens 502

ICELAND

Amnesty International
    Icelandic Section
PO Box 7124
127 Reykjavik

INDIA

Amnesty International
Indian Section
Vivekananda Vihar

c4/3 Safdarjung Development
    Area
New Delhi, 110016

IRELAND

Amnesty International
Irish Section
Liberty Hall
8th Floor
Dublin 1

ISRAEL

Amnesty International
Israel National Section
PO Box 37638
61 375 Tel Aviv

ITALY

Amnesty International
Italian Section
Viale Mazzini 146
00195 Rome

IVORY COAST

Amnesty International
Section Ivoirienne
01 BP 698
Abidjan 01

JAPAN

Amnesty International
Japanese Section
Daisan-Sanbu Building 3F
2-3-22 Nishi-Waseda
Shinjuku-ku
Tokyo 160

KOREA, REPUBLIC OF

Please send all correspondence via the International Secretariat

LUXEMBOURG

Amnesty International
    Luxembourg
Boite Postale 1914
Luxembourg-Gare

MEXICO

Senores
Ap. Postal No. 20-217
Mexico 20 DF

NEPAL

Amnesty International
Nepal Section
Post Box 918
21/94 Bagbazzar
Kathmandu

NETHERLANDS

Amnesty International
Dutch Section
Postbus 61501
1005 HM Amsterdam

NEW ZEALAND

Amnesty International
New Zealand Section
PO Box 11648
Manners Street
Wellington 1

NIGERIA

Amnesty International
Nigerian Section
7 Onayade Street
Fadeyi-Yaba
Lagos

NORWAY

Amnesty International
Norwegian Section
Rosenkrantzgatan 18
Oslo 1

PAKISTAN

Amnesty International
Pakistan Section
615 Muhammadi House
I.I. Chundrigar Road
Karachi

PERU

Senores
Casilla 2319
Lima

SENEGAL

Amnesty International
Section Senegalaise
B.P. 3813
Dakar

SPAIN

Amnesty International
Paseo de Recoletos 18, Piso 6
Madrid 1

Barcelona

Amnesty International
Boters 14, 2°
Barcelona 2

San Sebastian

Amnesty International
Apartado 1109
San Sebastian

SRI LANKA

Amnesty International
Sri Lanka Section
c/o E.A.G. de Silva
79/15 Dr C.W.W. Kannangara
   Mawatha
Colombo 7

SWEDEN

Amnesty International
Swedish Section
Surbrunnsgatan 44
S/113/48 Stockholm

SWITZERLAND

Amnesty International
Swiss Section
PO Box 1051
CH-3001 Bern

TURKEY

Please send all correspondence via the International
Secretariat

UNITED KINGDOM

Amnesty International
British Section
8-14 Southampton Street
London WC2E 7HF

USA

Amnesty International of the
   USA
304 West 58th Street
New York, NY 10019

Washington Office

Amnesty International of the
   USA
Washington Office
705 'G' Street, SE
Washington, DC 20003

Western Regional Office

Amnesty International of the
   USA
Western Regional Office
3618 Sacramento Street
San Francisco, CA 94118

VENEZUELA

Senores
Apartado 80909
Prados del Este
Caracas 1080-A

INDEX

Fontana Paperbacks : Non-fiction

Fontana is a leading paperback publisher of non-fiction, both popular and academic. Below are some recent titles.

- ☐ THE HELLENISTIC WORLD F. W. Walbank £2.95
- ☐ THE DIETER'S GUIDE TO SUCCESS
  Audrey Eyton & Henry Jordan £1.25
- ☐ LIFE ON EARTH David Attenborough £3.95
- ☐ THE VICTORIAN PROPHETS
  ed. Peter Keating £2.95
- ☐ THE REALITIES BEHIND DIPLOMACY
  Paul Kennedy £3.50
- ☐ TWOPENCE TO CROSS THE MERSEY
  Helen Forrester £1.75
- ☐ IRELAND: A SOCIAL AND CULTURAL HISTORY
  Terence Brown £3.50
- ☐ SOCIOBIOLOGY: THE WHISPERINGS WITHIN
  David Barash £2.50
- ☐ INEQUALITY IN BRITAIN: FREEDOM, WELFARE
  AND THE STATE Frank Field £2.50
- ☐ KARMA COLA Gita Mehta £1.50
- ☐ JOHN LENNON Ray Connolly £2.50

You can buy Fontana paperbacks at your local bookshop or newsagent. Or you can order them from Fontana Paperbacks, Cash Sales Department, Box 29, Douglas, Isle of Man. Please send a cheque, postal or money order (not currency) worth the purchase price plus 10p per book (or plus 12p per book if outside the UK).

NAME (Block letters)
_____

ADDRESS
_____

_____

_____

While every effort is made to keep prices low, it is sometimes necessary to increase prices at short notice. Fontana Paperbacks reserve the right to show new retail prices on covers which may differ from those previously advertised in the text or elsewhere.